JULES VERNE:
Narratives of Modernity

Liverpool Science Fiction Texts and Studies
General Editor DAVID SEED

Series Advisers I.F. Clarke, Edward James, Patrick Parrinder and Brian Stableford

JULES VERNE:
Narratives of Modernity

Edited by

EDMUND J. SMYTH

First published 2000 by
LIVERPOOL UNIVERSITY PRESS
Liverpool L69 7ZU

© 2000 Liverpool University Press

British Library Cataloguing-in-Publication Data
A British Library CIP record is available

ISBN 0-85323-694-1 (hardback)
ISBN 0-85323-704-2 (paperback)

Typeset in 10/12.5pt Meridien by
XL Publishing Services, Lurley, Tiverton
Printed by Bell & Bain, Glasgow

Contents

Contents

Contributors

WILLIAM BUTCHER was formerly Head of Languages at Hong Kong Technical College, and is now lecturing at the Hong Kong Institute of Education. He has written extensively on French literature and on natural language processing. He is the author of *Verne's Journey to the Centre of the Self* (1990), and five translations/critical editions of Verne, including *Journey to the Centre of the Earth*, *Around the World in Eighty Days*, and most recently *Twenty Thousand Leagues under the Seas*.

SARAH CAPITANIO is Principal Lecturer in French at the University of Wolverhampton. She has published on Zola and on the nineteenth- and twentieth-century novel and is currently preparing a book on the novel series in France, to be published in 2000.

DANIEL COMPERE is Professor of French at the University of Amiens. He is the author of *Jules Verne écrivain*, and numerous articles on Verne and other nineteenth-century writers.

ARTHUR B. EVANS is a Professor at DePauw University, Indiana, USA. He is the author of *Jules Verne Rediscovered*, and is the managing editor of *Science Fiction Studies*.

TERRY HALE is currently Senior Research Fellow at the Translation Performance Centre, University of Hull. He has published translations of some fifteen novels and collections of writings by the French avant-garde. His most recent publication is *The Dedalus Book of Nineteenth-Century French Horror*.

ANDREW HUGILL is a composer and Professor of Music at De Montfort University, Leicester. He has had a long-standing interest in French Surrealism and its precursors.

TREVOR HARRIS currently teaches at the University of Tours. He has published widely on nineteenth-century French literature, and is a specialist on the work of Guy de Maupassant.

DAVID MEAKIN is Senior Lecturer in French at the University of Bristol. He has worked on numerous nineteenth- and twentieth-century French writers, including the book *Hermetic Fictions: Alchemy and Irony in the Modern Novel*, and a critical study of Boris Vian's *L'Ecume des jours* and an edition of Robbe-Grillet's *Dans le labyrinthe*.

DAVID PLATTEN is lecturer in French at the University of Leeds. He has written a critical study of Philippe Djian's *37, 2 le matin*, and his book on Michel Tournier is being published by Liverpool University Press in 1999.

EDMUND SMYTH is Reader in French at Manchester Metropolitan University. His previous books include *Postmodernism and Contemporary Fiction* and *Autobiography and the Existential Self*. He is the editor of the Liverpool University Press series 'Modern French Writers'.

TIMOTHY UNWIN is James Barrow Professor of French at the University of Liverpool. His books include *Constant: 'Adolphe'*, *Art et Infini: l'œuvre de jeunesse de Gustave Flaubert*, *Verne: 'Le Tour du monde en quatre-vingts jours'*, and *The Cambridge Companion to The French Novel, from 1800 to the Present*.

1

Verne, SF, and Modernity: an Introduction

EDMUND J. SMYTH

1

In a series dedicated to the study of science fiction, it would seem to be more than appropriate to find a volume devoted to Jules Verne (1828–1905), who is widely credited as one of the founders of the genre. Numerous surveys of the evolution of science fiction pay tribute to his influence on successive generations of writers, with leading contemporary practitioners (such as Brian Aldiss, Ray Bradbury and Arthur C. Clarke) extravagant in their praise of Verne's 'fantastic' explorations of worlds known and unknown. Verne classed his texts under the collective title *Voyages extraordinaires*, with a sub-title *Les Mondes connus et inconnus*, signalling the preoccupation with exploration and discovery, which has come to be seen as the characteristic feature of his fictional universe. The first issue of Hugo Gernsback's landmark SF magazine *Amazing Stories* in 1926 had a drawing of Jules Verne's tomb at Amiens on its title page. According to the purist, however, less than a quarter of his sixty-four novels could be counted as 'genuine' SF; and there has been much argument surrounding whether 'scientific romance' may not be a more suitable designation. Of course, the term 'science fiction' itself did not exist until the 1930s; and, as Patrick Parrinder points out, Verne should be considered alongside other writers of 'scientific romance' in the nineteenth century, such as Poe, Mary Shelley, and H. G. Wells, in charting the continuity between the nineteenth-century tradition of scientific romance and twentieth-century science fiction.[1] Jules Verne's exploitation of the genre of the romance of adventure has profoundly affected the direction of science fiction. There has been as much debate concerning Verne's status within SF, as there has about his inclusion in the French literary canon. Nevertheless, it would be fair to state that in the popular imagination Verne and SF are seen as largely synonymous, even if modern science fiction has moved far beyond the narratives of travel and endeavour which are found in *Voyage au centre de la terre* (1864) and *Vingt mille lieues sous les mers* (1869). For the modern SF reader, Jules Verne's lunar novels—*De la Terre à la lune* (1865) and *Autour de la lune* (1869)—would appear somewhat quaint and technologically unsophisticated. However, as Andrew Martin states: 'Verne is less an individual than a style, a symbol, a mythology.'[2] A great deal of the controversy surrounding the academic legitimacy of SF can be attributed to the 'embarrassing' popularity of a writer like Jules Verne himself, despite the very conspicuous quotation of Vernian paradigms in contemporary French fiction by prominent 'mainstream' writers, such as Georges Perec in *W ou le souvenir d'enfance* (1975), and Michel Tournier in *Les Météores* (1975) and *Vendredi* (1967). In France, science fiction has continued to be relegated to the realms of 'paraliterary'; indeed the majority of Verne specialists prefer to downplay the SF dimension of Verne's *'romans scientifiques'* in order to facilitate his entry into the French literary canon. As Jean-Marc Gouanvic demonstrates in a recent study,[3] SF as a literary genre is regarded in France as an unwelcome American import, and is accorded a much lower status than the *récit policier*.

The posthumous publication in 1994 of *Paris au XXe siècle*, however, led to a reconsideration of Verne's status as a writer, even if much of the discussion so far has been concerned with the extent to which he had predicted certain cultural and technological developments in the modern world. Although this kind of debate is considered as naïve by conventional SF critics, the resulting publicity proved fertile in drawing attention once again to the importance of Verne as a key commentator on the anguishes of modernity, rather than as the over-enthusiastic promoter of the value of science and technology. It is certainly the case that, unlike Wells, Verne prided himself on his responsible scientific speculation, extrapolating from contemporary social and scientific trends. Of course, a rehabilitation (if any were needed) had been under way for some time, and *Paris au XXe siècle*, in many ways a classic example of 'la littérature d'anticipation' (the preferred term for SF), has come to be widely viewed as offering a prophetically dystopian vision of modern society.

It is the *nouveau romancier* Michel Butor who can be credited with drawing attention to the affinity between Verne and those writers who are more frequently cited as dramatizing the contradictions of the modern world and the instability of consciousness. Butor's long essay on Verne appeared in a collection entitled *Essais sur les modernes* (1960), which also contained chapters on Baudelaire, Dostoyevsky, Proust, Mallarmé, Roussel, Joyce, and Leiris.[4] Butor's interest in Verne's work is particularly significant, for Butor was an experimental novelist concerned with the renewal of narrative form, while Verne was not hitherto acknowledged as an innovator in the area of narrative technique. Most of his novels have a linear structure, and character psychology tends to be rudimentary. Indeed, for Roland Barthes, writing in *Mythologies* (1957), Verne's texts are unproblematically classic realist, not only in the sense that the narratives tend towards closure, but also because they reflect the social and cultural order in which they were produced ('Verne appartient à la lignée progressiste de la bourgeoisie: son œuvre affiche que rien ne peut échapper à l'homme, que le monde, même le plus lointain, est comme un objet dans sa main'[5]). For Barthes, Verne's works are therefore about bourgeois appropriation and containment, and ultimately demonstrate the rise of European colonialism and the politics of exploration: 'Verne ne cherchait nullement à élargir le monde selon des voies romantiques d'évasion ou des plans mystiques d'infini: il cherchait sans cesse à le rétracter, à le peupler, à le réduire à un espace connu et clos, que l'homme pourrait ensuite habiter confortablement.'[6] Michel Butor, however, conducts an admirably detailed analysis of a number of Verne's novels (but concentrating brilliantly on *L'Ile mystérieuse* (1874), perhaps the canonical text for contemporary readers), concluding that there can be detected a 'méfiance de Jules Verne vis-à-vis de la science'.[7] Butor is also at pains to emphasize that the poetic quality of Verne's descriptive writing bears comparison with Eluard, Lautréamont and Henri Michaux—thus making him more of an *écrivain* than an *écrivant*, to adopt Barthes's own dichotomy, in the sense that his writing is self-consciously wrestling with language itself, rather than being a vehicle for representation. It is the nature of the Vernian text which has come under scrutiny in recent years. In literary-historical terms, it would of course be scarcely credible to recruit Verne into modernism; however, a case can be made for asserting that he provides narratives of modernity, in that his texts both incorporate and perforate the modern, by encompassing the spirit of the scientific age and articulating some of its limitations and agonies. In Verne studies today, the scientific elements have tended to give way to an analysis of the social, cultural, mythical and ideological dimensions of his work.

It is undoubtedly true that Verne must initially be approached with due regard to the prevailing ideology of positivism which characterized his epoch. Roland Barthes is correct to point to the 'encyclopedic' aspect of Vernian discourse, with its reliance on documentation, catalogues and inventories. Barthes refers to Verne's obsession for plenitude: 'il ne cessait de finir le monde et de le meubler'.[8] The positivist context is apparent from the emphasis which seems to be placed on the role of science and technological progress generally—the product therefore of an era of determinism, scientific methodology and taxonomy, as evidenced in the writings of Auguste Comte, Hippolyte Taine and Ernest Renan. As Michel Serres says in his widely influential study *Jouvences sur Jules Verne* (1974):

'Au bout du compte, les *Voyages extraordinaires* sont le *Cours de philosophie positive* à l'usage de tous.'[9] At this level, his novels would appear to provide a perfect illustration of the literary ideal of factual documentation and objective detachment, which Emile Zola and others would carry over into naturalist fiction. As Patrick Parrinder has commented: 'Verne's fiction is a logical extension of the engineering mentality of the Age of Steam.'[10]

However, it is important to acknowledge the role played by his publisher Pierre-Jules Hetzel in fostering this particular reading. It was Hetzel who wrote the famous preface to the *Voyages extraordinaires* (originally accompanying *Les Voyages et aventures du capitaine Hatteras* (1866)), in which he states that Verne has created a new genre, encompassing all the knowledge amassed by modern science: 'l'heure est venue où la science a sa place faite dans le domaine de la littérature'.[11] Verne's novels do indeed contain a vast amount of information culled from the science of his day, including engineering, astronomy, physics, geology and oceanography. Much has been made of Verne's own working methods, based on the resources of research rather than the recourse to the artistic imagination: for example, *Voyage au centre de la terre* relies heavily on a manual of mineralogy, just as an accumulation of material on flora and fauna constitute the source of *Vingt mille lieues sous les mers*. In *De la Terre à la lune*, the rational, scientific basis can be seen in the elaborate calculations of escape velocity, weights, distances and ballistics. Hetzel's document is as important an aesthetic 'manifesto' in its way, as Balzac's 'Avant-Propos' to his own series of novels *La Comédie humaine*, or Breton's 'Manifestes du surréalisme', or the critical essays on the *nouveau roman* by Alain Robbe-Grillet in *Pour un nouveau roman* or Nathalie Sarraute in *L'Ere du soupçon*. As Gérard Genette has commented, a paratextual commentary of this kind will inevitably colour and condition the reading which results, determining the reception of literary texts.[12] Verne's stories initially appeared in the periodical *Le Magasin d'éducation et de récréation*, founded by Hetzel and Jean Macé in 1863, and were therefore viewed as in harmony with its programme of instruction and entertainment, in which fiction and scientific vulgarization existed alongside each other (and, in Verne's case, frequently within the same text). His publisher effectively appropriated Verne into a rhetoric of scientificity, extolling the prevailing ethos of progress. Hetzel typified in many respects the dominant ideology of Third Republic France, with its emphasis on secular, humanist values, and a belief in social and scientific progress, conveyed through a centralist, lay education system. Hetzel accepted *Cinq semaines en ballon* in 1863, and Verne would continue to write for him for the next forty years. It is Andrew Martin's contention, however, that Verne's writing 'will be conducted in a spirit of clandestine revolt against the paternalistic domination of

Hetzel'.[13] It is this subversive aspect of Verne which is particularly significant in assessing his relationship with modernity.

In focusing on the manner in which his work voices the ideology of the society and culture from which it emerged, as Marc Angenot has pointed out, Verne's work can be said to illustrate a liberal-capitalist utopia of free circulation.[14] Pierre Macherey devotes a large part of his seminal Althusserian Marxist book *Pour une théorie de la production littéraire* (1966) (*A Theory of Literary Production*) to an analysis of the immensely complex ideological resonances of the Vernian text. Macherey's discussion of Verne has been widely influential in the field of literary theory generally, as his aim is to examine the manner in which a literary text connects with ideology. For Macherey, the critic needs to tease out the differences within the work by demonstrating that it is other than it seems; despite the surface coherence and totalizing impulse, the text can in fact be shown to expose omissions, transgressions and absences. This is a deconstructive critical strategy, which concentrates on how the conditions of a text's production are inscribed 'silently' within the text itself. Verne's *L'Ile mystérieuse* is subjected to an intense reading along these lines, as Pierre Macherey demonstrates how the work subverts the Eurocentric, colonialist ideology which it otherwise seeks to endorse. For Macherey, there is a sense in which Verne's *Voyages extraordinaires* were 'commissioned' by the French bourgeoisie, coinciding with the crucial historical moment of the expansion of France's colonial empire. He argues that far from 'reflecting' this liberal-capitalist ethos in an unmediated and unproblematic way, the Vernian text provides a critique of its ambiguities and inconsistencies. Macherey is extremely critical of Barthes's cavalier dismissal of Verne, arguing instead that Verne provides a more fractured view of the dominant ideology of his society, 'unconsciously' articulating its contradictions:

> Si J. Verne a *senti* les contradictions de son temps ... et s'il a voulu donner quand même de ce temps une image non critique ... et qui se trouve en fait défaillante, c'est qu'il existe entre l'ensemble des contradictions historiques et le défaut propre à son œuvre un *décalage*, qu'il faut considérer comme le vrai centre de son œuvre.[15]

Macherey focuses on the 'discords' present in the text, those internal variations which puncture the totalizing narrative logic. As Catherine Belsey states, echoing this critical perspective: 'If Verne's nineteenth-century readers did not identify the repressed in the text, if they did not recognize the silence with which the work finally confronts its own ideological project, it was because they read from within the same ideological framework, shared the same repressions, and took for granted the same silences.'[16] Equally, as Andrew Martin remarks, 'if Verne's *œuvre* is in part a study of the growth of empire, it is also a diagnosis of its growing pains, of the upsets and disturbances to which the body politic is susceptible, and the strains that threaten to undermine its coherence'.[17] These comments indicate that the Vernian text is a much less seamless construction than many critics have asserted, and that, in some fundamental way, Verne is grappling with the problems associated with modernity.

It was Michel Butor who had identified Verne's ambiguous stance on science, emphasizing that in his novels: 'C'est tout le profond rêve peu à peu que portait avec elle la science de la fin du dix-neuvième siècle, et par lequel elle s'enracinait comme fait de civilisation et mentalité, qu'il révèle et qu'il juge.'[18] As Macherey states: 'Jamais Verne n'a voulu montrer qu'il *croyait* à l'efficacité de l'activité scientifique: ni qu'il croyait le contraire … C'est *l'image de la science* qu'il interroge, car il ne se contente pas de le représenter.'[19] According to this analysis, Verne is evoking the troubled relation of humanity to its technology, expressing fears about the modern world. Science is viewed ambivalently in a work such as *Robur-le-conquérant* (1886), for example. For Marc Angenot, 'Science is not described for its own sake, and never does the narrative focus on isolated gadgets. The referent of Vernian discourse is the *effect* of science.'[20] As William Butcher argues: 'the actual process of scientific/geographic discovery is shown as fraught with tremendous problems'.[21] The publication of *Paris au XXe siècle* in 1994 casts doubt on the view that disillusionment with science is a feature of the later Verne, as this text was written in 1863, before the *Voyages extraordinaires* got under way. Piero Gondolo della Riva comments in his critical edition that: 'Le pessimisme est donc présent dès le début de son œuvre.'[22] It is clearly necessary, therefore, to give a more nuanced account of the role of science in Verne's work: it is the specifically *textual* function of scientific discourse which should be scrutinized. In this light, 'science' is a text which will be reworked.

In considering the modernity of the Vernian text, it is evident that its composition is far more complex than is normally acknowledged. Michel Serres has examined the relationship between the incorporation of the scientific discourse and the world-view which produced it: 'Le grand impérialisme fin de siècle se reflète, chez Verne … dans cette mainmise du savoir sur l'univers.'[23] For Andrew Martin, Verne's novels are especially susceptible to being considered as a library of quotations: 'Few texts can ever have been quite so thoroughly permeated with other texts as Verne's. His novels are populated by proliferating references to novels, histories, treatises, journals, travel-writing, manuscripts of all kinds.'[24] Martin is especially attentive to the parallel which exists between both colonial and textual appropriation as evidenced by Verne's novels. In an important article devoted to Verne, Michel Foucault refers to the 'discours parasites' which trouble the surface of the Vernian text: for Foucault, the Vernian text is interesting because of the existence of discontinuities within it, of another voice which 'conteste le récit, en souligne les invraisemblances, montre tout ce qu'il y aurait d'impossible'.[25] Perhaps the most significant development in Verne studies in the past decade is this attention which has been paid to the polyphonic nature of the Vernian text. This can be seen in particular in *Jules Verne écrivain* (1991), in which Daniel Compère examines the manner in which Verne will 'incorporate' other texts: 'l'œuvre de Jules Verne brasse toutes les connaissances scientifiques, géographiques, littéraires de son temps, traverse différents genres romanesques, engrange une multitude de messages et d'opinions'.[26] Compère brings to bear on Verne's texts the developments in literary theory concerning intertextuality, inspired by Bakhtin and taken up by Julia Kristeva, Gérard Genette, Antoine Compagnon and others. It is possible, asserts Compère, to view the Vernian novel as an assemblage of discourses and quotations of other texts: 'L'énonciation vernienne se fait écho, commentaire, représentation du XIXe siècle. Elle orchestre une multitude de discours, textes littéraires certes, mais aussi documents scientifiques, journaux, récits de voyages, et même éléments verbaux (clichés, opinions, croyances, jargons, argots).'[27] According to Compère, Verne 'poetically' appropriates and transforms texts of various kinds. It may be legitimate to state that Verne provides a 'cornucopian text', in the manner that Terence Cave has analyzed in his study of Rabelais—another writer with a fascination for enumeration, the extraordinary, and the quotation and incorporation of other texts.[28]

It is this concern with the relationship between language and the literary text which has made Verne fascinating to contemporary writers and critics. It is significant that the Vernian cryptogram has been a particular source of interest to poststructuralist critics, alert to the manner in which the literary text betrays 'work on language', in addition to the notion of a 'decipherable' text. Michel Butor had drawn attention to this feature in his essay; but this was in many respects what originally attracted Raymond Roussel (whom Verne is said to have met) and the Surrealists to his novels earlier in the twentieth century. Raymond Queneau and, later, Georges Perec, both associated with the Oulipo (Ouvroir de littérature potentielle) group, were specifically interested in modes of textual organization derived from play with language, and have made reference to the significance of Verne's texts in this respect. For Compère, this ludic aspect constitutes an example of reflexivity, a feature which we would normally associate with more radical modernist works, such as Joyce's *Finnegans Wake*, the later *nouveau roman*, or those subversive fictions produced under the aegis of *Tel*

Quel in the 1970s. As William Butcher says: 'Verne's works contain an implicit critique of the continuity and verisimilitude of the "realist" novel. They secrete a self-reflexiveness and a self-referentiality which underline "faults" in the conventional system. They thus point the way to further experiments.'[29]

These readings point to the modernity of the Verne text. Although not quite attaining the dimensions of the multiple, heterogeneous, 'open text' as envisaged by Umberto Eco, it is evident that Jules Verne has produced works which are far from being as unproblematic as his detractors have claimed. These new approaches are fertile, and suggest the ways in which Verne will continue to fascinate successive generations of readers and critics. His novels will always be rediscovered, and new critical approaches will be brought to bear on them. The 'extraordinary' aspect of *Voyages extraordinaires* resides perhaps in the fact that these works overflow and transcend the boundaries of realism and naturalism, installing the fantastic and defamiliarizing the 'real'. It is the fictionality of the text which has to be considered: as Michel Butor signals, 'l'on ne peut plus savoir où se trouve la limite entre l'imaginé et l'appris'.[30] It is in the defamiliarization of reality that Jules Verne enjoys a profound relationship with twentieth-century science fiction, by providing a 'literature of cognitive estrangement', as science fiction has been described, which 'not only facilitates an imaginative "escape" from or transcendence of the given social environment, but sows the seeds of dissatisfaction with that environment, and of the determination and ability to change it'.[31]

2

The essays collected in this volume reflect the diversity of approaches being brought to bear on the work of Jules Verne. It is not the aim of this book to provide a definitive answer to the question of Jules Verne's status as a writer of science fiction, let alone to supply yet another 'justification' of his legitimacy as a serious writer. Rather, within the parameters of the debate concerning the nature of modernity, the contributors address those questions which have been exercising critics for some time, while indicating new directions for Vernian and SF research. Arthur B. Evans provides a detailed account of the relationship between Verne and the French literary canon, demonstrating the 'now-ineluctable trend towards rehabilitation and literary canonization'. Pursuing further the masterly analysis set out in *Jules Verne écrivain* (regrettably not yet published in English), Daniel Compère examines narrative technique, verisimilitude, defamiliarization, naturalization, and dialogism in his work. Timothy Unwin discusses the role of science and textual repetition, developing the enquiry into the nature of the Vernian text. Sarah Capitanio investigates the interface between realism, utopianism and science fiction in a number of Verne's novels. David Platten provides a sustained analysis of the controversial *Paris au XXe siècle*, one of the first major studies to be published on this novel. David Meakin looks at the alchemical richness of *Les Indes noires*, a work which is beginning to attract increasing attention. Trevor Harris examines the extent to which Verne writes against science, offering a challenging new perspective on this vexed question. Terry Hale and Andrew Hugill focus on the relationship between Verne and Surrealism, suggesting the repercussions for a modern reading of the writer. In an important new development for Verne criticism, William Butcher surveys the background to the posthumous, 'disturbingly modern' short story entitled 'Edom', which he sees as a rehearsal of the whole of *Voyages extraordinaires*.

Notes

1 P. Parrinder, *Science Fiction: its Criticism and Teaching* (Methuen, London and New York, 1980), pp. 4–10. For an account of Verne's influence on science fiction, see Peter Costello, *Jules Verne: Inventor of Science Fiction* (London, Hodder and Stoughton, 1978).

2 Andrew Martin, *The Mask of the Prophet. The Extraordinary Fictions of Jules Verne* (Oxford, Clarendon Press, 1990), p. 9.

3 Jean-Marc Gouanvic, *La Science-Fiction française au XXe siècle(1900–1968). Essai de socio-poétique d'un genre en émergence* (Amsterdam and Atlanta, Rodopi, 1994).

4 M. Butor, 'Le point suprême et l'âge d'or à travers quelques œuvres de Jules Verne', *Essais sur les modernes* (Paris, Gallimard, Collection 'Idées', 1960). Also in *Répertoire I* (Paris, Minuit, 1960). (This essay originally appeared in *Arts et lettres*, 15 (1949), 3–31.)

5 Roland Barthes, 'Nautilus et bateau ivre', in *Mythologies* (Paris, Seuil, Collection 'Points', 1957), pp. 80–2.

6 Ibid., pp. 80–1.

7 Butor, 'Le point suprême', p. 86.

8 Barthes, 'Nautilus et bateau ivre', p. 80.

9 Michel Serres, *Jouvences sur Jules Verne* (Paris, Minuit, 1974), p. 13.

10 Parrinder, *Science Fiction*, p. 7.

11 J. Hetzel, 'Avertissement de l'éditeur', in J. Verne, *Les Voyages et aventures du capitaine Hatteras* (Paris, Hetzel, 1866), pp. 1–2.

12 G. Genette, *Seuils* (Paris, Seuil, 1987).

13 Martin, *Mask of the Prophet*, p. 4.

14 M. Angenot, 'Jules Verne: the last happy utopianist', in *Science Fiction. A Critical Guide*, ed. P. Parrinder (London and New York, Longman, 1979), pp. 18–33.

15 Pierre Macherey, *Pour une théorie de la production littéraire* (Paris, Maspero, 1966), p. 220.

16 Catherine Belsey, *Critical Practice* (London, Routledge, 1980), p. 137.

17 Martin, *Mask of the Prophet*, p. 79.

18 Butor, 'Le point suprême', p. 39.

19 Macherey, *Pour une théorie*, p. 256.

20 Angenot, 'Jules Verne', p. 29.

21 William Butcher, *Verne's Journey to the Centre of the Self. Space and Time in the 'Voyages extraordinaires'* (New York and London, St. Martin's Press, 1990), p. 113.

22 J. Verne, *Paris au XXe siècle* (1863; Paris, Hachette, 1994), p. 23.

23 Serres, *Jouvences sur Jules Verne*, p. 12.

24 Martin, *Mask of the Prophet*, p. 30.

25 M. Foucault, 'L'Arrière-fable', *L'Arc (numéro spécial Jules Verne)*, 29 (1966), 5–13.

26 D. Compère, *Jules Verne écrivain* (Geneva, Droz, 1991), p. 11.

27 Ibid., p. 12.

28 T. Cave, *The Cornucopian Text: Problems of Writing in the French Renaissance* (Oxford, Clarendon Press, 1979).

29 W. Butcher, *Verne's Journey*, p. 131.

30 M. Butor, 'Le point suprême', p. 40.

31 P. Parrinder, *Science Fiction*, p. 72.

2
Jules Verne and the French Literary Canon

ARTHUR B. EVANS

1863–1905

The curious contradiction of Jules Verne's popular success and literary rebuff in France began during his own lifetime, from the moment his first *Voyages extraordinaires* appeared in the French marketplace in 1863–5 until his death in 1905. From the publication of his earliest novels—*Cinq semaines en ballon* (1863), *Voyage au centre de la terre* (1864), and *De la Terre à la lune* (1865)—the sales of Verne's works were astonishing, earning him the recognition he sought as an up-and-coming novelist. He was showered with enthusiastic praise from some well-known authors, prominent scientists, and even a small number of literary critics. For example, his first novel received the following book review in the prestigious *Revue des Deux Mondes* in 1863:

> Les grandes découvertes des plus célèbres voyageurs constatées et résumées dans un rapide et charmant volume de science et d'histoire—de l'imagination et de la vérité—voilà ce qui distingue le brillant début de M. Jules Verne. Son livre restera comme le plus curieux et le plus utile des voyages imaginaires, comme une de ces rares œuvres de l'esprit qui méritent la fortune des Robinson et de Gulliver, et qui ont sur eux l'avantage de ne pas sortir un instant de la réalité et de s'appuyer jusque dans la fantaisie et dans l'invention sur les faits positifs et sur la science irrécusable.[1]

George Sand is known to have written a letter to her (and Verne's) publisher Pierre Jules Hetzel saying: 'J'ai beaucoup de tes livres…mais je n'ai pas tous ceux de Jules Verne que j'adore, et je les recevrai avec plaisir pour mes petites et pour moi.'[2] And the following observations in 1866 by Théophile Gautier, when reviewing Verne's *Voyages et aventures du capitaine Hatteras*, were also among the first critical commentaries on Verne's works from the French literary community:

Il y a une volumineuse collection de voyages imaginaires anciens et modernes: depuis l'*Histoire véritable* de Lucien jusqu'aux *Aventures de Gulliver*, l'imagination humaine s'est complue dans ses fantaisies vagabondes où sous prétexte d'excursions aux contrées inconnues, les auteurs...développent leurs utopies ou exercent leur humeur satirique.

Les voyages de M. Jules Verne n'appartiennent à aucune de ces catégories. S'ils n'ont pas été réellement accomplis et si même ils ne sauraient l'être encore, ils offrent la plus rigoureuse possibilité scientifique et les plus osés ne sont que la paradoxe ou l'outrance d'une vérité bientôt connue. La chimère est ici chevauchée et dirigée par un esprit mathématique. C'est l'application à un fait d'invention de tous les détails vrais, réels, et précis qui peuvent s'y rattacher de manière à produire l'illusion la plus complète...

M. Jules Verne, dans son récit exact et minutieux comme le livre de bord, fait naître l'absolue sensation de la réalité. La technicité maritime, mathématique et scientifique employée à propos et sobrement imprime un tel cachet de vérité à ce fantastique *Forward* qu'on ne peut se persuader qu'il n'a pas accompli son voyage d'exploration. ...En outre, M. Jules Verne, qui ne néglige pas le côté humain et cordial, sait faire aimer ses personnages.[3]

From the ranks of the French scientific community, the following review by the geographer Saint-Martin is quite representative. It appeared in the popular scientific journal *L'Année Géographique*:

Il est bien difficile que la science et la fiction se trouvent en contact sans alourdir l'une et abaisser l'autre; ici elles se font valoir par une heureuse alliance que met en relief le côté instructif de la relation tout en laissant son attrait au côté d'aventures. Les plus habiles y trouvent à apprendre, et la masse des lecteurs y puisera presque à son insu, des notions irréprochables que bien peu auraient été chercher dans des livres d'un aspect plus sévère. J'ajouterai, et c'est là pour moi le plus grand mérite des compositions de M. Verne, que loin d'éloigner des lectures plus graves, elles y attirent plutôt d'acquisitions variées dans les récits d'un voyageur instruit qui est en même temps un conteur spirituel.[4]

Lastly, a small number of literary critics contemporary to Verne also commended his works. One of the most interesting and detailed is Marius Topin's *Romanciers contemporains* (1876), a 417-page collection of literary discussions about such celebrated authors as Hugo, Balzac, Dumas, Flaubert and Zola. The following selection of excerpts gives a reasonable idea of Topin's opinions concerning Verne's œuvre:

Voici maintenant le roman scientifique...le genre dont M. Jules Verne est l'incontestable inventeur. Assurément bien d'autres avant lui s'étaient efforcés de mêler dans leurs récits, avec une juste mesure, l'utile et agréable, et d'être à la fois instructifs par la portée sérieuse de leur œuvre et piquants par l'invention ingénieuse. Mais nul n'y a réussi comme M. Verne.[5]

Toutes les combinaisons...tous les artifices que les romanciers ordinaires imaginent pour nouer et dénouer une situation, M. Verne les a empruntés à la science. Aux merveilles usées de la féerie, il a substitué les merveilles réelles de la nature; aux crimes accumulés du roman d'aventure, il a substitué des procédés dont les notions récentes de la science font les frais.[6]

M. Verne est le romancier le plus populaire de notre temps et, nous l'ajoutons avec joie, le plus justement populaire. Il est de ceux qui honorent leurs lecteurs, car rien n'est sorti de sa plume qui ne soit sain, substantiel, et élevé...dans ses œuvres le beau moral resplendisse dans tout son éclat à côté du vrai scientifique.[7]

It is also interesting to note that Topin's discussions of Verne's *Voyages extraordinaires* seem more textually oriented than most critics from this period; the majority appear to deal almost exclusively with Verne's personal life. Consider, for example, Adolphe Brisson's chatty discussion of Verne in his *Portraits intimes*,[8] Georges Bastard's newspaper account in 'Célébrités contemporaines: Jules Verne en 1883' where he describes the author's physionomy, his yacht, and his work habits,[9] and Jules Clarétie's accurate but strictly biographical *Jules Verne* of the same year[10] (the first of many Vernian biographies to be published in the years to follow). In surveying most of the early criticism and reviews of Verne's novels, it is often evident that his growing popularity as a writer seems to have produced more interest in him as a public figure than in his actual works.

In this context, mention must also be made of two additional popularizers of Verne's novels in France which eventually brought him more public recognition (and certainly more wealth) than his texts themselves: those theatrical productions adapted from his novels and two early experiments in the new art of cinematography. The former include *Le Tour du monde en 80 jours* which Verne co-produced with Adolphe d'Ennery in 1874 (a huge box-office success, eventually chalking up over fifty years of performances at the Châtelet Theatre), *Le Docteur Ox* in 1877 (with music by Jacques Offenbach), *Les Enfants du capitaine Grant* in 1878 and *Michel Strogoff* in 1880 (both also with d'Ennery), and *Voyage à travers l'impossible* in 1882 (a fanciful pastiche of a variety of Vernian 'voyage' motifs—some found in his earlier novels, others not). The latter included two silent movies by Méliès in 1902 and 1904: *Voyage dans la lune* and *Voyage à travers l'impossible* respectively. These films are of particular importance when considering the phenomenal success of those cinematic adaptations of Verne's works that appeared in America during the mid-twentieth century and which functioned as the prime popularizers of the *Voyages extraordinaires* (and the myth of 'Jules Verne, the Father of Science Fiction') in the United States. Thus, both French theatre and early cinema contributed to enhancing further Jules Verne's reputation as a highly successful 'popular' author.

But the word 'popular' in French literary circles is a two-edged term. It was undoubtedly due to his 'popularity' that Verne was systematically shunned by the French literary and university establishment as being 'a mere writer of children's stories'. Very representative, for example, were the views of Emile Zola who repeatedly dismissed both Verne and his novels as totally non-literary:

> un aimable vulgarisateur, M. Verne obtenait des succès énormes avec ses livres qui succédaient aux contes de Perrault, entre les mains des enfants. Les féeries d'il y a trente ans étaient tirées de ces contes; il devenait logique que les féeries d'aujourd'hui fussent tirées des livres de M. Verne.[11]

> Si les *Voyages extraordinaires* se vendent bien, les alphabets et les paroissiens se vendent bien aussi à des chiffres considérables... [Ils sont] sans aucune importance dans le mouvement littéraire contemporain.[12]

Verne's lack of 'official' literary status is also reflected in the strange irony of the Académie Française's 'crowning' the *Voyages extraordinaires* in 1872 (along with the poetry of Coppée)—an award which Verne's publisher Hetzel thereafter unfailingly mentioned in the frontispiece of each of Verne's novels—whereas their author, Jules Verne himself, was consistently snubbed and never offered membership of this prestigious assembly. It perhaps should be noted, however, that Verne apparently never expended much energy toward soliciting such an appointment. Time and time again, his publisher and friends encouraged him to push his own candidacy more insistently, and to be more sensitive to the political and social amenities that were prerequisite to such a nomination. But Verne invariably refused to do so. One wonders, in retrospect, if Verne's reluctance was a product of his disinterest, or, as is more likely the case, a question of pride coupled with a fear of overt rejection. Verne's correspondence indicates that he repeatedly discussed with Hetzel his chances of entering the Académie—several letters even show a great deal more than just passing interest in such a possibility. But, as Verne himself admitted in one such letter, the very genre itself of his *Voyages extraordinaires* would probably preclude any chance of his being nominated:

> Je ne vous ai parlé de l'Académie qu'à propos des genres de littérature, et je n'ai pas dit autre chose que ceci: dans l'échelle littéraire, le roman d'aventures est moins haut placé que le roman de mœurs. Aux yeux de tous les critiques, Balzac est supérieur à Dumas père, ne fût-ce que 'par le genre'.[13]

And Verne then goes on to say, in a very rare and revealing commentary on his own literary beliefs:

> Je ne dis pas autre chose, grand dieu! que ce que je fais! ... Je crois d'une grande façon générale, et question de forme à part, que l'étude du cœur humain est plus littéraire que les récits d'aventures. Ces récits peuvent réussir davantage, je ne dis pas non. Mais il vaut mieux avoir fait *Eugénie Grandet* que *Monte-Christo* [sic]...[14]

As excerpts from these letters clearly show, Verne was well aware of how his scientific-adventure tales were viewed within the dominant literary ideology of his society. And, *homme de lettres* himself (and being well-schooled in French literary history), he shared these fundamental values. Nevertheless, despite his self-deprecating remarks about the overall worth of his own efforts, Verne must have also realized that the Académie Française was not the exclusive reserve of writers of *romans de mœurs*, and his correspondence suggests that he continued to hope that he might someday be recognized as having made an important contribution to his country's *belles lettres* and eventually be awarded his place in the history of French literature. But he was to be bitterly disappointed in this regard. The Académie Française—although willing to acknowledge the popularity and 'wholesomeness' of his *Voyages extraordinaires*—was adamant in its unwillingness to acknowledge Jules Verne as a writer of 'real' literary merit. Even the most noted educators and literary historians of the time such as Ferdinand Brunetière, Emile Jaquet, Jules Lemaître and René Doumic never once mentioned Jules Verne or his *romans scientifiques* in their respective reference books on French literature—a silence more damning than the worst reviews, and more painful than the Académie's refusal to recognize him personally.

But what were the underlying social reasons for Verne's lack of 'official' recognition? First, although quite difficult to pinpoint in retrospect without venturing into anachronistic revisionism, one obvious factor seems to have been the rigid and hierarchically defined notion of *littérature* itself during this period: a very deeply rooted social concept in France—consecrated not only by time and ideology, but also by the French educational system—and one founded on a deep nationalistic pride in the 'great works and great men' of the centuries-old French literary tradition. Literary canonization was (and continues to be) the result of a three-fold social process of initial triage, curricular institutionalization and publishing practices. First, literary critics are given the responsibility of identifying those works of 'merit' according to the litmus-test of *le Beau* and *le bon goût*: 'c'est le goût qui choisit…selon les règles immuables, identiques, également souveraines dans tous les arts'.[15] Then, professional educators and academics ratify such choices by allowing only those properly sanctioned literary texts into the French classroom (for pedagogical purposes of linguistic modelling and cultural training).[16] Finally, an important and often-overlooked accomplice in this canonization process, book publishers provide extended longevity to those selected texts, reprinting various editions of the same titles year after year for successive generations of teachers and students. This canonization loop, operating as it does between these mutually dependent entities, is a closed one and highly resistant to change. And, since Verne's particular genre belonged to no identifiable tradition within the French literary heritage, his *Voyages extraordinaires* could not pass beyond the first stage of this canonization process. Those same hierarchical standards long used by literary critics to discern 'high art' from 'low' and 'major works' from 'minor' were insufficient and inappropriate for judging such a radically new literary form. Thus, Verne's *romans scientifiques* were classified as 'secondary' literature or, even worse, 'paraliterary'. And once rejected from the loop, Verne's works were subsequently not taught in the schools, unabridged reprints of his works were not published on a regular basis, Verne was not cited in literary reference books, and the entirety of the *Voyages extraordinaires* continued to remain outside the 'official' French literary canon.

Second, as the notion of what truly constituted a *roman* was itself slowly evolving, the widespread belief still persisted in nineteenth-century France that its primary subject-matter should continue to be a psychological portrayal of human love. In the words of one critic:

> [Verne] n'est pas à proprement parler un romancier, car l'amour, base de tous les romans, brille par son absence dans la plupart de ses ouvrages. La femme y est presque toujours réléguée au second plan … ses héros n'ont pas de temps à perdre aux doux propos du petit dieu malin.[17]

From a twentieth-century perspective, of course, this convention seems rather quaint and ironic. And it seems even more so when viewed historically—i.e., when considering the difficulty that the *roman* (romance) had originally encountered in becoming an acceptable literary genre in the first place, precisely *because* of its subject-matter!

Third, there was the inevitable question of style. Echoing the pejorative comments of Zola, Charles Lemire paraphrases the reactions of most late nineteenth-century French *littérateurs* who condemned Verne's works as follows:

> Jules Verne? ...un conteur de contes de fées à prétentions pseudo-scientifiques! Un amuseur de collégiens! ...un tissu d'invrais-emblances sans psychologie et sans style! ...Littérairement, cela n'existe pas![18]

Verne himself was very sensitive to this prerequisite for literary respectability, and he laboriously reworked his compositions time and time again to improve their style. At one point, he confided in his publisher and friend Hetzel (who often acted as his sounding-board on such questions), saying:

> Ce que je voudrais devenir avant tout, c'est un écrivain, louable ambition que vous approuvez pleinement. Vous me dites des choses bien aimables et même flatteuses sur mon style qui s'améliore... Rien ne m'a donc fait plus de plaisir qu'une telle approbation venant de vous... Tout ceci, c'est pour vous dire combien je cherche à devenir un styliste, mais sérieux; c'est l'idée de toute ma vie.[19]

But Verne's efforts to conform his writing style to historical expectations were obviously doomed from the start: his very subject matter dictated a kind of style which had never before been attempted. In creating his *romans scientifiques* Verne was combining two very different sorts of discourse— scientific and literary—traditionally viewed as mutually exclusive. As Roland Barthes has observed:

> Il est bon ton aujourd'hui de contester l'opposition des sciences et des lettres... Mais du point de vue du langage...cette opposition est pertinente; ce qu'elle met en regard n'est d'ailleurs pas forcément le réel et la fantaisie, l'objectivité et la subjectivité, le Vrai et le Beau, mais...des lieux différents de parole... [L'écriture] vise le réel même du langage; elle reconnaît que le langage est un immense halo d'implications, d'effets, de retentissements, de tours, de retours, ... L'écriture fait du savoir une fête.[20]

But Verne's own stylistic 'fête du savoir'—his plays on words, anagrams, cryptograms and double-entendres, his complex juggling of narrative voice and point of view, his revolutionary creation of technological and scientific exoticism—this entire critical perspective on his *Voyages extraordinaires* was totally alien to and ignored by the critics of his time. From a typically nineteenth-century and purely quantitative frame of reference, Verne was labelled an author who simply did not have 'enough style'. And, considered with the other evidence described above, he was promptly and irrevocably classified as a writer of mere 'popular' fiction.

There are three other social reasons why Verne's works could not be recognized as canonical during the latter half of the nineteenth century: certain changes taking place within the French literary establishment itself, the continuing conflict between the Catholic Church and the forces of anti-clericalism, and the progressive rise of anti-scientism among the French public itself.

The first of these concerns the emergence of a new ideological mandate for writers of 'true' literature in France during this period: they were expected to write *in opposition to* their (presumably bourgeois) reading public. In reaction to the growing presence of what Sainte-Beuve had earlier castigated as *la littérature industrielle*[21] (i.e., mass-produced and inexpensive books churned out in ever-increasing quantities) as well as to the oppressive bourgeois social climate of the Second Empire, a new literary and artistic aesthetic took shape in the world of French letters around the middle of the century: *l'Art pour l'Art*. As Sartre described this unique development in his *Qu'est-ce que la littérature?*:

> A partir de 1848, en effet, et jusqu'à la guerre de 1914, l'unification radicale de son public amène l'auteur à écrire par principe *contre tous ses lecteurs*. Il vend pourtant ses productions, mais il méprise ceux qui les achètent, et s'efforce de décevoir leurs vœux; c'est chose entendue qu'il vaut mieux être méconnu que célèbre, que le succès, s'il va jamais à l'artiste de son vivant, s'explique par un malentendu. Et si d'aventure le livre qu'on publie ne heurte pas assez, on y ajoutera une préface pour insulter. Ce conflit fondamental entre l'écrivain et son public est un phénomène sans précédent dans l'histoire littéraire.[22]

All literary works viewed as having some 'useful' function to society in practical, moral or educational terms immediately became suspect. Any novel, short story, collection of poetry, or theatrical play that was believed to harbour any intentions toward public edification was dismissed by the intellectual élite as intrinsically non-literary. For them, true literature must focus, to the exclusion of all else, on a portrayal of *le Beau* and on the primacy of form over content. Judged according to these criteria, Verne's *Voyages extraordinaires*—overtly didactic and strongly referential—were obviously not 'true' literature.

Secondly, there is the question of *Voyages extraordinaires* and the Catholic Church. The intense religious debates in France during the second half of the nineteenth century are familiar to any who have studied the history of that time. One issue of violent contention was the question of public education: lay versus Catholic, science curricula versus 'letters' curricula, etc. Although Verne's publisher Hetzel made great efforts to maintain a neutral religious position in his publications, there was often no middle ground acceptable to both sides. For example, Hetzel's popular periodical *Magasin d'éducation et de récréation* (in which most of Verne's novels first appeared) was condemned in 1868 by the Catholic bishop Dupanloup. Monseigneur Dupanloup was recognized as one of the leading educational experts of the day, and he was a vigorous proponent of the superiority of Catholic parochial schools and their 'humanist' curricula which systematically excluded all science instruction. Hetzel's reaction to this condemnation, in an eight-page letter to Dupanloup, stands as a true testament to tongue-in-cheek editorial diplomacy:

> Monseigneur,
> J'ai lu avec une douloureuse surpise à la suite d'une lettre que vous avez publiée récemment une note relative au *Magasin d'éducation et de récréation* dont j'ai seul la direction. Je ne vois qu'un moyen de convaincre votre conscience qu'elle s'est méprise ou qu'on l'a abusée, c'est de mettre sous vos yeux l'ouvrage dont vous parlez et que vous réprouvez cette note. Je regrette extrêmement, Monseigneur, de ne pouvoir vous épargner de lire les huit volumes dont se compose le *Magasin* que vous avez condamné. Pour un enfant ce serait tout profit et tout plaisir peut-être. Pour Votre Grandeur, ce sera une pénitence. Si vous l'avez un peu méritée, vous me pardonnerez de désirer vous l'imposer.[23]

Verne himself, because of his immense popularity, was not immune to concern by religious authorities. Although his novels are teeming with references to *Dieu, la Providence* and *le Créateur*, they just as often cite *le hasard, le destin* and *la fatalité* as the hidden forces governing the actions of his heroes and villains. This particular narrative trait, while not meriting him a total condemnation by the Church, nevertheless earned him the following warning by the powerful Catholic journalist Louis Veuillot (in a letter addressed to Hetzel):

> Je n'ai pas encore lu les *Voyages extraordinaires* de M. Verne. Notre ami Aubineau me dit qu'ils sont charmants, sauf une absence...qui désembellit tout et qui laisse les merveilles du monde à l'état d'énigme. C'est beau mais c'est inanimé. Il manque quelqu'un...[24]

Needless to say, the *quelqu'un* referred to in this letter—the one who, according to Veuillot, seemed conspicuously absent from Verne's *Voyages extraordinaires*—was God and/or Jesus Christ.

Finally, another reason for Verne's rebuff seems to have been more sociological than literary or religious. Verne was one of the first novelists in France to attempt to bridge a deep cultural chasm that divided French society as a whole throughout the nineteenth century. On the one side were the progressive and energetic Positivists who, taking full advantage of the tools of the Industrial Revolution and a Guizot-type laissez-faire brand of governmental capitalism, were rapidly industrializing the French countryside in the name of Progress and Science. On the other were the partisans of anti-scientism and the practitioners of *l'Art pour l'Art* (both sometimes in uneasy coalition with the Catholic Church) who viewed this unrestricted technological growth as a direct threat to human values. This age-old struggle—as exemplified in the twentieth century, for example, by C. P. Snow's celebrated 'Two Cultures' debates[25] and by New Criticism's stinging denunciation of Science as 'the villain of history which has...made man the alienated, rootless, godless creature that he has become in this century'[26]—was particularly acute in France throughout the mid-to-late nineteenth and early twentieth centuries. From the works of respected writers like Michelet,[27] Vigny,[28] Flaubert[29] and the Goncourt brothers,[30] to the post-war Dada and Surrealists, French *littérateurs* continually attacked the positivistic precepts and false hopes of France's social engineers Auguste Comte, Ernest Renan, Hippolyte Taine and others. Note, for example, Brunetière's catchy slogan popularized during the 1890s where he speaks of the demonstrated 'faillite de la Science',[31] or Marcel Schwob's demand that all 'descriptions pseudo-scientifiques, l'étalage de psychologie de manuel et de biologie mal-digérée' be permanently banned from the French novel.[32] Despite the attraction that modern technology held for a few (initially) 'non-mainstream' writers like the poet Apollinaire and the satirist Alfred Jarry, such public sentiments of anti-scientism in France reached a zenith immediately after the cataclysm of World War I. And although dozens of French literary works and paintings from the 1920s might be cited as examples of this prevailing public attitude, it is perhaps fitting that the French novelist and caricaturist Albert Robida be singled out. As the well-known humoristic proselytizer of scientific progress and technological gadgetry during the 1880s and 1890s—in such popular novels as *Le Vingtième siècle* and *La Vie électrique*—Robida became in 1918 one of their most ferocious critics in his (appropriately titled) novel *L'Ingénieur von Satanas*:

> le débordement d'horreurs apportées par ce qu'on appelait Science et Progrès, Civilisation et autres fadaises écroulées, illusions noyées dans les fleuves de sang ...
>
> Où nous a-t-elle conduits cette Science haïssable? ... Oui, l'engin est tout, et la valeur de l'homme, son esclave, rien, ou presque rien...

Dans quel gouffre sanglant nous a-t-il précipités, ce fameux Progrès dont nous étions si fiers, quand nous nous rengorgions bouffis d'admiration pour nous-mêmes, ce Progrès qui a permis soudain la démolition rapide et complète, l'écroulement subit d'une civilisation illusoire, laquelle en réalité n'était qu'un dégénérescence, et une maladie mortelle?[33]

Consequently, amid such rapidly rising tides of anti-scientism in France during the late nineteenth and early twentieth centuries, it is hardly any wonder that Jules Verne's *romans scientifiques* might be viewed somewhat unfavourably in certain circles.

Thus, it appears to have been a convergence of many different factors which dictated that Jules Verne, despite the enormous popular success of his *Voyages extraordinaires*, was not recognized as an important literary figure in France during his lifetime. Of course, no simple answers can be given to such a complex question. In the preceding pages, I have discussed several different hypotheses to account for why I believe Jules Verne did not (or could not) become part of the late nineteenth-century French literature canon. But two facts are inescapable: Verne's works were indeed rebuffed by the French literary establishment of his time, and the author himself was painfully aware of this rejection. As Verne explained it to one of his American interviewers in 1894:

The great regret of my life is that I have never taken any place [sic] in French literature... A little more justice to me from my own countrymen would have been prized by me... That is what I regret and always shall regret... Dumas used to say to me when I complained that my place in French literature was not recognized: 'You should have been an American or an English author. Then your books, translated into French, would have gained you enormous popularity in France and you would have been considered by your countrymen as one of the greatest masters of fiction.' But, as it is, I am considered of no account in French literature.[34]

1905–1955

The evolution of Verne's literary reputation during the period of 1905 to 1955 in France is characterized by three developments: his public enshrinement as a popular cultural icon, a sharp decline in the publishing and sales of his *Voyages extraordinaires* themselves (particularly the original unabridged versions) and the beginnings of an underground 'Jules Verne cult' composed of youngsters seeking adventure, adults a sort of nostalgic escapism, and writers a new vision of the world. One modern Verne biographer has described this period as follows:

c'est la traversée du désert. Hetzel (fils), sans prévenir Michel [Verne], cède en 1914 ses droits exclusifs sur les *Voyages extraordinaires* aux editions Hachette, qui laissent épuiser la plupart de ses titres. Jules Verne est considéré comme un auteur pour enfants passé de mode. Les précieuses éditions polychromes 'au phare' se couvrent de poussière dans les greniers ou dorment dans les bibliothèques. Des temps en temps, un jeune garçon curieux grimpe en haut de la tour, se pique au fuseau, et alors c'est le grand réveil, parfois l'éblouissement, qui décide d'une vocation: celle des aviateurs Byrd, Wright, Bréquet; du chimiste Georges Claude, etc. Jules Verne, c'est aussi le mot de passe, la référence secrète des plus grands artistes de Tolstoi à Apollinaire, de Raymond Roussel à Michel Tournier.[35]

The enshrinement of Jules 'Verne the man' as a kind of French folk hero was propagated by two highly reverential biographies published soon after his death: Charles Lemire's *Jules Verne*[36] and Marguerite Allotte de la Fuÿe's supposedly authoritative *Jules Verne: sa vie, son œuvre*.[37] The former, a resident of Verne's adopted hometown of Amiens, spared no effort in eulogizing Verne's mythical life with almost venerational discussions of his personal habits, his family, his friends and his wide popularity—all continually punctuated with homages paid to the author by other writers and journalists from his time. But Lemire's well-meaning biography also tampered with established historical fact, 'touching up' Verne's public image for posterity. The following small but all too typical example shows the effects of such distortions: C. P. Cambiare's otherwise fine 1927 study of Edgar Allan Poe's influence in France contains the following statement:

> As Verne knew English very well, he did not need to have recourse to translations. Speaking of him, Charles Lemire writes: 'Ses livres de prédilection étaient Walter Scott, Fenimore Cooper, et Dickens qu'il lisait en leur langue et citait souvent...'[38]

In this passage, some twenty years after Lemire's biography originally appeared, one witnesses the inevitable aftermath of Lemire's myth-making. Henceforth, Jules Verne would be known as able to read English fluently—whereas, as the author himself had stated on several occasions (to his Anglo-American interviewers among others): 'Unhappily, I read only those works which have been translated into French... Owing to my unfortunate inability to read English, I am not so familiar as I would like to be with Mayne Read and Robert Louis Stevenson...'[39] And Lemire's biography was only the first to attempt to 'improve' on Verne's life with such laudatory fabrications—others would be much worse.

Such creative embellishments on Verne's life had no greater practitioner than Marguerite Allotte de la Fuÿe. As Verne's great-niece and one who had access to many previously unpublished documents kept within Verne's family, her 1928 biography was immediately hailed as the first 'authoritative' and 'canonical' biography on the legendary author of the *Voyages extraordinaires*. And her book retained this (unwarranted) distinction for generations of readers and researchers—yielding the limelight only in 1973 when Verne's grandson Jean Jules-Verne decided to set the record straight with an updated and more accurate biography of his grandfather.[40] While Allotte de la Fuÿe's text contained much documented material unknown to earlier readers and critics of Verne, it also sought to further idolize him in the public's mind by liberally 'embroidering' on the facts of Verne's life—to such an extent, in fact, that modern Vernian critics are still sorting out her truths, her half-truths, and her inventions.[41]

Ironically, while his enshrinement as a national legend was making a cultural hero of him, Verne's *Voyages extraordinaires* sank deeper and deeper into oblivion. Hetzel fils sold his rights to the novels to the large publishing house Hachette in 1914. And, to remedy a sluggish sales problem, Hachette decided to revamp Verne's most popular novels and launch their famous series called the 'Bibliothèque Verte': severely abridged and watered-down versions of Verne's original works, adapted specifically to young boys (a counterpart to their 'Bibliothèque Rose' series intended for young girls). Sales immediately picked up, the strategy was seen as an unqualified business success, and the two series continue today. As a direct result, educators and literary historians now discussed less often the question of Verne's appeal to adults versus children and more often the question of his appeal to young boys versus young girls. Consider, for example, the following observations by Marie-Thérèse Latzarus in her 1924 book on children's literature in France:

> Les petites filles aiment, sans doute, les romans de Jules Verne; pourtant elles les apprécient généralement moins que ne le font les petits garçons. Le plus souvent, elles lisent rapidement les pages dans lesquelles sont décrits les appareils. ... Elles sont plutôt attirées par le but poursuivi; les petits garçons, eux, s'intéressent en général à toutes les questions de mécanique...[42]

And while this and other studies[43] consecrated Jules Verne as a writer of fine children's stories, the French literary establishment gradually forgot about him altogether. Erudite literary critics persisted in panning his works (convinced, no doubt, of the wisdom of their *fin-de-siècle* predecessors), academics shunned any mention of his contribution to French literature, and publishers discontinued printing full-length versions of the *Voyages extraordinaires*. It is quite significant that the 1920s and 1930s are extremely meagre in Vernian criticism, with one important exception: the birth of the *Société Jules Verne* and its *Bulletin de la Société Jules Verne* (1935–8), founded by Jean Guermonprez. The *Société*—the first official 'club of learned amateurs' devoted to Jules Verne—published in its *Bulletin* many articles on Verne's life and works, excerpts from Verne's correspondence, various eye-witness testimonies, and accounts of his literary status in other countries. In so doing, the *Bulletin de la Société Jules Verne* kept alive the flame of Vernian scholarship during an otherwise very lean period. Its exhortations to 'Propagez la lecture des *Voyages extraordinaires*!' and 'Faites de la propagande en faveur de la *Société Jules Verne*!' must surely have had some modest effect, but its brief existence was unfortunately cut short by World War II. The *Bulletin* was not to reappear until some thirty years later in 1967.

Another important constituency within this growing 'Jules Verne cult' during the first half of the twentieth century was a number of young French writers who had been weaned on the *Voyages extraordinaires* during their formative years. Many went on to become celebrated *littérateurs* in France's most élite literary circles—authors like Jean Cocteau, Paul Claudel, François Mauriac, Blaise Cendrars, Raymond Roussel, Antoine Saint-Exupéry, Jean-Paul Sartre, Marcel Aymé, René Barjavel, Claude Roy, Michel Carrouges, Michel Butor and Roland Barthes among others.[44] And they ultimately paved the way for the sudden renaissance of public interest in Jules Verne and the scholarly (re)discovery of the *Voyages extraordinaires* in France during the 1960s and 1970s. Defying many decades of canonical repression and politico-literary correctness, they unabashedly proclaimed their admiration for Verne and his 'prodigieuse puissance de faire rêver'.[45] Raymond Roussel, for example, repeatedly sang the praises of Verne's 'genius' in his own fiction and personal correspondence, saying:

> Je voudrais aussi…rendre hommage à l'homme d'incommensurable génie que fut Jules Verne. Mon admiration pour lui est infinie. Dans certains pages de *Voyage au centre de la terre*, de *Cinq semaines en ballon*, de *Vingt mille lieues sous les mers*, de *De la Terre à la lune* et *Autour de la lune*, de *L'Ile mystérieuse*, et d'*Hector Servadac*, il s'est élevé aux plus hautes cimes que puisse atteindre le verbe humain…[46]

> Demandez-moi ma vie mais ne me demandez pas de vous prêter un Jules Verne! J'ai un tel fanatisme pour ses œuvres que j'en suis jaloux. … C'est Lui, et de beaucoup, le plus grand génie littéraire de tous les siècles; il 'restera' quand tous les autres auteurs de notre époque seront oubliés depuis longtemps.[47]

And, in Roussel's case at least, one astonishing fact emerges: Verne's influence on him was just as often stylistic as it was thematic. Roussel's constant borrowing from the *Voyages extraordinaires* (his 1926 *Etoile au front*, for example), his use of Verne-like cryptograms, enumerations, exotic and rare vocabulary, technicisms, and double-entendres (his 1913 *Locus Solus*) establish a palpable link between these two authors so seemingly distant from one another in French literary studies.

During the late 1940s and early 1950s, several new critical studies on Verne and his *romans scientifiques* appeared from within the very heart of the French literary community. The soon-to-be-famous author Michel Butor and the respected critic Michel Carrouges spearheaded this seminal avant-garde with two articles entitled 'Le Point suprême et l'âge d'or à travers quelques œuvres de Jules Verne'[48] and 'Le Mythe de Vulcain chez Jules Verne'[49] published in the 1949 edition of *Arts et Lettres*. In the former, Butor shrewdly and sensitively analyzes many of the leitmotifs in Verne's opus: primordial initiation rites and the human quest for rebirth, the use of symbols and cryptograms, the Earth's elements, the role of Providence, etc. In these recurring themes throughout the *Voyages extraordinaires* Butor finds many parallels to André Breton's hypothetical 'point suprême' described in the latter's *Seconde manifeste du Surréalisme*, to Henri Michaux's hallucinatory visions, to Lautréamont's oxymoronic juxtapositions, and to the haunting images of Henri Rousseau and Max Ernst. In the latter, Carrouges examines Verne's apparent obsession with volcanoes and eruptive islands—especially as they relate to humanity's age-old mythic battle with the forces of Nature, its descent into subterranean netherworlds, and its heroic rebirth. Whereas Butor integrates Verne solidly into the French literary heritage, Carrouges links Verne to the mythological origins of all Western literatures and concludes his richly suggestive psycho-historical study of these human archetypes thus:

> Chez Jules Verne, la mythologie anthropomorphique du type greco-latine antique est évacuée au profit d'exposés scientifiques, mais à travers ces descriptions positives, tous les éléments du vieux mythe vulcanien reparaissent rénoués, laïcisés, mais intacts. D'une façon générale, on peut dire que les grands romans d'aventure modernes représentent un mode profane de transposition des vieilles épopées sacrées.[50]

These ground-breaking analyses by Butor and Carrouges contributed to a growing impetus for a complete reappraisal of Jules Verne and his works in literary and academic circles throughout France. But yet another critical work (published the following year) provided further credentials to Verne's slowly growing stature in literary history: Jean-Jacques Bridenne's *La Littérature française d'imagination scientifique*.[51] Bridenne's detailed, historical survey served to define a scientifico-literary lineage for Verne

and his *Voyages extraordinaires*. It identified Verne as a literary descendant
of the *voyages imaginaires* of Lucian, Cyrano de Bergerac and Voltaire, as a
direct offspring of the scientific and mystery tales of Edgar Allan Poe, and
as a powerful precursor to the two twentieth-century genres of science
fiction and the detective novel in the works of authors like J.-H. Rosny
aîné, H. G. Wells, Albert Robida, Gaston Leroux, Conan Doyle *et al.*
Bridenne characterizes Verne as the first important writer of these types
of 'scientific' literature, and he castigates the 'pontiffs and snobs' of the
French literary establishment, saying:

> L'indifférence ou l'antipathie de pontifes et de snobs à l'égard de la
> littérature d'imagination scientifique a empêché le créateur de
> Phileas Fogg et du capitaine Nemo d'être un Wells avant la lettre, un
> répondant moderniste à Villiers de l'Isle-Adam, un Loti technicien.[52]

> Quelles que soient les réserves s'imposant et qui, en bonne justice,
> ne doivent pas être automatiquement portées à son débit, Jules
> Verne, premier romancier véritable de la Science, n'est pas plus
> méprisable littérairement que scientifiquement, il. s'en faut de
> beaucoup.[53]

And finally, in 1953 and 1955, the pathway toward more extensive
scholarship on Verne was permanently opened by several more influential
studies. Parménie and Bonnier de la Chapelle published the personal
correspondence of Verne's publisher P.-J. Hetzel,[54] casting an entirely new
light on the editorial environment in which Verne worked and clarifying
many previously unknown aspects of Verne's private life, stylistic concerns
and literary opinions. One of the first modern, scholarly, and non-
biographical books of literary criticism on Verne, *Voyage au monde de Jules
Verne* by René Escaich was published two years later and discussed Verne's
sources, his major themes, his fictional characters and his treatment of
history, nationalism and geography.[55] And, during the same year, two pre-
eminent French literary journals—*Livres de France*[56] and *Europe*[57]—made
the decision to dedicate an entire issue to Verne and his works, in
celebration of the fiftieth anniversary of the author's death. The former
included a variety of essays by recognized figures like Georges Duhamel,
Marguerite Allotte de la Fuÿe, Bernard Frank (who had earlier published
a rather undistinguished biography on Verne[58]) and Jean Guermonprez
of the *Société Jules Verne*, as well as excerpts from Verne's correspondence
and various homages to Verne by famous public figures (like the Emperor
William II of Germany, among others). *Europe* offered a considerably
more sophisticated selection of critical articles by Pierre Abraham,
Georges Fournier, Georges Sadoul and Pierre Sichel and covered
topics such as Verne's public versus private life, his political leanings, his

portrayal of Nature, the illustrators of the *Voyages extraordinaires*, modern cinematic adaptations of Verne's works and his status in countries like Hungary and Russia (where Verne had always been held in high 'literary' esteem).

In the wake of this sudden influx of scholarly and semi-scholarly publications into the French *belles lettres* marketplace, Verne and his *Voyages extraordinaires* began gradually to emerge from hallowed oblivion. And, as the 1960s and 1970s approached—years which were to witness a veritable explosion of renewed interest in Verne in all segments of French society—it was already evident that Jules Verne's reputation in his native land was undergoing a cultural metamorphosis that could be described as nothing short of extraordinary.

1955–1978

This sudden *prise de conscience* and reassessment of Jules Verne in the French literary canon during the 1960s and 1970s was undoubtedly the result of the convergence of a great many social and historical forces. Among them, one might include the following:

1. the acceleration of technological development in France during this period, and the accompanying—perhaps subliminal—need to revisit those fictional works that portrayed, in more simple terms, the relationship between human beings and machines.

2. the unprecedented achievements in space exploration and deep-sea research, recalling the best-known *topoi* of Verne's fictional universe, and suddenly bringing him back into the public's eye.

3. the progressively non-mimetic and self-conscious tendencies in modern French fiction, creating a kind of backlash revival of more highly referential forms of literature.

4. the increase in popularity of science fiction in the French marketplace, sparking an interest in this genre's historical antecedents.

5. certain developments in French literary criticism itself throughout this period which acted as the catalyst for a comprehensive reappraisal of Verne's *Voyages extraordinaires*.

With the advent of structuralist and semiotic literary analysis—along with the competing schools of Marxist socio-critical and Freudian psychoanalytical criticism—the very notion of what comprised 'literariness' and literary canons suddenly became the focal-point of intense scholarly attention. And Verne's *Voyages extraordinaires* proved to be a perfect testing-ground for the demonstration of such literary theories. As one critic has explained this unexpected (re)valorization of Verne's works:

> Cette œuvre offre en effet un remarquable terrain d'études pour les *techniques d'analyse des textes* les plus actuelles: lecture mythologique, psychanalytique, idéologique, politique, initiatique, épistémologique; analyse structurale du récit, du discours, voire 'analyse textuelle'. Par ailleurs, maints *contextes* s'y croisent: échos de la littérature générale, scientifique, politique de l'époque; domaines, complémentaires, de la littérature 'marginale'; littérature pour la jeunesse, récit d'aventures, d'anticipation ou de terreur, roman populaire; influences contemporaines...sur des écrivains aussi divers que Roussel ou Cendrars, Cocteau ou Saint-Exupéry, Butor ou Le Clézio.[59]

But the question is a bit more complex than it might appear at first glance. For example, the first stirrings of this renewed interest in Jules Verne and his *romans scientifiques* came neither from the universities nor from those more sophisticated literary scholars later to be associated with Vernian criticism. It came, rather, from the French public at large, from private groups of Verne enthusiasts, and from the French publishing industry itself. At the outset of this Jules Verne revival, one reviewer for *Le Figaro Littéraire*, for instance, made the following observation about Verne's burgeoning popularity: 'Il est lu, traduit, célébré comme les plus grands, mais sa position littéraire ne va pas s'améliorant.'[60] And another popular science-fiction writer and critic, while acknowledging the broad-based appeal which Verne's *Voyages extraordinaires* seemed to be enjoying, nevertheless complained of an almost total lack of 'serious' university study of Verne's texts:

> Plus surprenante encore est l'abstination de la critique et en particulier de la recherche universitaire. Les bons ouvrages sur Jules Verne sont rares et, à ma connaissance, aucune thèse de lettres ne lui a été consacrée. La Sorbonne le juge-t-elle trop scientifique? Ou bien trop populaire et, par là, trop suspect? Que faudra-t-il pour que nos savants professeurs découvrent enfin que la littérature n'est pas une collection d'œuvres arbitrairement, sinon capricieusement, définies mais ce qui se lit?[61]

But this critical 'time-lag' was relatively short-lived. The often stodgy French *universitaire* community eventually joined the French reading public in its renewed enthusiasm for Verne's *Voyages extraordinaires*, and by 1978 Verne was comfortably ensconced in the French university curriculum.

Let us take a closer look at the details of this Vernian renaissance in France during the 1960s and 1970s. It appears to have occurred in two successive waves, peaking in the years 1966 and 1978. The first crescendo seems to have been generated by two scholars in particular: Roland Barthes and Marcel Moré. Perhaps inspired by the 1955 quindecennial celebrations and the popular interest in Verne's works that resulted from it, Roland Barthes included in his 1957 collection of articles called *Mythologies* an insightful essay titled 'Nautilus et bateau ivre'.[62] This essay, when viewed in retrospect as part of the history of literary criticism, was profoundly prophetic:

> L'œuvre de Jules Verne (dont on a fêté récemment le cinquantenaire) serait un bon objet pour une critique de structure: c'est une œuvre à thèmes. Verne a construit une sorte de cosmogonie fermée sur elle-même, qui a ses catégories propres, son temps, son espace, sa plénitude, et même son principe existentiel.[63]

Although many years would pass before Barthes would return to Verne's oeuvre and actually sketch the outlines for just such a comprehensive structural analysis—in the scholarly journal *Poétique*[64]—and although even more years would pass before Verne would finally receive serious university study, Barthes was nevertheless among the very first to recognize Verne's *Voyages extraordinaires* as ideal narrative corpus for advanced literary exegesis. Marcel Moré's contribution to the re-examination of Verne's novels was even more provocative. He created an immediate public controversy with two psycho-thematic studies, his *Le Très Curieux Jules Verne*[65] in 1960 (referring to Mallarmé's 1874 cryptic comments on Verne) and, three years later, his *Nouvelles explorations de Jules Verne*.[66] Moré not only traced Verne's possible sources and influences in a totally unorthodox manner (e.g., Huysmans, Dostoievsky, Wagner, Nietszche *et al.*) but also convincingly analyzed many apparent obsessions present in the *Voyages extraordinaires*: the search for a father-figure (recalling Verne's 'curious' relationship with his own father and with his surrogate father Hetzel), the need for brotherly love (i.e., Verne's rapport with his brother Paul) and others. Moré's study was one of the first to apply Freudian psychoanalytic methods to Verne's life and works and, by slicing through many of the established myths surrounding Verne's patriarchal and grandfatherly image—even hinting at latent homosexual tendencies in this revered cultural icon—Moré's publications caused a small scandal in France.

The door for a more profound examination of Verne's life and works was now opened. As 1966 dawned, the literary journals *L'Arc*,[67] *Arts et Loisirs*[68] and *Nouvelles Littéraires*[69] devoted special issues to Jules Verne, featuring an astonishingly rich variety of essays by several well-known French writers and scholars: Michel Foucault, Michel Serres, Marcel Brion, J.-M.-G.- Le Clézio, Marcel Schneider, Marc Soriano, Georges Borgeaud, René Barjavel, Pierre Versius, Marcel Lecomte, Francis Lacassin, Pierre-André Touttain and even Michel Butor and Marcel Moré. Other critical works of 1966 include those by the Marxist critic Pierre Macherey who offered a materialist-sociological interpretation of Verne in his *Pour une théorie de la production littéraire*[70] and by Simone Vierne who dared to question the true authorship of several novels in Verne's *Voyages extraordinaires* in her 'Authenticité de quelques œuvres de Jules Verne'.[71] Further, in the 1966 publishing market, Livre de Poche decided to print (in unabridged format with original *gravure* illustrations) one million copies of Verne's ten most popular novels—a decision which dramatically increased the availability of Verne's original texts at reasonable cost. And the Swiss publisher Editions Rencontre took the unprecedented step of publishing (in unabridged hard-cover editions, with original illustrations, and with scholarly prefaces by Charles-Noël Martin and Gilbert Signaux) the *entire* series of Verne's *Voyages extraordinaires*—an accomplishment not equalled since the original Hetzel editions and the short-lived Hachette facsimiles of the 1920s. Suddenly Verne's entire opus, including his short stories and posthumous works, was fully accessible to all. And Parisian journalists of periodicals covering the literary scene like the *Quinzaine Littéraire*,[72] *Le Figaro Littéraire*[73] and *Lectures pour tous*[74] soon began to acknowledge a true 'Jules Verne revival'.

The impetus given to the study of Verne by the many events of 1966 continued to the end of the decade and into the next. As the republication of his *Voyages extraordinaires* continued unabated, the *Bulletin de la Société Jules Verne* was resuscitated in 1967 through the efforts of Joseph Laissus, Olivier Dumas and other 'amateur scholars'. The *Bulletin* immediately reprinted in toto their earlier pre-World War II issues and then continued their quarterly publication of articles and current-events information about Verne's life, works and international status. Of particular value were the efforts made to establish a comprehensive bibliography for Verne's many works.[75] The *Bulletin* rapidly became the leading continuing source for serious scholarship on Verne's *Voyages extraordinaires*; many years before the universities in France began to consider Verne as an appropriate author for advanced literary study, scholars like Jean Chesneaux, Daniel Compère, Piero Gondolo della Riva, Simone Vierne, Pierre Terrasse, François Raymond, Robert Taussat and others were already widening and deepening the scope of Vernian criticism. And work of the *Société Jules Verne* (and its international counterparts[76]) continues today. For example, adding to those archival and research possibilities offered by the Musée Jules

Verne, the Archives Jules Verne, and the Centre universitaires de recherches verniennes founded in 1965–7 by the city of Nantes (Verne's birthplace), the *Société* also established a Centre de documentation Jules Verne in the author's adopted city of Amiens. Housed in Verne's former residence, the Centre contains an impressive collection of over six thousand items relating to Verne and his works, all indexed and cross-referenced.

The final years of the 1960s and early 1970s continued this now-ineluctable trend toward Jules Verne's popular rehabilitation and eventual literary canonization. For example, an early harbinger of things to come, Jules Verne and his *Voyages extraordinaires* were cited for the first time in 1967 and 1971 in two academic anthologies of French literary history: Paul Guth's *Histoire de la littérature française*,[77] and the authoritative sixteen-volume Arthaud series entitled *Littérature française*.[78] Following a successful 1965–6 exposition in Nantes celebrating the centennial of Verne's prophetic *De la Terre à la lune* , Paris's Ecole Technique Supérieure also held in 1967 an elaborate exposition called 'Jules Verne et le courant scientifique de son temps'. The Apollo moon flight in 1969 and Neil Armstrong's comments in Paris years later[79] further served to heighten international interest in Verne as a technological visionary. French university scholars and various 'learned amateurs' found their book-length studies on Verne immediately accepted for publication: Ghislain de Diesbach's *Le Tour de Jules Verne en quatre-vingts livres* (1969),[80] Jean Chesneaux's very influential *Une Lecture politique de Jules Verne* (1971),[81] Marie-Hélène Huet's *L'Histoire des* Voyages extraordinaires (1973),[82] Simone Vierne's myth-oriented *Jules Verne et le roman initiatique* (1973),[83] the long-awaited 'authoritative' biography on the author by Jean Jules-Verne entitled simply *Jules Verne* (1973),[84] and finally Michel Serres' highly structuralist *Jouvences sur Jules Verne* (1974).[85] And French radio and television, as well as the French film industry, began further to popularize this unusual cultural phenomenon by broadcasting literary discussions on Verne's works, televising dramatizations of some of his *Voyages extraordinaires*, and producing full-length films of several of his novels.[86]

It was toward the end of the 1970s in France, during the heyday of the French Structuralist movement in literary criticism, that Jules Verne definitively shed his 'paraliterary' image within the French *Academe* and intellectual élite. For example, the prestigious *Revue des Lettres Modernes* in 1976 began to publish, under the direction of François Raymond, an on-going series called *Jules Verne*.[87] This series was to become the scholarly forum for serious university-level critical analyses of Verne's texts from a wide variety of methodological perspectives and academic disciplines. In another valuable support-structure for advanced Vernian research (and sponsored by the *Société Jules Verne*), Piero Gondolo della Riva published in 1977 a detailed *Bibliographie analytique de toutes les œuvres de Jules Verne*,[88] the most authoritative listing to date of all Verne's primary texts, providing Vernian researchers with top-notch reference material for studying this very prolific author. But it was during the year 1978—in celebration of the 150th anniversary of Verne's birth—that this increasing academic study of Jules Verne was consummated by two important events: his novel *Voyage au centre de la terre* was placed on the Agrégation reading-list within the French university system (precipitating a rush of undergraduate and graduate theses on this and other novels of the *Voyages extraordinaires*), and, that same year, Jules Verne was chosen as the topic for one of several academic colloquia held at Cérisy-la-Salle.[89] These two symbolic gestures seemed to do more for the acceptance of Jules Verne within the French university literary establishment than all the previous studies of Verne's works published throughout the prior two decades combined. As expected, an explosion of Vernian criticism accompanied these two events: Christian Robin's *Un Monde connu et inconnu*,[90] Marc Soriano's psychoanalytical *Jules Verne*,[91] Charles-Noël Martin's excellent *La Vie et l'œuvre de Jules Verne*[92] and Jean-Michel Margot's computer-assisted listing of all secondary materials on Verne titled *Bibliographie documentaire sur Jules Verne*,[93] to name but a few. Three international colloquia in Amiens were sponsored by the Université de Picardie in 1975, 1978 and later in 1985, and the texts of those scholars presenting papers there appeared in *Nouvelles recherches sur Jules Verne et le voyage*,[94] *Jules Verne: filiations, rencontres, influences*[95] and *Modernités de Jules Verne*.[96] Literary journals once again devoted special issues to Verne: one of the more important was (again) *Europe*, which offered a rich collection of previously unpublished essays by Verne experts like Marc Soriano, Daniel Compère, François Rivière, Philippe Mustière, Alain Buisine, Francis Lacassin, Christian Robin and François Raymond. The French publishing industry itself joined this anniversary salute to Jules Verne: Hachette announced its intention to publish (for the first time since the Rencontre editions of 1966) a complete and unabridged series of Verne's *Voyages extraordinaires*, and the publishing house of Michel de l'Ormeraie made a similar announcement for the creation of a deluxe facsimile edition of Hetzel's original red-and-gold versions of Verne's novels. And two years later, within the French university system, a development of great significance took place: the completion of the first *Doctorat d'Etat* dissertation on Jules Verne,[97] the capstone of academic respectability.

Thus, three quarters of a century after his death, Jules Verne finally gained the literary recognition denied him during his own lifetime. Although perhaps not (yet) viewed as being of the literary stature of a Baudelaire or a Zola, his place in the history of French literature was nevertheless secured. His *Voyages extraordinaires* were finally recognized as an important literary monument, and he was now an 'official' part of the French literary canon.

Addendum

Verne's literary canonization in France during this period had important repercussions on international Vernian scholarship. Prior to the 1970s and 1980s, English-language studies on Verne were based (for the most part) on hackneyed and severely bowdlerized translations from the French; it is only recently that accurate English-language translations have begun to appear in the Anglo-American marketplace.[98] As a result, the many myths attributed to Verne—which had become, over time, deeply embedded in the American and British public's consciousness by virtue of Hollywood cinema, Disneyland and the popularity of science fiction—continued to cling tenaciously to his literary reputation. One American bibliographer, for example, characterized the state of pre-1980 Anglophone scholarship on Verne as follows:

> In English language criticism to date, for instance, the same basic four notions seem to be repeated over and over.
>
> First, Verne is thought of as a writer of adventure novels for children. Unlike *Gulliver's Travels*, 'Rip Van Winkle', or *Frankenstein*, however, Verne's works do not repay rereading as an adult...
>
> Second, Verne is thought of as unreservedly pro-science and pro-technology... In a world which has found more relevance in the dystopian vision, Verne simply seems old-fashioned.
>
> Third, much English language criticism of Verne contrasts him with the great science fiction writer who preceded him, Edgar Allan Poe, and with the one who followed him, H. G. Wells ... Verne took from Poe the nuts-and-bolts, realistic, plausible dimension that has earned him such titles as 'the poet of hardware' and 'the Father of Hard Science Fiction', but this quality too has seemed less appealing to modern readers than Wells' 'soft' social science fiction. While Verne was writing 'Facts Every Boy Should Know' and mechanically writing thrillers to the end of his life, Wells has a sense of social injustice and thus performed a social mission...
>
> Fourth, Verne, who said 'What one man can imagine, another man will someday be able to achieve', has been thought of as a prophet whose careful, scientific presentations have caused imagination to become reality by inspiring others to great scientific achievements ... True as these statements are, prophetic skill is not

a good literary criterion, and Verne's literary currency has faded as the science and technology he foresaw has advanced.

Thus, English language criticism has not passed beyond the sterile and superficial level. There are few provocative overviews, few close analyses of individual works, and the pessimistic dimension to his works are virtually unknown ...the main insights of English language criticism are relatively undeveloped and scattered in diverse places.[99]

But during the mid to late 1980s, partly due to this renaissance of French interest in Verne during the previous two decades, his literary reputation suddenly began to improve in Great Britain and America as several university scholars completed their PhDs on his *Voyages extraordinaires*: Andrew Martin at Cambridge in 1982, William Butcher at Queen Mary College in 1985 and myself at Columbia University also in 1985. All these doctoral dissertations on Verne were subsequently published as books[100] and constituted the first serious English-language scholarship on Verne in several decades, paving the way for more advanced study of this French author in the United States and England.

As we now enter the new millennium, the flow of both French- and English-language Vernian criticism has not diminished. The discovery and publication by Hachette in 1994 of Verne's 'lost novel' *Paris au XXe siècle* (translated and published in English by Random House in 1996 as *Paris in the Twentieth Century*) drew unparalleled worldwide attention to Verne and to his often-misunderstood literary legacy. In France, the efforts of scholars like Simone Vierne,[101] Olivier Dumas,[102] Daniel Compère,[103] the late François Raymond,[104] Piero Gondolo della Riva,[105] Jean-Paul DeKiss,[106] Michel Lamy,[107] Christian Robin,[108] and those participating in the Colloque d'Amiens[109] have provided sophisticated bibliographical, biographical and analytical commentary on Verne and his works. For Anglo-Americans, the 1990s have witnessed the birth of the North American Jules Verne Society (1993–4, Arthur Edwards, president) as well as a flood of new English-language studies and reference texts on Verne including those by Lawrence Lynch,[110] Peggy Tweeters,[111] myself and Robin Miller,[112] and, perhaps more significantly, those by Brian Taves and Steve Michaluk[113] and Herbert R. Lottman,[114] whose encyclopedia and biography (respectively) of Verne are important watersheds in English-language Vernian scholarship. Finally, for both Francophone and Anglophone aficionados of Verne of the late 1990s, the Internet and cyberspace[115] has rapidly become an important public site for all things Vernian—a particularly appropriate tribute to an author whose *romans scientifiques* sought to popularize through fiction both the wonders and the dangers of modern technology.

Notes

1 L. M., 'Bibliographie', *Revue des Deux Mondes* 43 (1863), 769.

2 Letter to P.-J. Hetzel. Reprinted in P.-A. Touttain, 'Verniana', *Cahiers de l'Herne* 25 (1974), 343.

3 Théophile Gautier, 'Les voyages imaginaires de M. Jules Verne', *Moniteur Universel* 197 (16 juillet 1866). Reprinted in P.-A. Touttain (ed.), *Cahiers de l'Herne* 25 (1974), 85–7.

4 Vivien de Saint-Martin, 'Histoire du capitaine Hatteras', *Année Géographique* (1864), 270.

6 Ibid., p. 382.

7 Ibid., pp. 395–6.

8 Adolphe Brisson, *Portraits intimes* (Paris, Armand Colin, 1899), pp. 111–20.

9 Georges Bastard, 'Célébrités contemporaines: Jules Verne en 1883', *Gazette illustré* (8 septembre 1883). Reprinted in P.-A. Touttain (ed.), *Cahiers de l'Herne* 25 (1974), 88–92.

10 Jules Clarétie, *Jules Verne*. Paris, A. Quantin, 1883.

11 Emile Zola, 'Adolphe d'Ennery', in *Œuvres complètes* (Paris, François Bernouard, n.d.), p. 271.

12 Emile Zola, 'Jules Verne in *Le Figaro litteraire* (Dec. 22, 1878), Rpt. in his *Romanciers Naturalistes* (Paris, 1881), pp. 356–7.

13 Letter reprinted in Charles-Noël Martin, *La Vie et l'œuvre de Jules Verne* (Paris, Michel de l'Ormeraie, 1978), p. 221.

14 Letter reprinted in ibid., p. 222.

15 Topin (384).

16 For an interesting analysis of the ideological dynamics of how language and literature is taught in the French public schools, see France Vernier, *L'Ecriture et les textes* (Paris, Editions Sociales, 1974) and Renée Balibar, *Les Français Fictifs* (Paris, Hachette, 1974).

17 Charles Raymond, 'Jules Verne', *Musée des Familles* 42 (1875). Reprinted in Jean Jules-Verne, *Jules Verne* (Paris, Hachette, 1973), p. 329.

18 Charles Lemire, *Jules Verne* (Paris, Berger-Levrault, 1908), p. 107.

19 Letter to P.-J. Hetzel. Reprinted in Martin, *La Vie et l'œuvre*, pp. 138–9.

20 Roland Barthes, *Leçon* (Paris, Seuil, 1978), p. 20.

21 C.-A. Sainte-Beuve, 'De la littérature industrielle', *La Revue des Deux Mondes* (1 septembre 1839), 675–91.

22 Jean-Paul Sartre, *Qu'est-ce que la littérature?* (Paris, Gallimard, 1978), p. 148.

23 Letter reprinted in Parménie and Bonnier de la Chapelle, *Histoire d'un éditeur et de ses auteurs, P.-J Hetzel* (Paris, Albin Michel, 1953), p. 491.

24 Letter reprinted by Ghislain de Diesbach in *Jules Verne: Le Tour du monde en 80 livres* (Paris, Julliard, 1969), p. 199.

25 C. P. Snow, *The Two Cultures and the Scientific Revolution* (Cambridge University Press, 1960).

26 As quoted in René Welleck 'The New Criticism: Pro and Contra', *Critical Inquiry* 4:4 (1978), 619.

27 Michelet, for example, railed against the heartlessness of science proclaiming: 'Science barbare, dur orgeuil, qui ravale si bas la nature animée, et sépare tellement l'homme de ses frères inférieurs!' Jules Michelet, *Le Peuple* (Paris, Didier, 1946), p. 80.

28 Alfred de Vigny, in his poem 'La Maison du berger' (1844), nostalgically evoked the loss of spontaneity and of the unknown which science had seemed to banish from everyday life:

> La distance et le temps sont vaincus. La science
> Trace autour de la terre un chemin triste et droit.
> Le Monde est rétréci par notre expérience
> Et l'équateur n'est plus qu'un anneau trop étroit.
> Plus de hasard. Chacun glissera sur sa ligne,
> Immobile au seul rang que le départ assigne,
> Plongé dans un calcul silencieux et froid.

Alfred de Vigny, 'La Maison du berger' in *Poèmes antiques et modernes* (Paris, Ernest Flammarion, n.d.), p. 273.

29. See Gustave Flaubert's stinging satire of science in *Bouvard et Pécuchet*, where he parodied Positivism by portraying two comically inept office clerks who, in blind veneration of Science, attempt to assimilate and apply the entirety of human knowledge by systematically putting into practice their readings of the scientific books of their day—with invariably catastrophic results.

30 The Goncourt brothers, well-known partisans of *l'Art pour l'Art*, greeted with tongue-in-cheek praise (and unknowing foresight) the scientific tales of Edgar Allan Poe, saying: 'Quelque chose que la critique n'a pas vu, un monde littéraire nouveau, les signes de la littérature du XXeme siècle. Le miraculeux scientifique, la fable par A plus B... Plus de poésie; de l'imagination à coup d'analyse: Zadig juge d'instruction, Cyrano de Bergerac élève d'Arago. Quelque chose de monomaniaque. Les choses ayant plus de rôle que les hommes, l'amour cédant la place aux déductions...la base du roman déplacée et transportée du cœur à la tête et de la passion à l'idée, du drame à la solution.' Edmond and Jules Goncourt, *Journal*, I (Paris, Flammarion, n.d.), p. 108.

31 Ferdinand Brunetière, 'La Renaissance de l'idéalisme', in *Discours de Combat* (Paris, Perrin, 1914), p. 16.

32 Marcel Schwob, 'Préface' to *Cœur Double* in *Œuvres complètes*, II (Paris, Bernouard, 1928), p. x.

33 Alfred Robida, *L'Ingénieur von Satanas* (Paris, Renaissance du Livre, 1919), p. 270.

34 R. H. Sherard, 'Jules Verne at Home', *McClure's Magazine* 2:2 (January 1894), 115–21.

35 Marc Soriano, *Jules Verne* (Paris, Julliard, 1978), p. 323.

36 Charles Lemire, *Jules Verne* (Paris, Berger-Levrault, 1908).

37 Marguerite Allotte de la Fuÿe, *Jules Verne: sa vie, son œuvre* (Paris, Simon Kra, 1928; repr. Paris, Hachette, 1966).

38 C. P. Cambiare, *The Influence of Edgar Allan Poe in France* (New York, NY, Stechert, 1927; repr. New York, NY, Haskell, 1970), p. 242.

39 Marie A. Belloc, 'Jules Verne at Home', *Strand Magazine* (February 1895), 208.

40 Jean Jules-Verne, *Jules Verne* (Paris, Hachette, 1973).

41 See, for example, Olivier Dumas, 'Quand Marguerite se contredit', *Bulletin de la Société Jules Verne* 64 (1982), 312.

42 Marie-Thérèse Latzarus, *La Littérature enfantine en France dans la seconde moitié du XIXeme siècle* (Paris, PUF, 1924), pp. 227–8.

43 See M. Lahy-Hellebec, *Les Charmeurs d'enfants* (Paris, Baudinère, n.d.).

44 See 'Verniana' in P.-A. Touttain (ed.), *Jules Verne : Cahiers de l'Herne* 25 (1974), 343–7.

45 Ibid., 346.

46 Raymond Roussel, *Comment j'ai écrit certains de mes livres* (Paris, Pauvert, 1963), p. 26.

47 Letter from Roussel to Eugène Leiris. Reprinted in *Arts et Lettres* 15 (1949), 100–1.

48 Michel Butor, 'Le point suprême et l'âge d'or à travers quelques œuvres de Jules Verne', *Arts et Lettres* 15 (1949), 3–31. Reprinted in his *Répertoire* (Paris, Minuit, 1960), 130–62.

49 Michel Carrouges, 'Le Mythe de Vulcain chez Jules Verne', *Arts et Lettres* 15 (1949), 32–58.

50 Ibid., 53–4.

51 Jean-Jacques Bridenne, *La Littérature française d'imagination scientifique* (Lausanne, Dassonville, 1950).

52 Ibid., p. 135.

53 Ibid., p. 138.

54 A. Parménie and C. Bonnier de la Chapelle, *L'Histoire d'un éditeur et ses auteurs, P.-J. Hetzel* (Paris, Albin Michel, 1953).

55 René Escaich, *Voyage au monde de Jules Verne* (Paris, Ed. Plantin, 1955). This book was first published four years earlier in Belgium under the title *Voyage à travers le monde vernien* (Brussels, Ed. 'La Boétie', 1951).

56 *Livres de France* 5 (1955), 3–16.

57 *Europe* 33: 112–13 (avril–mai, 1955), 3–125.

58 Bernard Frank, *Jules Verne et ses voyages* (Paris, Flammarion, 1941).

59 François Raymond, 'Pour une espace de l'exploration', in *Jules Verne I: Le Tour du monde* (Paris, Minard, 1976), p. 1.

60 Robert Kanters, 'Situation de Jules Verne', *Le Figaro littéraire* (21 avril 1966), 5.

61 Gérard Klein, 'Pour lire Verne', *Fiction* 197 (1970), 137.

62 Roland Barthes, 'Nautilus et bateau ivre', *Mythologies* (Paris, Seuil, 1957), pp. 80–92.

63 Ibid., p. 80.

64 Roland Barthes, 'Par où commencer?', *Poétique* (1970), 3–9.

65 Marcel Moré, *Le Très Curieux Jules Verne* (Paris, Gallimard, 1960).

66 Marcel Moré, *Nouvelles explorations de Jules Verne* (Paris, Gallimard, 1963).

67 *L'Arc* 29 (1966).

68 *Arts et Loisirs* 27 (1966).

69 *Nouvelles littéraires* 44 (24 mars 1966).

70 Pierre Macherey, 'Jules Verne ou le récit en défaut', in *Pour une théorie de la production littéraire* (Paris, Maspero, 1966), pp. 159–240.

71 Simone Vierne, 'Authenticité de quelques œuvres de Jules Verne', *Annales de Bretagne* 73 (1966), 445–58.

72 Bernard Gheerbrant, 'Jules Verne ressuscité', *La Quinzaine littéraire* (21 avril 1966), 16–17.

73 Kanters, 'Situation de Jules Verne', 16–17.

74 Charles Guider, 'Jules Verne, plus jeune que jamais', *Lectures pour tous* 150 (1966), 16–17.

75 Olivier Dumas *et al.*, 'Bibliographie des œuvres de Jules Verne', *Bulletin*

de la Société Jules Verne(*BSJV*) NS 1 (1967), 7–12; NS 2 (1967), 11–15; NS 3 (1967), 13; NS 4 (1967), 15–16.

76 It is worth noting, for example, the new *North American Jules Verne Society* which was recently founded in the autumn of 1993–4 through the efforts of non-university North American Verne enthusiasts like Arthur Edwards of Quincy, Massachusetts, USA, Betty Harless of Indianapolis, Indiana, USA and Andrew Nash of Toronto, Ontario, Canada.

77 Paul Guth, *Histoire de la littérature française*, II (Paris, Fayard, 1967), p. 538.

78 *Littérature française* (Paris, Arthaud, 1971).

79 'Lorsque j'ai posé le pied sur la Lune et que j'ai vu la Terre flottant comme un ballon bleu dans le ciel obscur, j'ai tout de suite pensé à Jules Verne...' Reprinted in Igor and Grichka Bogdanoff, *L'Effet science-fiction* (Paris, Laffont, 1979), pp. 66–8.

80 Ghislain de Diesbach, *Le Tour de Jules Verne en quatre-vingts livres* (Paris, Julliard, 1969).

81 Jean Chesneaux, *Une Lecture politique de Jules Verne* (Paris, Maspero, 1971).

82 Marie-Hélène Huet, *L'Histoire des* Voyages extraordinaires (Paris, Minard, 1973).

83 Simone Vierne, *Jules Verne et le roman initiatique* (Paris, Ed. Sirac, 1973).

84 Jean Jules-Verne, *Jules Verne* (Paris, Hachette, 1973). Translated by Roger Greaves as *Jules Verne: A Biography* (New York, NY, Taplinger, 1976).

85 Michel Serres, *Jouvences sur Jules Verne* (Paris, Minuit, 1974).

86 See, for example, Daniel Compère's articles 'Jules Verne à la radio et à la télévision' in *BSJV* 31–2 (1974), 189–90; *BSJV* 33–4 (1975), 48; *BSJV* 35–6 (1975), 95–6; *BSJV* 39–40 (1976), 190; and *BSJV* 41 (1976), 32. See also his 'Filmographie des œuvres de Jules Verne' in *BSJV* 12 (1969), 82–4; *BSJV* 16 (1970), 137, and *BSJV* 21 (1972), 123.

87 François Raymond (ed.), *Jules Verne I: Le Tour du monde* (Paris, Minard, 1976).

88 Piero Gondolo della Riva, *Bibliographie analytique de toutes les œuvres de Jules Verne* (Paris, Société Jules Verne, 1977).

89 See *Jules Verne et les sciences humaines*. Centre culturel international de Cérisy-la-Salle (Paris, UGE, '10/18', 1979).

90 Christian Robin, *Un Monde connu et inconnu* (Nantes, Centre universitaire de recherches verniennes, 1978).

91 Marc Soriano, *Jules Verne* (Paris, Julliard, 1978).

92 Charles-Noël Martin, *La Vie et l'œuvre de Jules Verne* (Paris, Michel de l'Ormeraie, 1978).

93 Jean-Michel Margot, *Bibliographie documentaire sur Jules Verne* (Ostermundigen (Suisse), Margot, 1978).

94 *Nouvelles recherches sur Jules Verne et le voyage*, Colloque d'Amiens I (Paris, Minard, 1978).

95 *Jules Verne: Filiations, rencontres, influences*, Colloque d'Amiens II (Paris, Minard, 1980).

96 *Modernités de Jules Verne*, Colloque d'Amiens III (Paris, PUF, 1988).

97 Jean Delabroy, 'Jules Verne et l'imaginaire' (Université de Paris III (Sorbonne), 1980); and Charles-Noël Martin, 'Recherches sur la nature, les origines, et le traitement de la science dans l'œuvre de Jules Verne' (Université

de Paris VII (Jussieu), 1980).

98 See, for example, Walter James Miller's pioneering efforts in his *The Annotated Jules Verne: Twenty Thousand Leagues under the Sea* (New York, NY, Crowell, 1976) and his *The Annotated Jules Verne: From the Earth to the Moon* (New York, NY, Crowell, 1978), Sidney Kravitz's excellent but as yet unpublished translation of *Mysterious Island* (1986), Emanuel K. Mickel's *The Complete Twenty Thousand Leagues under the Sea* (Bloomington, Indiana University Press, 1992) or William Butcher's superb translations of *Journey to the Centre of the Earth* (London, (Oxford University Press, 1992) and of *Around the World in Eighty Days* (London, Oxford University Press, 1995).

99 Edward J. Gallagher *et al.* (eds), *Jules Verne: A Primary and Secondary Bibliography* (Boston, G. K. Hall, 1980).

100 See Arthur B. Evans, *Jules Verne Rediscovered* (Westport, CT, Greenwood Press, 1988), Andrew Martin, *The Mask of the Prophet* (London, Oxford University Press/Clarendon Press, 1990), and William Butcher, *Jules Verne's Journey to the Centre of the Self* (London, Macmillan, 1990).

101 Simone Vierne, *Jules Verne* (Paris, Balland, 1986) and *Jules Verne, mythe et modernité* (Paris, PUF, 1989).

102 Olivier Dumas, *Jules Verne* (Lyon, La Manufacture, 1988). Dr Dumas is also the very active president of the Société Jules Verne in France and the editor-in-chief of the very authoritative *Bulletin de Société Jules Verne*.

103 Daniel Compère, *Jules Verne écrivain* (Geneva, Droz, 1991) and *Jules Verne: parcours d'une œuvre* (Amiens, Encrage, 1996).

104 François Raymond (ed.), *Série Jules Verne* (Paris, Minard, Lettres Modernes, 1976–93).

105 Piero Gondolo della Riva, *Bibliothèque de toutes les œuvres de Jules Verne, 2e ed.* (Paris, Société Jules Verne, 1985).

106 Jean-Paul DeKiss, *Jules Verne: le rêve du progrès* (Paris, Gallimard, 1991).

107 Michel Lamy, *Jules Verne, initié et initiateur* (Paris, Payot, 1994).

108 *Cahiers du Musée Jules Verne* (Nantes, Amis de la Bibliothèque, 1981–93).

109 The papers given at this important Verne conference are now published in a new collection entitled *Revue Jules Verne*, Revue du Centre de Documentation Jules Verne d'Amiens (1, nouvelle série: 1er semestre 1996).

110 Lawrence Lynch, *Jules Verne* (New York, NY, Twayne, 1992).

111 Peggy Tweeters, *Jules Verne: The Man Who Invented Tomorrow* (New York, NY, Walter & Co., 1992).

112 Arthur B. Evans and Ron Miller, 'Jules Verne: Misunderstood Visionary', *Scientific American* (April 1997), 92–7. See also my recent articles 'The "New" Jules Verne', *Science-Fiction Studies*, vol. 22, 65 (1995), 35–46, 'Literary Intertexts in Jules Verne's *Voyages extraordinaires*', *Science-Fiction Studies*, vol. 23, 69 (1996), 171–87, and 'The Illustrators of Jules Verne's *Voyages extraordinaires*', *Science Fiction Studies* vol. 25 (July 1998), 241–71.

113 Brian Taves and Steve Michaluk, Jr., *The Jules Verne Encyclopedia* (Lanham, MD, Scarecrow, 1996).

114 Herbert R. Lottman, *Jules Verne: An Exploratory Biography* (New York, NY, St Martin's, 1996), translated and published in French as *Jules Verne* (Paris, Flammarion, 1996).

115 The most important of these Internet sites is the one by Zvi Har'El at http://www.math.technion.ac.il/~rl/Jules Verne.

3

Jules Verne and the Limitations of Literature

DANIEL COMPERE

Jules Verne appeared on the French literary scene in 1863, with his first novel *Cinq semaines en ballon*. In the middle of the nineteenth century he both witnessed and participated in, the evolution of literature, due in particular to the increasing number of readers and changes in publishing techniques. New genres were born, such as serialized novels, detective stories, and futuristic novels. Verne was to try to impose one of his own, the 'scientific romance'[1] as he called it, 'for the want of a better name'.

The 1867 edition of *Voyages et aventures du capitaine Hatteras* begins with an 'Editor's Note', stipulating the guidelines that Verne was to follow:

> What is more, Jules Verne's novels have reached their pinnacle. Seeing an eager public rushing to conferences organized all over France, and seeing that alongside art and theatre critics, we have had to make room in our newspapers for the reports of the *Académie des Sciences*, it has to be said that *art for art's sake* is no longer relevant in our day and age; the time has come for science to take its rightful place in literature...
>
> Verne's new works will be successively added to this edition which will always be updated with the utmost care. In this way, the works already published, and those to be published, will represent the intentions of the author who has subtitled this work *Voyages dans les mondes connus et inconnus*. His aim is, in fact, to bring together all the *geographical*, *geological*, *physical* and *astronomical* elements known to modern science, and to retell, in his own attractive and picturesque form, the history of the universe.

Two slightly conflicting points of view emerge from this preface written by Verne, and revised by the publisher. One undeniably corresponds with Hetzel's intentions: 'to bring together all the ... elements known to modern science'. The emphasis is placed on education, but in an 'attractive and picturesque form'. The second point of view is that of Verne himself, and shares the ideas of Flaubert, Zola and Hugo on the subject of literature being exposed to its period, thus in contrast with *romantic* theories: 'for science to take its rightful place in literature'. On several occasions, Verne defended this idea, as in 1875 for example, before the Académie d'Amiens ('Literature has widened its scope, and science and art are nowadays becoming part of it'[2]), and again, in an interview which he gave to an American journalist at the end of the nineteenth century: 'People always used to say that politics and science do not belong to the realm of art. It seems to me that there is nothing more fit for the imagination of a poet than science; and as for politics, it surely could be done.'[3]

It is interesting to see how this *widening* of literature is accomplished through the insertion of science. I shall not discuss the different processes used by Verne to make scientific writing merge into his novelistic works. These range from quotations retaining the original voice, to allusions which exclude it from the field of speech.[4] In this study, I am interested in general by what indicates this opening up of a literary text into a non-literary one, and in particular its opening up to science.

Narrative Technique

Since the text that we are dealing with is novelistic, it will be opened up to science if it is given a narrative role. The facts are inserted during the narrative, as certain episodes occur. In this way, things that might seem tedious are slipped into the action and the readers do not notice as they pass from reality to fiction. Verne, for example, likes to introduce everyday physical events into exceptional situations. In *Une ville flottante*, a storm breaks out while characters are engaged in a duel. The traitor's sword acts as a conductor, and he is electrocuted. Mathias Sandorf and his companions, whilst trapped in the Pisino fortress, discover who denounced them, thanks to an acoustic peculiarity. Verne often introduced what he called 'an extraordinary, but perfectly explicable phenomenon' (*Mathias Sandorf*).

Here we can see a marked difference from the popularization that sometimes portrays science as fiction, or stories. Verne goes one step further and removes all limits between the real and the imaginary. I believe that there is no need to dwell on this point, since it is not particularly specific to Verne's writing.

Verisimilitude

As in all fiction, Verne's novels try to retain the reader's interest. They move between the probable, the expected and the unexpected. Science is therefore used in a 'game' between the known and the unknown, the likely and the unlikely. On one hand, science refers to a reality with which we are familiar and gives us a guarantee of truth. Scientific knowledge is, in this case, playing a traditional role as an 'element of reality'.[5] On the other hand, science is used to justify the bizarre. This is one example of Verne's originality: he uses the features of the adventure story, but all mysteries are given scientific explanations. In *Voyages et aventures du capitaine Hatteras* for example, Verne explains that the mirages and ghostly visions experienced by the sailors as they travel towards the North Pole are optical illusions. Likewise, fantastic machines are justified by contemporary research. In *Vingt mille lieues sous les mers*, Verne combines several inventions to create Captain Nemo's *Nautilus*: Fulton's *Nautilus* (1802), including the 1857 semi-submersible craft of Jean-François Conseil (who Verne met, and whose name he gave to one of the book's characters), and the cigar-shaped submarine developed in Britain in 1864. Ponton d'Amécourt's helicopter of 1863 became the *Albatros* of *Robur-le-conquérant* in 1886. On this subject, it is important to note how much Verne considered his works to be different from the science fiction which appeared at the end of the nineteenth century, with particular reference to H. G. Wells, whom he called 'a purely imaginative writer'. Verne considered that he himself did not invent things: 'I have always made a point in my romances of basing my so-called inventions upon a groundwork of actual fact, and of using in their constructions methods and materials which are not entirely without the pale of contemporary engineering skill and knowledge. ... The creations of Mr Wells belong unreservedly to an age and degree of scientific knowledge far removed from the present.'[6]

Defamiliarization

Another sign of Verne's opening up of texts to scientific writing is the defamiliarization effect which was defined by Chklovski and the Russian Formalists at the beginning of the twentieth century: 'In order to transform an object into an artistic event, it has to be taken out of its series of everyday events.'[7] Taken out of its context, scientific information is made strange ('étrangées') and becomes a literary object. The names of different types of mosquitoes take on an eerie resonance: 'Le moustique gris, le velu, la patte-blanche, le nain, le sonneur de fanfares, le petit fifre, l'urtiquis, l'arlequin, le grand nègre, le roux des bois' (*La Jangada*, part 1, ch. 11). Here one can feel a different pleasure in language: the pleasure of assembling words which sometimes sound curious when put together. Verne also shows a taste for the heterogeneous, so characteristic of the nineteenth century, but which, in some aspects, seems to herald poetic works such as those of Michaux.

Even so, science clearly risked losing its status as an objective source on reality, thus becoming a subjective one, i.e., relating to a particular speaker, in a specific place and moment in time. Furthermore, Verne rarely relied on the register of defamiliarization, because he knew that it might jeopardize the verisimilitude.

Naturalization

Another indication in Verne's works of the insertion of scientific writing is its *naturalization*, that is to say when information is transferred to another environment (Verne's text) which then appropriates it. The documentation is, in fact, never recopied *verbatim*, but rearranged and rewritten so that it smoothly follows the thread of Verne's narrative. Science becomes part of Verne's writing. He seemed to derive pleasure from writing about anything, and from attempting the impossible, incorporating into his texts the most diverse, and least literary of elements—figures, technical terms and the contents pages of scientific books.

He also tried to use the poetic function in scientific discourse, emphasizing the formal aspect of language, something unheard of in discourse of this type. On this subject, I shall simply mention the comments made by Michel Butor and Alain Buisine[8] who stress the stylistic effects in *Vingt mille lieues sous les mers*, particularly where the names of shellfish are transformed into true poetry. So, when Aronnax stares through the glass panels of the *Nautilus* he sees

> d'amirables tellines sulfurées, de précieuses espèces de cythérées et de vénus, le cadran treillissé des côtes de Tranquebar, le sabot marbré à nacre resplendissante, les perroquets verts des mers de Chine, le cône presque inconnu du genre *Coenodulli*, toutes les variétés de porcelaine qui servent de monnaie dans l'Inde et en Afrique, la 'Gloire de la Mer', la plus précieuse coquille des Indes orientales; enfin des littorines, des dauphinules, des turritelles, des janthines, des ovules, des volutes, des olives, des mitres, des casques, des pourpres, des buccins, des harpes, des rochers, des tritons, des cérites, des fuseaux, des strombes, des ptérocères, des patelles, des hyales, des cléodores, coquillages délicats et fragiles, que la science a baptisés de ses noms les plus charmants (part 1, ch. 11).

In addition to an 'element of reality' as mentioned earlier, these scientific articles are the object of a writer's work: not only does Verne show his lexical skill (in the variety of his vocabulary), but he also asserts his linguistic talent (in his ability to make words count).

Dialogism

Finally, science is integrated into the literary work in so far as learning is the responsibility of fictional characters whose professions justify such knowledge: doctors, geographers, engineers, journalists, teachers and technicians. In *Vingt mille lieues sous les mers*, the naturalist Pierre Aronnax, Conseil, his servant and assistant (who was obsessed by classification), and the sailor Ned Land are looking at the diversity of marine life through the porthole of the submarine *Nautilus* (which they have been taken aboard), and are identifying them according to their respective skills:

> Un baliste, avais-je dit.
> —Et un baliste chinois! répondait Ned Land.
> —Genre des balistes, famille des sclérodermes, ordre des plectognathes, murmurait Conseil.
>
> Décidément, à eux deux, Ned et Conseil auraient fait un naturaliste distingué … Notre admiration se maintenait toujours au plus haut point. Nos interjections ne tarissaient pas. Ned nommait les poissons, Conseil les classait, moi, je m'extasiais devant la vivacité de leurs allures et la beauté de leurs formes. (part 1, ch. 14).

In this way, scientific discourse which is univocal finds itself multiplied since the scientific information integrated into Verne's writing is taken on by several voices: the narrative voice and the characters' voices. It should be noted, in passing, that this text attributes a discourse on reality to fictitious creatures, and thus raises questions about the authenticity of this 'reality'. But it is precisely by giving his characters these professional credentials that Verne tries to remove the fictitious nature of these creatures; they are a genuine representation of knowledge in the text. Beyond the balance between verisimilitude and defamiliarization, this naturalization combined with the use of dialogism is what truly unites science and Verne's novels.

As can be seen, Verne used a variety of very effective methods to introduce science into the literary field. This is one of his particularities which contemporary critics were quick to discover. As early as 1876, Marius Topin noted that 'his novels are not only scientific due to the descriptions which they contain, and the aims that they pursue; they are also scientific due to the very means used to excite the reader continually and to renew his interest'.[9]

This opening up to science did, nevertheless, have paradoxical consequences: instead of bringing Verne's work closer to the great authors of the Modernity (such as Baudelaire, Rimbaud and Flaubert), it was instrumental in his exclusion from the literary field. His works also suffered from being considered literature for the young. For a long time in fact, these works, although widely read, were not recognized by authoritative sources such as the Académie Française (Verne was never accepted as a member), and textbooks and critical works on the nineteenth-century novel.

Verne was not concerned with creating a new novelistic genre. On the contrary, he was a willing successor to Daniel Defoe or Edgar Allan Poe. What really interested Verne was the possibility of creating a literary work accessible to his contemporaries. It has taken until the last decades of the twentieth century for his success to be finally recognized.

Translated from the French by M. Donovan

Notes

1 Taken from an interview with Marie C. Belloc: 'Jules Verne at Home' in *The Strand Magazine* 9 (February 1895).

2 Welcoming speech given to Gustave Dubois at the Académie d'Amiens on 8 January 1875. This speech is reproduced on p. 225 of *Textes oubliés* (Paris, UGE, '10/18' collection, 1979).

3 Undated interview, reprinted as 'Jules Verne is Dead. Used Science in Romance', *The Evening Post* (Chicago), 25 March 1905.

4 D. Compère, *Jules Verne écrivain*, ch. 4 (Geneva, Droz, 1991).

5 D. Compère, 'Le jeu avec les références scientifiques dans les romans de Jules Verne', in *De la science en littérature à la science-fiction* (Paris, Comité des travaux historiques et scientifiques, 1996).

6 Interview with Gordon Jones: 'Jules Verne at Home', *Temple Bar* (London, June 1904).

7 'La construction de la nouvelle et du roman', p. 184 of *Théorie de la littérature*: Russian Formalist texts translated and presented by T. Todorov (Paris, Seuil, 1965).

8 Michel Butor, 'Le point suprême et l'âge d'or à travers quelques œuvres de Jules Verne' in *Essais sur les modernes* (Paris, Gallimard, 'Idées' collection, 1964). Alain Buisine, 'Un cas limite de la description: l'énumération' in *La Description* (Presses Universitaires de Lille, 1974).

9 Marius Topin, *Romanciers contemporains* (Paris, Charpentier, 1876, p. 382).

4

The Fiction of Science, or
the Science of Fiction

TIMOTHY UNWIN

Writing in the great Realist tradition, Verne is an avid consumer of written sources. In a more obvious manner than Flaubert or even Zola, he restates, rewrites or recycles knowledge gleaned in the scientific, geographical and historical reviews of the day, and his narrative style is almost instantly recognizable by its long digressions designed to instruct, to enlighten or to initiate.[1] This pedagogical dimension is clearly in keeping with the aims and objectives of Hetzel's *Magasin d'éducation et de récréation* in which the *Voyages extraordinaires* were serialized. However, it also at times takes the novel to the extreme limit of its possibilities, and Verne himself was not the only one to see that, if the function of the novel were to become essentially documentary, informative or indeed scientific, then it would almost certainly be surpassed by other media.[2] In a 1902 interview with the *Pittsburgh Gazette*, published under the title 'Le Roman disparaîtra bientôt', Verne had this apparently pessimistic statement to make about the future of the novel:

> Les romans ne sont pas nécessaires et dès maintenant leur mérite et leur intérêt déclinent ... Les journalistes ont si bien appris à donner des événements de tous les jours un récit coloré qu'en lisant ce qu'ils ont décrit, la postérité y trouvera un tableau plus exact que celui que pourrait donner un roman historique ou descriptif. (*TO*, 383)

Yet even as Verne points to the crisis of confidence which results from extreme Realism and Naturalism in the novel, it is also clear that his own fictions revel in the enchantment of the verbal and that they are anything but 'threatened' or even self-conscious. While he sets out to describe and to depict objective realities of the world, Verne finds his tone and his authority as a novelist precisely in the pleasure of verbal creativity which he never shows signs of wishing to surpass. In passages where he is apparently at his most 'pedagogical', it is the linguistic exuberance and the fascination of exotic or technical terms which strikes us, or indeed the energetic enumerations and taxonomies. As Michel Butor pointed out, Verne's descriptions are invested with an immense poetic power where the richness and strangeness of words themselves is underlined.[3]

The interplay in Verne's writings between the objective and the poetic, the scientific and the fictional, is the subject of the present chapter. How does Verne, even as he seems to take the novel away from its status as 'novel' and ever further towards an ostensibly scientific or documentary text, manage to complete the circle and return to the taste for verbal invention that was his starting point? How does he turn science back into fiction even as he turns fiction into science? If he founds his narrative style on the recorded and the factual, the objective and the documented, then where does the almost rhapsodic poetry of his approach fit in? Herein lies, it seems, one of the central paradoxes for the reader of Verne. Science fiction in Verne becomes not the creation of new and barely recognizable worlds inhabited by strange beings, but the larger-than-life fictions of science itself. Verne stages and dramatizes the scientific, giving it power and mystery through the cumulative impact of his language. Even as natural phenomena are tamed, understood and classified by language, they are endowed with a compelling otherness. Nowhere, perhaps, is this paradoxical equivalence more simply revealed than in the full title of Verne's collective series of novels, *Voyages extraordinaires dans les mondes connus et inconnus*. The known and the unknown are here side by side. The unknown, by dint of its being explored and exposed, becomes the known; and by the same token, the known takes on something of the mystique of the unknown. The essential impetus of Verne's fiction may be an act of taming and appropriation,[4] yet it is precisely here that the strangeness of our world and of our means of comprehending it seem also to be exposed, as language joyfully dramatizes the encounter between human thought and external reality. Verne's fiction may not draw attention to itself in a self-conscious manner (he is far from problematizing explicitly, as for instance Flaubert does, the issue of language and its power to express) yet everywhere it rejoices in its own procedures, in its power to create mystery out of the real or reality out of the mysterious. Was Verne perhaps, notwithstanding what Barthes once said of Voltaire, 'le dernier des écrivains heureux'?[5]

Much has been made of the so-called 'futuristic' element of Verne's novels yet, as modern commentators point out with almost equal relentlessness, what is genuinely unknown and unexplored is given only the briefest of mentions in his work.[6] In *Cinq semaines en ballon*, the journey deviates from its quest to locate the source of the Nile, as the balloon is transported across the African continent. In *Voyage au centre de la terre*, the centre of the earth is never reached. And in *Autour de la lune*, the dark side of the moon is only briefly apprehended by Verne's astronauts before known realities take centre stage once again. Verne has been hailed as a prophet of space-travel, and his lunar novels are probably the first to envisage a journey to the moon as a real possibility—but the launching of the Columbiad in Florida and its eventual touchdown in the Pacific are not the visions of a prophet who foresaw the Apollo space programme. They are based on known and, for Verne, readily available calculations of the moon's movement around the Earth and of the most favourable launching opportunities. As Simone Vierne laconically observes in her introduction to the lunar novels, Verne is anything but the 'chantre du progrès technique' that he is sometimes seen as (*TL, AL*, 22). Far from being a fiction of futuristic visions, Verne's brand of science fiction (if indeed the term 'science fiction' fits at all) is a restatement of the known, an almost nostalgic recycling of the past and indeed most often the creation of a myth.[7] The machines and inventions of Verne's stories are rickety contraptions which seem to have been put together with the incomplete means at the novelist's disposal, a clumsy but charming *bricolage* which will often strike us as rather old-fashioned. The steel elephant of *La Maison à vapeur*, powered by steam, amphibious, and drawing two carriages is one such example. The flying machine of *Robur-le-conquérant* is another: it is a combination of ship and helicopter, powered by electricity, with multiple propellors. This quaint design (the novel is published in 1885) is Verne's contribution to a topical debate between the partisans of lighter-than-air flying machines and the heavier-than-air lobby. In this sense, it is not futuristic but very contemporary, just as is Verne's most famous travel machine of all, the *Nautilus*, a vehicle literally 'built' from current and available knowledge. And there are, of course, inevitable mistakes, such as the electricity supply which powers the *Nautilus* or, in the case of the lunar excursion, then novelist's failure to take account of weightlessness when Michel Ardan pours out wine for his fellow-travellers (the wine miraculously stays in the glasses). However, such errors do little to detract from the very solid basis of scientific research that underpins Verne's novels. Moreover, given that he bases his stories on what Claude Bernard called 'l'état actuel de nos connaissances', those very errors and lacunae in fact lend substance and credibility to his scientific method.

It is true that, often in Verne's stories, the solemnity or the objectivity of science is counterbalanced by the deliberate introduction of an element of fantasy, the two coexisting and counterbalancing each other. During Phileas Fogg's journey across the American continent, the train in which he travels is extolled as a symbol of the ultimate comfort and flexibility of the modern machine (*TDM*, 198–9). It contains every possible convenience, with carriages of all kinds, and in the evening Fogg's own carriage is effortlessly transformed into a bedroom. Thus the intrepid British traveller is (like the inmates of the *Nautilus*) spared the grimy discomfort of real travel. But Fogg's train is truly magical, for it is capable of leaping across an open chasm at Medicine Creek, blatantly and triumphantly defying the laws of locomotion and gravity. The machine here takes on the pent-up and explosive power of human beings, and is in that sense the symbolic displacement of emotions which the impassive Fogg forever fails to display. But often in Verne's fiction, the distribution of characters itself performs this oppositional function. The impassive and apparently 'rational' Fogg is counterbalanced by the imaginative and quirky Passepartout, an arrangement which has the effect of moving the story between the twin poles of reason and passion, the objective and the fanciful. It is Fogg who calculates, ledger-style, the passage of space and time as he pursues his course around the globe. But it is Passepartout who, against all reasoned estimates, discovers the error of his master's calculations and enables him to win his bet. And yet, by a further irony, this flouting of the rational becomes the pretext to introduce scientific knowledge into the novel once more, as the question of why there was an unseen extra day is explained and resolved by the narrator in the dying stages of the text. Science is replaced by fiction or by fantasy, but fantasy invariably leads back to science in this never-ending relay.[8]

The introduction of quixotic or extravagant characters, counter-balancing the judicious or the rational, is itself a frequent tactic in Verne. The impassioned and cantankerous Lidenbrock in *Voyage au centre de la terre* provides the human complement to the serious scientific investigation of the mysteries of the earth, and indeed powers the debate between the two main characters about what is to be found at the Earth's core. The coexistence of antagonistic (but perhaps complementary) world-views is one of the principal motivating factors too in the lunar novels, where the character of Michel Ardan is fantasy personified. He flouts science and calculation in every way possible, and is from the outset the devil's advocate against anything which smacks of reason, good sense or indeed scientific proof. When asked what he will do about the absence of air on the moon, he replies with preposterous simplicity: 'une fois rendu là-haut, je tâcherai de l'économiser de mon mieux et de ne respirer que dans les grandes occasions!' (*TL*, 183) Ardan is the epitome of the challenge against the impossible, the already known, the proven, and thus he is the fictional character *par excellence*, notwithstanding his having been inspired by the very real figure of Nadar. He symbolizes that coexistence in the lunar novels between scientific calculation and fictional inventiveness. *De la Terre à la lune* in particular must rank as one of Verne's most exuberant and rhapsodic

texts, even as it brings the notion of a lunar excursion within the real reach
of man. Alongside the scientific calculation of the moon's position and
movements (as in the scientifically serious and precise 'Réponse de
l'Observatoire de Cambridge' which makes up chapter 4 of the novel) there
is humour, excess, buffoonery, and a strong taste for the absurd. The project
to send a missile to the moon comes not from the scientists at the Cambridge
Observatory, but from the ghastly, war-mongering misfits of the Baltimore
Gun-Club. The novel seems at once to oscillate between these extremes
and to play them off against each other.

Yet the pattern of complementary and opposing elements in Verne's
novels leaves a question. Do the scientific and the fictional cohabit uneasily,
or is there a real merging of the apparently disparate elements? Does the
scientific become fictional by association with it, with the fictional similarly
gaining some scientific credibility in the process? It must be said that,
beyond the movement of oscillation there is a further process at work. This
process can be seen in the very detail and precision of Verne's descriptions
where, by a further paradox, the literal denotation of objective reality itself
assumes, through the accumulation of its own words, a poetic and
incantatory force. Apollinaire is reported to have said admiringly of Verne:
'Quel style! rien que des substantifs!'[9] Though this is clearly something of
an exaggeration, the comment points to the sharpness of focus in Verne's
style and to the richness of his vocabulary. Objective description shades
off into poetic invocation, a process nowhere more apparent than in *Vingt
mille lieues sous les mers*, where the classifications and taxonomical precision
of the scientific style end up not by appropriating the aquatic world and
reducing it to comprehensible proportions, but by doing the opposite:
highlighting its strangeness and its mystery, and foregrounding the
intoxicating effect of descriptive words themselves. Under the gaze of the
Vernian narrator, the world fragments and dissolves. Verne is perhaps one
of the few writers before Ponge to convey so powerfully both the plasticity
and the ultimate resistance of the real. Thus Verne achieves what the
Russian Formalists considered one of the essential properties of the
literary—defamiliarization—and the process seems to be exactly the
opposite from the movement towards reduction and closure that Barthes
diagnoses (see n. 4). Indeed, Verne's mimesis is expansionist rather than
reductionist.[10] He aims not to convey the essence of the real, like Balzac
for example, but potentially to say everything about everything. The world
is infinite, but then so too is writing in its fundamental gesture of reaching
out into the whole of reality in order to discover or to recover it. For Verne,
this is a never-ending process, and completion or closure is only the
chimera which sustains it. For a novelist such as Balzac, the world is
ultimately 'lisible' since it is itself a novel, and the novelist himself (or such

at least is the conceit upon which his narrative approach is premised) is merely the secretary who finds, observes and writes down the story. For Verne, on the other hand, the world is infinitely 'scriptible'. It contains multiple realities, and forces the novelist into a never-ending inventory of its properties. This is, of course, an impossible wager with the infinite, for as Barthes tells us in *S/Z*,[11] the logical conclusion of the 'scriptible' is precisely the impossibility both of writing and of reading: there is no closure, no point of entry into the text or the word, no single approach or path through, and no exit from them. Verne's approach moves, then, from 'mimesis' to 'mathesis'. It is an approach that is premised at once not only on its ultimate powerlessness, but also on an extraordinary sense of vitality, as it chases the ever-receding horizon.

Verne's strange fictions arise, then, less out of the imagined possibilities or situations to which science or reality may lead, but out of the actual, the known, the present—even if there are characters in his fiction who deliberately and preposterously challenge the real. Any transcendent or 'supernatural' dimension which Verne's writing introduces is achieved from within. The only alien force in his texts is the immanent power of the real to astonish and to undermine all attempts at recuperating it. Although there is speculation in Verne's work (what is on the moon, what is at the centre of the earth and so on) there are no *external* agents disrupting the forces of nature. If an apparently supernatural phenomenon manifests itself, it soon becomes comprehensible—at the beginning of *Vingt mille lieues sous les mers* the *Nautilus* turns out to be a man-made machine, and in *Robur-le-conquérant* the unidentified flying object is similarly revealed to be a scientifically constructed means of transport. In *L'Île mystérieuse*, the providential force which protects the castaways turns out to be Captain Nemo himself. Nature does not play supernatural tricks, for in Verne's vision, it has quite enough power within its own laws to unleash acts of vengeance, wrath or even occasional justice. Like Phileas Fogg, it is impassive on the exterior, but within, it is often volcanic and explosive, likely to destroy, to disrupt or to transform at any moment. It functions almost bodily. Axel and Lidenbrock are expelled from the bowels of the Earth, the *Nautilus* is swallowed up in the maelstrom, Lincoln Island is destroyed by a volcanic eruption. The earth alternately produces wind, water or even fire to help the good or destroy the evil. There is little need in the Vernian cosmology to look beyond the forces that are actually present in known reality, and indeed as Michel Butor points out, there is in Verne's novels a sense in which man is ultimately protected by the inherent properties of nature; in his godless world, it is as though there is none the less some secret force of providence.[12] Even as the unknown becomes known, so too does the known take on the extraordinary power of the unknown. Nature is itself the immanent, terrifying yet ultimately consoling and presence of God. It is an almost Spinozistic vision in which creation and the creator are logically indivisible, united in infinite oneness.

In an essay on Edgar Allen Poe, Verne once wrote admiringly of the American author's ability to create a sense of the fantastic not by going beyond the real, but precisely by entering further into it. Here is how he sees Poe's tales of the fantastic:

> Qu'il me soit permis maintenant d'attirer l'attention sur le côté matérialiste de ces histoires; on n'y sent jamais l'intervention providentielle; Poe ne semble pas l'admettre, et prétend tout expliquer par les lois physiques, qu'il invente même au besoin; on ne sent pas en lui cette foi que devrait lui donner l'incessante contemplation du surnaturel. Il faut du fantastique *à froid*, si je puis m'exprimer ainsi, et ce malheureux est encore un apôtre du matérialisme; mais j'imagine que c'est moins la faute de son tempérament que l'influence de la société purement pratique et industrielle des Etats-Unis; il a écrit, pensé, rêvé en Américain, en homme positif. ('Edgar Poe et ses œuvres', *TO*, pp. 151–2)

The fantastic is achieved, then, in a 'materialistic' fashion, by emphasis on the laws of reality and the concrete presence of phenomena rather than by appeal to external forces. The interesting classification of Poe's approach as a national characteristic, typical of American materialism, does nothing to detract from Verne's admiration of his literary technique and his vision. Indeed, this passage stands not only as an analysis of Poe, but more obviously as a self-diagnosis by Verne, and if not a statement of intention, at least a revelation of his own manner; Verne achieves precisely the sense of, if not the supernatural, at least the 'otherness' of the natural world by going ever further into the observable and classifiable realities of it. His ambition in this respect is vast, and dwarfs even the gigantic enterprises of Balzac or of Zola. If it was Balzac's wish to write the social history of his generation, Zola's to write the history of a Second Empire family, Verne's is ultimately to write about the whole of the known world, nothing more and nothing less. As Hetzel wrote in the famous preface to *Voyages et aventures du capitaine Hatteras*, the novel which had been serialised in the first issue of Hetzel's own *Magasin d'éducation et de récréation* in 1864: 'Son but est...de résumer toutes les connaissances géographiques, géologiques, physiques, astronomiques, amassées par la science moderne, et de refaire, sous la forme attrayante et pittoresque qui lui est propre, l'histoire de l'univers.' Some twenty-five years later, confirming phlegmatically that his ambition, though diminished perhaps from the 'universe' to the 'Earth' is otherwise undaunted, Verne writes to Hetzel fils on 19 September 1889:

'Je n'ai pas fini l'œuvre de ma vie, dépeindre toute la terre.'[13] This must be as clear a statement as any that Verne's essential gesture is one of expansion rather than reduction. Fiction exists not despite its adherence to the known realities of our universe, but through and within those realities. They justify and sustain it, for they are themselves the ultimate, infinitely self-regenerating narrative.

There is scarcely a better example of Verne's fictional science, or scientific fiction, than the fifth chapter of *De la Terre à la lune*, significantly entitled 'Le roman de la lune'. The chapter comes immediately after the answers sent to the Baltimore Gun-Club by the Cambridge Observatory, in which a number of precise issues to do with launching conditions are dealt with soberly and scientifically. 'Le Roman de la lune' (*TL*, 74–80) is by contrast a visionary, poetically evocative chapter written at once with pedagogical precision and great verbal resourcefulness. The narrator sets out by imagining an impossible situation: 'Un observateur doué d'une vue infiniment pénétrante, et placé à ce centre inconnu autour duquel gravite le monde, aurait vu des myriades d'atomes remplir l'espace à l'époque chaotique de l'univers.' The imagined observer—of such infinite perspicacity and transcendent status—maintains his presence throughout the chapter. He is the essential device through which Verne introduces the human dimension as he discusses the chaotic mass of the universe, the formation of celestial bodies, the galaxies and the solar systems, before he moves in and focuses on our own world, the sun, the Earth, the planets and—last but of course not least—the moon. Through his observer, the narrator is thus able to project a fascinated gaze onto reality. But the allure and mystery of the real is expressed in other ways too, for the novelist's vocabulary and sentence-construction are at once straightforward and controlled, yet almost reverently relishing the process they reveal: 'Mais peu à peu, avec les siècles, un changement se produisit; une loi d'attraction se manifesta, à laquelle obéirent les atomes errants jusqu'alors; ces atomes se combinèrent chimiquement suivant leurs affinités, se firent molécules et formèrent ces amas nébuleux dont sont parsemées les profondeurs du ciel.' The series of (mainly reflexive) verbs, all in the *passé simple*, give sharpness of focus to the description, and their denotation of change contrasts paradoxically with the sense of immutable natural law which is conveyed. Stasis and movement thus combine in a single vision, and the inversion at the end of this sentence ('dont sont parsemées les profondeurs du ciel') elegantly rounds off the opening paragraph with another timeless and static snapshot of the infinite. Yet, despite the obvious enjoyment of his linguistic medium exhibited by the novelist, and despite the ironies which the human observer of the universe uncovers ('une étoile de quatrième ordre, celle qui s'appelle orgueilleusement le Soleil'), the chapter progresses soberly and pedagogically towards its eventual focus on the moon. Precision and exuberance move side by side, and it is no surprise to find a poetic homily to the moon, as the narrator compares it to the blinding and overpowering splendour of the sun: 'La blonde Phœbé, plus humaine au contraire, se laisse complaisamment voir dans sa grâce modeste; elle est douce à l'œil, peu ambitieuse, et cependant, elle se permet parfois d'éclipser son frère, le radieux Apollon, sans jamais être éclipsée par lui.' This mood of reverence, highlighting the traditional view of the moon as feminine, allows the narrator to move on and describe the worship of the moon by humans from ancient times to the present, and then to the progressive attempts to understand it and to draw up a map of its visible surface. The poetic invocation begets once more the scientific account, yet at no time does the narrator depart from his pedagogical mission, even as his descriptions of mankind's relationship with the moon become indeed the 'roman' that the chapter title has promised. The text highlights its own nature as text, not only by its reference to and relaying of the known accounts of the moon, nor even by its dramatization of man's relationship with that celestial body, but also and perhaps most of all by its own linguistic energy. Science here—or at least the science of lunar investigation—is itself presented by Verne as one of the greatest and most compelling of all fictions. Put the other way round, this means that it is precisely fiction, in its broadest sense, that motivates and underpins science. There is, it is suggested, no such thing as objective and rational investigation outside of the human subject. The fictions of the human mind are what produce science, and without that fictitious 'human' observer of the universe from whose perspective this chapter is written, there would be no science in any case. Precision of knowledge thus arises from speculation and indeed invention, as one theory replaces another in the never-ending quest for truth: 'Ainsi Thalès de Milet, 460 ans avant J.-C., émit l'opinion que la Lune était éclairée par le Soleil. Aristarque de Samos donna la véritable explication de ses phases. Cléomène enseigna qu'elle brillait d'une lumière réfléchie.' Human endeavour is here incorporated completely into the Vernian cosmology, and the description of the moon becomes precisely the equivalent of the enumeration of the different attempts to understand it. Reality and our knowledge of reality unite in the single space of language, and the novel itself becomes a privileged mode of engagement, the ultimate scientific 'instrument'.

    Although Verne appears not to problematize explicitly the issue of the subjective or limited reflector of reality, it is none the less possible to detect in his fiction the presence of what some might call 'the Flaubertian problem'. Flaubert's limited registers of human experience perceive reality through the clichés or the illusions of their own minds. They are mistaken, and yet their engagement with the world is entirely dependent on the limited and distorted means at their disposal. If the narrator is able to undercut and expose ironically the defects of their understanding, then he clearly does so at the cost of his own detachment, for he too is ensnared by language and by the omnipresence of cliché. His irony thus turns in on itself and exposes its own baselessness. No objective, language-free evaluation of the real is possible. We are all enveloped in fictions, and the writer who tries to write his way out is merely another, perhaps the ultimate, victim of the fictional. But if Flaubert is pessimistic about this problem, Verne seems positively to rejoice in it. Nothing is more proper, in his view, than the invention of fiction—a strange paradox indeed for a writer so scientific. Fiction is the royal road to knowledge, and even if it is a wrong fiction, it is still the means of engaging pragmatically with the world. Like Ardan, who finds himself sneering at the laws of nature (for they themselves are no more than fictions—'La distance est un vain mot, la distance n'existe pas!' he says (*TL*, 174)—Verne asserts the primacy of the fictional, yet on condition that it is part of an ongoing process of the acquisition of knowledge. Error itself is of no consequence if it produces results, and there is in any case no guarantee that the refusal of fiction and subjectivity can help to avoid error. In *Les Enfants du capitaine Grant*, the story of the search for the missing sea captain is motivated precisely by error. The cryptogram that sets the story moving (in the form of a message in a bottle) is read in three different ways by the travellers, and each of the three readings corresponds to one volume—and one geographical location—of the novel. The story that unfolds arises out of reading, and thereby attests its own fictional status. The eccentric Paganel, secretary of the Société de Géographie and a clear literary relative of characters like Passepartout or Ardan, finds himself on board the search vessel by error (when he had been heading for another part of the globe) and indeed despite his encyclopedic knowledge he occasionally makes huge geographical mistakes, such as forgetting the existence of a continent through sheer absent-mindedness. But this seems to be extolled by Verne as the 'best' form of knowledge, and Paganel meets his equal when faced with the distorted geographical perceptions of the young Aboriginal, Toliné, in chapter 13 of the second volume of the novel. A perfect 'mise en abyme' of the narrative of distorted knowledge, this chapter shows that young recipient of first prize in geography at a Melbourne school giving all the wrong answers to Paganel's questions. But in his ingenuous eccentricity, the boy upstages even the French geographer. For Toliné has been taught an exclusively Anglocentric geography. Oceania belongs entirely to the English, he believes. There are no French possessions or settlements. But nor are there any in Africa or in America, and France itself, he asserts, is a British province ruled by a governor, Lord Napoleon, whose residence is in Calais! Increasingly exasperated, Paganel then asks if perhaps the moon itself is a British territory: '—Elle le sera, répondit gravement le jeune sauvage' (*ECG*, II, 143). Now clearly, one of the functions of this passage is to make an ironical comment on the British. Yet Verne—especially at the time this novel is published (1868)—is far from being a detractor of the British and of their colonising spirit.[14] Toliné is, in fact, an example of the noble quest for knowledge for its own sake, however wrong it may be, and he represents a symbolic reminder that the knowledge of those more sophisticated than he is perhaps ultimately no more reliable. After his questioning by Paganel, he is offered a book by Glenarvan, head of the expedition. The book is 'le *Précis de géographie* de Samuel Richardson, un ouvrage estimé en Angleterre, et plus au courant de la science que les professeurs de Melbourne' (*ECG*, II, 143). Another English book on geography? The point is implicitly made that, despite its reputation, it may perhaps be offering just as distorted a knowledge as that which Toliné has received and relayed. And the same point is reinforced at the end of the chapter. During the night, Toliné disappears, slipping the Richardson volume into Paganel's coat pocket before he departs. Perhaps Paganel himself will have something to learn from the Anglocentric view, if only because it provides the antidote to his equally Francocentric vision. Toliné, on the other hand, clearly does not need further manipulation of his ideas.

The book that Toliné leaves behind is, in another sense, a very obvious reminder that knowledge is textual. Our apprehension of the world, far from transcending words and books, is intimately bound up with them. Science *is* fiction in the sense that we are obliged to use words and books to learn it, to understand it, and to share and communicate it. Despite the initial impression that Verne's novels may sometimes give of offering a 'window' on reality, and of suggesting that the relationship between word and world is uncomplicated and direct, there are many explicit or implicit references to the text within the text. Although the *Voyages extraordinaires* may seem to take us on an imaginary armchair tour of the continents and the seas, we are constantly returned to the book and to the bookish. Text is everywhere. It is not only in the narrator's own visionary descriptions of the universe, it is itself thematized within the text. The book is revived, it returns as a constant symbolic reminder of the medium through which science is transmitted, just like that volume in Paganel's coat pocket. And Paganel himself is one of the arch-recyclers, in Verne's fiction, of bookish knowledge. He revels in his textual medium, regaling his fellow travellers with accounts of the history, development, customs or features of the countries they visit, and has a memory that might put even Julien Sorel to shame. This highlighting of 'text' within the text often assumes a ludic dimension, as when the travellers are approaching the Australian continent and Paganel makes a bet with Mac Nabbs that he will be able to mention fifty names of individuals who have explored Australia or influenced its colonization. The fifty names are reeled off, the dizzying list being held together with a loose and improvised narrative. Just for good measure Paganel adds another twenty-one names before the momentum of his narrative slows down. He is 'telling the story' of Australia, but of course it is the story that has been told many times over, and Paganel is essentially repeating and recycling, echoing the names rote-style from his memory, delighting in the text that has been handed down to him by history, which he is yet able to make his own by improvisations around the repetition.

As has often been pointed out[15] Verne's texts frequently require another text to get them going: this is most obviously the case with the cryptograms which start, for example, *Voyage au centre de la terre* or *Les Enfants du capitaine Grant*. But the more general foregrounding of the very notion of text within the text itself reveals the modernity of this author who for so long was dismissed as somewhat old-fashioned and naïve. Every Vernian text is an intertext, and the promise of total knowledge is always founded on the paradoxical premise of absolute indebtedness. The textual journey, to be complete and to achieve its ultimate goal of appropriation, must be a perfect copy. Thus the journey into unknown worlds ends up by being a triumphant return to the known, as it is written down and recorded in available texts. Fiction itself is repetition and citation of other texts, but repetition is, as Compagnon has so convincingly argued in his study of citation, a rewriting.[16] And just as Paganel recycles the story of Australian explorers, so too in a much larger way does Verne recycle the knowledge available to him in published form. In some cases this leads to a form of writing which is near-plagiarism,[17] yet it also evidences his pleasure in the verbal, particularly where exotic or unusual terms are used. In the end, the whole world is a text for Verne, and despite his central theme of quest for the discovery of new places and new worlds, he returns again and again to recorded information and the book. Even Barbicane, as he addresses the Gun-Club in Baltimore to explain his plans for a space mission, will feel compelled to remind his audience of that most literary of inspirations, Edgar Allan Poe, and of the story of Hans Pfaal and his journey to the moon. For Verne, if fiction feeds on science, then science also feeds on fiction, for fiction is what motivates science. Science fiction in the Vernian text is not only the fictionalization of science. It is the realization that fiction is literally everywhere, that it has expanded to fill the whole universe, and that we are sure to come across it even in the places we had least expected to find it.

Notes

The following abbreviated titles for Verne's texts are used in this chapter:
AL (*Autour de la lune* (1869; Paris, Garnier-Flammarion, 1978)); *ECG* (*Les Enfants du capitaine Grant* (1868; Paris, Hachette, 1928)); *TDM* (*La Tour du monde en 80 jours* (1872; Paris, Garnier-Flammarion, 1978)); *TL* (*De la Terre à la lune* (1865; Paris, Garnier-Flammarion, 1978)); *TO* (*Textes oubliés*, recueillis et présentés par Francis Lacassin (Paris, Union générale d'Editions, 1979)).

1 For a detailed discussion of Verne's methods and of his preferred sources, see Daniel Compère, *Jules Verne écrivain* (Geneva, Droz, 1991), pp. 33–53. On the subject of Verne's preference for written sources over practical observation, Compère quotes the Chicago *Evening Express* interview of 25 March 1905, in which Verne states: 'Je pense qu'une lecture attentive des ouvrages les plus documentés sur n'importe quel sujet nouveau vaut mieux que l'expérience concrète, du moins lorsqu'il s'agit d'écrire des romans' (p. 45).

2 This point about the impending redundancy of the genre was elegantly restated by Michel Butor ('Le roman comme recherche', repr. in *Répertoire I* (Paris, Editions de Minuit, 1960), pp. 7–11). Butor stresses, however, the difference between the verifiable 'récit' of other forms of documentation, and the unverifiable nature of the novelistic 'récit'. The novel's due and proper role is therefore, he maintains, to explore and examine the functioning of our modes of narration.

3 Butor, 'Le point suprême et l'âge d'or à travers quelques œuvres de Jules Verne', repr. in *Répertoire I* , pp. 130–62.

4 As Barthes wrote in his famous *Mythologies* article, 'le geste profond de Jules Verne, c'est…incontestablement l'appropriation' ('Nautilus et bateau ivre', in *Mythologies* (Paris, Seuil, 1957), p. 81). In Barthes' view, this reflex to appropriate therefore leads Verne into an epistemology of closure, and ultimately a bourgeois desire for comfort and de-alienation. Thus, 'Verne ne cherchait nullement à élargir le monde selon des voies romantiques d'évasion ou des plans mystiques d'infini: il cherchait sans cesse à le rétracter, à le peupler, à le réduire à un espace connu et clos' (ibid.) The present discussion takes precisely the opposite view, by arguing that the very process of appropriation re-alienates reality.

5 'Ce qui nous sépare peut-être de Voltaire, c'est qu'il fut un écrivain heureux. Nul mieux que lui n'a donné au combat de la Raison l'allure d'une fête' ('Le dernier des écrivains heureux', repr. in *Essais critiques* (Paris, Seuil, 1964), p. 99).

6 See, for example, Andrew Martin, 'The Scientific Fictions of Jules Verne', in *The Knowledge of Ignorance: from Genesis to Jules Verne* ((Cambridge, Cambridge University Press, 1985), p. 155.

7 Butor ('Le point suprême') is especially convincing on the mythological aspect of Verne's work; see also Simone Vierne, *Jules Verne: mythe et modernité* (Paris, PUF, 1989).

8 See Timothy Unwin, *Verne: 'Le Tour du monde en quatre-vingts jours'* (Glasgow University, 1992), pp. 74–7 for further remarks on the complementary structure of character roles in *Le tour du monde*.

9 Quoted in Martin, 'The Knowledge of Ignorance', p. 151. This author unfortunately fails to give the source of the Apollinaire quotation which may,

it appears, be apocryphal.

10 Cf. Martin, *The Knowledge of Ignorance*, pp. 134 ff.

11 'Le texte scriptible, c'est *nous en train d'écrire*, avant que le jeu infini du monde (le monde comme jeu) ne soit traversé, coupé, arrêté plastifié par quelque système singulier (Idéologie, Genre, Critique) qui en rabatte sur la pluralité des entrées, l'ouverture des réseaux, l'infini des langues' (*S/Z* (Paris, Seuil, 1970), p. 11).

12 Butor, 'Le point suprême'.

13 Unpublished letter quoted in Vierne, *Jules Verne*, p. 54.

14 Interesting remarks about Verne's evolving attitude towards the British and their methods of colonial domination are made by Chesneaux, *Une lecture politique de Jules Verne* (Paris, Maspero, 1971) p. 110; for a fuller survey of Verne's evolving attitude towards the British see Ghislain de Diesbach, *Le Tour de Jules Verne en quatre-vingts livres* (Paris, Julliard, 1969), pp. 63–74.

15 For example, Butor, 'Le point suprême', or Andrew Martin, *The Mask of the Prophet* (Oxford, Clarendon Press, 1990), pp. 27–54.

16 'La citation tente de reproduire dans l'écriture une passion de lecture, de retrouver l'instantanée fulgurance de la sollicitation, car c'est bien la lecture, solliciteuse et excitante, qui produit la citation. La citation répète, elle fait retentir la lecture dans l'écriture: c'est qu'en vérité lecture et écriture ne sont qu'une seule et même chose' (Antoine Compagnon, *La Seconde Main ou le travail de la citation* (Paris, Seuil, 1979), p. 27).

17 There are many detailed examples in current critical studies of Verne's use of source material, and the comparison of his final text with the material he uses often yields interesting results. In the writing of *Mistress Branican*, for example, Verne is heavily reliant on the use of Désiré Charnay's *Six mois en Australie* for his description of the three Australian cities of Melbourne, Sydney and Adelaide, to the point where Charnay's material is sometimes directly transcribed in the novel. I have discussed this instance of Verne's use of source material in a publication, entitled 'Plagiarist at Work? Jules Verne and the Australian City' (John West-Sooby (ed.), *Images of the City in Nineteenth-century France* (Mount Nebo, Boombana Publications, 1998), pp. 183–99.

5

'L'Ici-bas' and 'l'Au-delà' … but Not as they Knew it. Realism, Utopianism and Science Fiction in the Novels of Jules Verne

SARAH CAPITANIO

The nineteenth century in France is, as we all know, the Golden Age of the Realist novel. However, other Golden Ages existed in the nineteenth century in the form of a number of textual utopias (one thinks immediately of Saint-Simon and Fourier); and it is the era which saw the burgeoning of the narrative form science fiction.

The above statements appear to suggest that we are dealing with three distinct modes of narrative discourse; in fact their interpenetration is considerable at a number of levels in writings of the nineteenth century, and the works of Jules Verne provide an unrivalled example of this phenomenon, as the title of this essay seeks to suggest. In the following pages I aim to examine the interface between Realism, utopianism and science fiction in a number of Verne's novels. These novels, whatever one's judgement of them in terms of 'great literature', provide an interesting case study of the way in which a particular vision of society is constructed from a number of different nineteenth-century perspectives. Such a fictional vision may well have appeared to readers of the time to be not the world 'as they knew it'; however, from a distance of over a hundred years and from the perspective of narratology, it is possible to see how this vision relies for its being on the conventions and ideologies of Realism and utopianism, genres which were to live on in science-fiction narratives of the twentieth century.

Although I shall examine separately the various formal, thematic and ideological aspects of these different genres in Verne's novels, I shall at the same time point to ways in which they interact. This study makes reference to only a relatively small number of Verne's most widely read works (and which, it must be noted, cannot be seen as representative of the whole corpus); it nevertheless adopts an approach which allows us to go beyond the habitual dismissal of Verne's works as mere forerunners of one specific paraliterary genre (science fiction), and to read them within a broader and more complex nineteenth-century literary historical context.

'L'Ici-bas'

At first sight, it seems perverse to link Verne with Realism. Comparisons, however superficial, with Balzac, Stendhal, Zola, Flaubert or Maupassant do not really seem in order and are in fact rare. This is hardly surprising from one point of view: in terms of content, the latter are preoccupied principally with a society which portrays itself as historically, sociologically and topographically verifiable, circumscribable and subject to classification in various ways. The principal characters whose trajectories move within this context are representative of social classes or professional groups. These characters play a large part at the outset in the creation of the referential illusion: the highly referential present tense in the opening pages of *Le Père Goriot* firmly situates not only the Maison-Vauquer but also its fictitious owner within a cartographically verifiable *faubourg*.[1] Characters can only be read within the confines of the recognizable society in which they are fixed. Furthermore, the characters' trajectories are closely bound up with the evolution of that society: the Realist protagonist either swims with the social current (Rastignac, Lucien de Rubempré) or falls foul of it through Romantic rebellion (Julien Sorel, Emma Bovary in different ways), or through circumstances largely beyond his/her control (Gervaise Macquart, Jeanne de Lamare). Realism thus vaunts itself in various forms as that famous Stendhalian 'miroir qui se promène sur une grande route',[2] a phrase which neatly sums up the essentially Realist notions of unproblematical spatio-temporal mimesis.

The 'programme' followed by Verne's characters is different from that of their counterparts in traditional Realist novels: their actions and thoughts are usually bound up with a feat or an experience which projects, creates, or at the very least suggests an ideal or alternative way of living ('une réalité autre' in the words of Froidefond[3]), usually made possible by technological advances in a particular field. Alternatively, characters present themselves as representatives of the whole of humanity (a representation that is underscored by the didactic voice of the narrator): 'Représentants de la Terre, de l'humanité passée et présente qu'ils résumaient en eux, c'est par leurs yeux que la race humaine regardait ces régions lunaires et pénétrait les secrets de son satellite' (*AL*, 148[4]).

Nevertheless, there is a sense in which Verne's novels derive very clearly from the context of the second half of the nineteenth century: nearly all

the journeys (by land, sea or air) are framed by events which are as
historically verifiable as any to be found in the works of the Realist novelists:
the American Civil War is one privileged point of anchorage (for example
in *L'Ile mystérieuse* and *De la Terre à la lune*). The characters function
collectively as a means of representing contemporary society, hence their
classification as socially representational types—'l'ingénieur' (Cyrus
Smith, *L'Ile mystérieuse* ; James Starr *Les Indes noires*; Murchison, *De la Terre
à la lune*), 'le marin' (Pencroff, *L'Ile mystérieuse*), 'l'overman' (Simon Ford,
Les Indes noires), 'le professeur' (Lidenbrock, *Voyage au centre de la terre*), to
name but a few; more irritatingly for the modern reader, they also function
collectively as over-simplistic national or racial stereotypes—Americans
(*TL*, 2, 3, 5; *RC*, 9), for example, or black people (Frycollin in *Robur le
conquérant*).[5] Classification operates too in spatial contexts: 'Est-ce un
continent? Est-ce un archipel? Est-ce une mer paléocrystique...?' the
narrator of *Robur-le-conquérant* asks with regard to Antarctica (187). Hence
the enormous importance attached to the naming of newly discovered
places (*L'Ile mystérieuse*, *Voyage au centre de la terre*), for naming is a means
of defining (and hence classifying) perceived phenomena and, in an age
in which signifier and signified are readily conflated, constitutes a textual
convention which theoretically allows the reader unmediated access to the
referent.

There is also more convergence than divergence between Verne's novels
and those of his contemporaries in terms of narrative structure. Two
particular areas are worth studying in this connection: structural opposition
and the modalities of the description. Both of these inevitably point to the
particular ideology that subtends the texts.

Opposition is the mainstay of Realist fiction, as it is of drama/melodrama
with which it has considerable affinities.[6] Oppositions abound in the novels
of Realist writers such as Balzac and Zola, engendering dramatic suspense
and conflict through character, space and narrative structure. Such
oppositions are equally present in Vernian texts. *De la Terre à la lune* is a
prime example of a novel in which oppositions are constantly introduced;
they act as a counter to what is essentially a didactic, pedagogical text in
which consensus is stressed at every point (and is indeed vital to the whole
nature of the feat of financing, building and launching a rocket to the
moon). Firstly, Nichols emerges as a rival to the Gun-Club president,
Barbicane; rivalry arises between Texas and Florida to host the construction
and launch of the *Columbiad*; Michel Ardan, a physical and temperamental
opposite to Barbicane, then appears on the scene. The Cité de l'Acier and
France-Ville and their respective 'rulers' exemplify a more fundamental
structural opposition in *Les 500 Millions de la Bégum*.[7] The fact that these
oppositions are nearly always finally resolved is, however, a point to be

borne in mind, and it is one to which I shall return in the next section.

Description is perhaps the area in which there is most similarity between Verne and the Realists. The amount of detail in Verne's descriptions, and their internal organization, follow the Realist model; they are ordered in a particular way (such as the description of Abomey, *RC*, 155–6), they contain statistics, repetition, *feuilletonesque* 'rappels' and reformulations; above all, they contain enumeration, frequently of technical substantives, thus reinforcing the importance at the textual level of the 'naming' process just noted. The result is that the often fantastic nature of the elements that form the subject matter of the descriptions is eclipsed by modes of narration which follow Realist conventions of writing (and thus call on parallel modes of reading), lending these elements a particular type of credibility. The proairetic and cultural (or referential) codes identified by Barthes in *S/Z* predominate, thus maximizing 'lisibilité' of the text.[8] The visual support provided by frequent illustrations reinforces the process through interaction with the text. More evidently mathetic than those of his contemporaries,[9] Verne's texts take to an extreme the nineteenth-century Realist tendency to represent a world that is *a priori* circumscribable, causal and explicable in a way that frequently blurs the boundaries between novel and scientific or technical manual (*VCT*, 172–4, 183–4 and 306–8;[10] *IN*, 18–26; *RC*, 66–72); technical footnotes almost invariably strengthen this process.[11] Ideologically, it is clear that Verne's descriptions are motivated by the same sort of impulse as that which drove the Goncourts and Zola (and, to different ends, Flaubert) to document their texts and to represent society in an ordered and apparently exhaustive way.[12] In short, like most of his Realist contemporaries, Verne 'décrit pour donner à voir et à savoir'.[13]

Over and above the extreme mathesis of the descriptions, however, one also finds devices which 'naturalize' or justify the latter in narrative terms. Thus, a specialist/initiated character explains or shows to one or more uninitiated characters the nature of a particular element or the way in which a process works; the place in which this explanation or demonstration is given facilitates this activity: it is usually bathed in light (real or artificial), and the description takes place from a privileged vantage point (doors, windows or their equivalent).[14] At times this device is taken to more than one narrative degree: after Nemo's exposition to Aronnax of the way in which marine raw materials provide the clothing of the *Nautilus'* crew (*VMLM*, 103), Aronnax explains the process in similar terms (this time in reported speech) to his manservant Conseil (155). In cases such as this, the redundancy that so evidently operates at the level of the zero degree narrator-focalizer in many of the novels (such as the constant reminder of the opposing seasons in the southern and northern

hemispheres in *Robur-le-conquérant*, and even more so in *L'Île mystérieuse*)
is attenuated by being integrated into the fabric of the diegesis.

Inevitably, this 'naturalization' process leads to a particular typology of
characters, places and situations. To take but one example, the presence
of the poetical, whimsical character of Michel Ardan is a necessary pretext
for the long technical and scientific explanations by Barbicane and Nicholl
concerning the speed of the rocket, the relative temperatures of the Earth,
moon and sun, the Earth's atmosphere and the topography of the moon;
the spacecraft and its 'windows' are the vectors of their attention, and their
'imprisonment' in the rocket for several days on its voyage provides the
opportunity for long discussions and explanations (*AL*, 60–72, 82–7,
90–100, 163–90, 239–53). Above all, what is being described, explained
or shown is assumed to be of interest, for, inevitably, the engagement of
one character by another is at the same time engagement of the reader in
this didactic process. The reader's engagement in the text (albeit in an
implicit way) was, of course, vital given the 'cahiers des charges' imposed
on Verne by Hetzel who signed him up in 1862 as a contributor to his
'encyclopédie de l'enfance et de la jeunesse', entitled *Magasin d'éducation
et de récréation*.[15]

Verne's adherence to contemporary representational conventions
clearly reflects a particular ideological standpoint that places a premium
on knowledge of the world. Again, the character of Michel Ardan is
important in that his 'fantaisie' is implicitly rejected (he is frequently made
fun of, though in a more gentle way than the secretary of the Gun-Club,
J.-T. Maston—see *AL*, 129–33, 244–5, 262–3) in favour of the solid body
of scientific knowledge that Nicholl and Barbicane can draw on and the
positivistic rationalism that they are able to apply to it.[16] As is the case with
Zola,[17] the highest value is placed on the character of the 'savant' or his
technological counterpart in Verne, the 'ingénieur'.[18] The real spaces to be
conquered are all those relating to 'l'inconnu', 'l'incompréhensible',
'l'inexplicable' (see, *inter alia*, *AL*, 138; *IN*, 210, 212; *RC*, 55, 144, 222; and
the opening chapters of *Vingt mille lieues sous les mers* and *Robur-le-
conquérant*). Once ignorance, or its corollary 'mystification', has been
overcome, progress ('une des lois de ce monde'—*RC*, 243) is unstoppable.
It is in this respect that the underlying assumptions that pervade most of
Verne's novels place him quite firmly within the socio-cultural context of
his time. Even more overtly than in works by his contemporaries, the quest
for and exploitation of knowledge provides a highly 'lisible' narrative
structure (unknown—>known, mystery—>clarification, impossibility—
>possibility).[19] Although at the end of a few texts some element of mystery
may remain (such as the true identity of Captain Nemo—*VMLM*, 616), this
is frequently dispelled in later texts (in this case in *L'Île mystérieuse*, 802 ff.).

Even in cases where science may seem to err, these errors will eventually lead to the truth; all nature's 'merveilles' are ultimately explicable by the laws of physics; *in extremis* even the inexplicable need not stop the forward-thrust of progress: these are the optimistic messages of one of Verne's first novels, *Voyage au centre de la terre* (249, 302, 327) as of many later ones.

Nearly all Vernian texts ultimately work towards a central solution and resolution—indeed the word 'centre', so frequent in Verne's works, deserves special attention in thematic, narratological and even epistemological terms, as Butor has shown.[20] The resultant overriding optimism distances his corpus ideologically from the often more ambiguous nineteenth-century classic Realist novel in France, even if many of the narratological means by which the central message is conveyed are analogous. Contributing to that ideological distance are other elements of discourse, not the least of which pertain specifically to utopian writing. It is to this aspect of Verne's writings that we shall now turn.

'L'Au-delà'

Utopianism is the ultimate textual construct.[21] It is also an inherently paradoxical and hybrid form of writing. From the two acknowledged archetypes of utopian writing, Plato's *Republic* and More's *Utopia*, which rely on dialogue and reported speech, through to works in which the heroes' adventures become important in themselves,[22] utopian discourse inevitably relies heavily on description. The descriptions are framed by narrative—which stands as a kind of textual 'rite of passage', providing access to the imagined utopia—but narrative itself inevitably plays a minor role, for narrative is diegesis, that is, it has a spatio-temporal dimension. Utopia is therefore largely incompatible with History; utopian writing is *a fortiori* incompatible with Realist novelistic discourse.[23]

Critics are usually wary of classifying Verne as a writer of utopias, rejecting the designation in favour of other types of generic classification: 'romans d'anticipation', 'robinsonnades', 'romans d'aventures', 'romans scientifiques'. However, even these critics admit the presence in Verne's writings of certain codes found in textual utopias.

Utopian writing constitutes a vast and controversial subject of critical discussion and, like so many genres, lacks clear definition. However, one useful starting-point is provided by Trousson:

> On pourra ... parler d'utopie lorsque, dans un cadre narratif ... , se voit animée une collectivité ... fonctionnant selon certains principes politiques, économiques, moraux, restituant la complexité d'une

existence sociale … qu'elle soit située dans un lointain géographique ou temporel et enclavée ou non dans un voyage imaginaire.[24]

We might further refine these general outlines by enumerating the themes and symbols codified in utopian discourse against which we can then set those to be found in Verne's writings.

Utopias contain a number of well-defined themes: access to the utopia is via a journey or a dream; the utopia is generally isolated in an imprecise spatio-temporal locus; it is organized socially, along urban lines, but the urban space opens onto some elemental space, usually water—sea, lake or river.[25] This surrounding elemental space serves a triple purpose: firstly, it protects the utopia from possibly harmful outside forces; secondly, it ensures that 'life' in utopia is self-contained and therefore organized without recourse to any kind of existence outside itself; thirdly, it allows the inhabitants of the utopia a distant contact with and hence knowledge of a spiritually comforting, timeless elsewhere from which they originally came and to which, implicitly at least, they will return.[26]

The citizens of utopia are traditionally (and paradoxically) involved in agricultural activity within this clean, geometrically arranged urban environment; the fruits of their labours are shared, but there is a hierarchy amongst them, sages and philosophers holding the pre-eminent positions in society; men and women are generally separated and the role of the latter as mother effaces that of sexual partner. Above all, utopia is fixed in an eternal present, of necessity outside evolution with its attendant notions of imperfection, evil and, above all, death.[27]

Many of the codes of utopian writing that I have outlined above are present in the novels of Verne. The most obvious element is the space within which the *fabula* is set. Rockets, submarines, hot-air balloons, desert islands are the isolated, protected, self-contained loci propitious for the formation of a utopian social organization, like that of the *Albatros*: 'A bord, on vivait d'une existence commune, d'une vie de famille, en gens heureux qui ne se cachaient pas de l'être' (*RC*, 162–3); this type of social organization can also exist in isolated communities on land—the parallels between the features of a utopian existence enumerated above and those to be found in France-Ville are particularly striking (*CCMB*, 143–59). Time in these places is almost obsessively modelled on the calendar time of the framing narrative, with frequent references to the date and the duration of the journey (or other experience); nevertheless, there is a pervading sense of the timelessness of existence within (or on) them. Spatially they are either in ceaseless motion or in a no-man's land—'un monde à part';[28] in this respect the calculation of the exact geographical location of 'l'île mystérieuse' by Cyrus Smith (I, 426), accurate though it may be, is of purely academic value. This is also true of the 'real time' data of the

American Civil War from which the principal characters have escaped as prisoners of the Confederates and which has ended by their return to America at the end of the novel (*IM*, I, 11–25; II, 864).[29] Socio-historical space and time are thus largely effaced, but not to the extent of giving way to their allegorical counterparts in purely utopian discourse. Verne's texts stand at a crossroads between the empirical time–space nexus of Realist texts and that of an 'ailleurs' which is never granted complete autonomy.

On a more banal level, the great importance attached to eating has been commented on by more than one critic;[30] sickness and disease, on the other hand, are largely absent; exceptions are fevers, often the result of extreme thirst, a fall or gunshot wounds (Axel, *VCT*, 186 and 227 and ff.; Harbert, *IM*, 682 and ff.). Sex and death (so often closely linked in nineteenth-century literature) are both banished for reasons of propriety; the odd animal might meet an unfortunate end (like the dog Satellite, *AL*, 101 and illustration, 99), but in doing so becomes more an object of light comedy than of tragedy.

If some conditions for the creation of a utopia appear to be present in Verne's novels, one fundamental element is missing: a break with the existing social order which traditionally underlies the creation of a utopian space (in its widest sense). In Verne's novels, the utopia aspired to in many cases is precisely a *perfection* of nineteenth-century values and phenomena, most notably, of technical and scientific advances.[31] It is true that some of the staple elements of contemporary Western society are absent: Verne very largely neglects references to an orthodox Judaeo-Christian God and organized religion.[32] On most counts, however, it is now almost commonplace to stress the extent to which he is not only a product of late nineteenth-century France but also a propagandist for its values, most notably capitalism in its most potent manifestations of mercantilism and feats of engineering. Furthermore, as Unwin has pointed out, the almost undiluted praise for capitalism goes hand-in-hand with the bourgeois principles of Verne's time which uphold particular class values, gender distinctions and a belief in the total supremacy of Western man's (and exclusively man's!) civilization.[33] Thus, if the various loci of Verne's stories—rockets, submarines and desert islands—are the sites of a utopian, universalizing vision, such a vision is, paradoxically, firmly geared towards the 'ici-bas' of nineteenth-century life and *Weltanschauung*. These utopias are timeless, but they are also historically determined in an explicit way. The world to which the protagonists return may be imperfect for the present; however, the possibility of realizing an ideal form of society has been glimpsed in the loci in which an experimental utopia has been provisionally played out. As in all utopias, contradiction or opposition (between characters, beliefs, technical means) are ultimately resolved and uniformity of viewpoint reigns. The difference is that here such uniformity does not exclude or even satirize contemporary empirical reality, rather, it embraces it; in Noiray's phrase, Verne's corpus presents itself overall 'comme panorama idéalisé de son siècle'.[34]

Vernian novelistic discourse stands in an awkward and probably unique relationship to Realism. It is still generally considered that Verne's contemporaries, Balzac, Zola and (in different ways) Flaubert provide an important insight into the socio-historical conditions and mentalities of their time. In Verne's case, it is the latter, the *Zeitgeist*, which is clearly the most prominent; and although his novels do not lead to the varying degrees of satirical or ironic questioning of social mechanisms that are the hallmark of these other novelists, collective attitudes are reflected (even caricatured) in the social microcosms which present themselves through an imaginative extension of contemporary scientific and technological advances. Moreover, although description plays a very important part in the novels— one thinks of the lengthy didactic descriptions of the appearance and functioning of the *Columbiad* (*TL*, 76–119, 173–207, 296–309), of the mine (*IN*, 31–2, 34–7) and of the *Albatros* (*RC*, 66–71) which tend in parts to render the novels 'illisible'—narrative too is important, as we shall see in the following section.

There are thus a number of ways in which Verne's work can be placed ideologically and narratologically at the crossroads of the dominant discourse of Realism and of utopian writing. This is particularly the case with the recently discovered *Paris au XXe siècle*, which I discuss in the final section. This work, first published in 1994, is thought to have been written in 1863;[35] it offers a new angle on the discussion of Vernian utopias, for the futuristic dystopia it represents provides an interesting counterpoint to the mini-utopias of the mainstream novels. Moreover, *Paris au XXe siècle* is further evidence of the fact that by the second half of the nineteenth century, utopianism as a genre was itself evolving into its present-day form, science fiction. Verne's novels clearly play an essential part in this evolution.

...but Not as they Knew it

By common consent, Verne is famous above all as the precursor of the science fiction genre.[36] In this respect too he is a child of his time, for, as Gattégno says, 'il ne peut y avoir science-fiction (même baptisée "anticipation scientifique") tant qu'il n'y a pas de science, et même science appliquée ... la science-fiction naît avec la science, elle appartient au même univers.'[37] In an age of positivism in which many areas of human activity (such as medicine and the natural sciences) were being placed under the remit of science rather than art, it is not surprising that the novel should reflect these new currents; science could be portrayed in fictional narrative as the means whereby the laws governing the universe could be demystified (and to a large extent de-mythified). Thus, where Poe *'présente le mystère insondable ... Jules Verne l'explique'* in a spirit of 'optimisme scientiste'.[38]

Verne's concern for scientific plausibility is thus an extension of the 'vraisemblance littéraire' that all Realist fiction strives to achieve.[39] That said, one needs to define the precise parameters of the science fiction mode within which Verne's texts operate. The first point to note is that the vast majority of Verne's fiction is not futuristic. Apart from *Paris au XXe siècle* and, to a far lesser extent, *Robur-le-conquérant*, apparently set in the mid-to-late 1990s,[40] Verne's novels are all more or less contemporaneous with their publication. However, as Alkon has pointed out, temporal displacement of narrative time into the future, although enhancing the possibilities of science fiction, is not a prerequisite.[41] It is, of course, principally the nature and the perceived potential of the machines employed by the characters of Verne's novels that lend them a futuristic air; however, whilst these machines hover at times on the edge of fantasy, they very rarely leave the rational confines of what was technically possible at the time.

There are at least two other senses in which Verne's novels are closer to science fiction than to utopian writing. The first relates to the ideology of the content. Like most science fiction—at least until very recent times—his novels present in largely Manichaean fashion contemporary concerns and/or conflicts on an international or cosmic level: imperialism of some kind, Western-style industrialization and its consequences, and armaments and their use against the enemy are the stuff of a great deal of twentieth-century science fiction from Wells onwards. The second element of common ground lies in the narrative form of the novels; the situations created by the above-listed subjects offer scope for diegetic evolution of the storyline without losing sight of an ideal, that ideal being a microcosm of society whose functioning relies on the full potential offered by science and technology. The balance is a delicate one between narrative (plot, suspense and an unexpected *dénouement*) and diegetic stasis, characterized by long passages of scientific pedagogy. Nevertheless, seen as a whole, Verne's narratives give at least the impression of conveying a series of actions and adventures.

Moreover, just as Verne skirted round the future while still colliding with it in its widest sense, so, without introducing strange or alien life (another of those essential ingredients of science fiction) he nevertheless manages to capture some sense of the exotic. There are first of all Verne's monsters (the giant octopus of *Vingt mille lieues sous les mers*, the antediluvian creatures of *Voyage au centre de la terre*), popularized, as Raymond notes, by the cinema.[42] Perhaps less obviously, there are Verne's characters whose frequent foreignness seems rarely to have attracted critical attention. One reason for the inclusion of Americans must surely be that they (who appear to predominate in the *Voyages extraordinaires*) are seen to possess the 'génie inventif' (or 'pratique', 'audacieux', 'industriel'—or quite simply 'américain')[43] which is the characteristic *par excellence* of the scientist or the engineer who is necessary, as we have seen, both to enable the fantastic journey to take place and to give it credibility. Then there is the comic effect produced by the figure of the hapless, stupid negro (Frycollin in *Robur-le-conquérant*). Yet at the same time one should surely not neglect the fact that one of the effects of introducing 'foreigners' is to 'exoticize' the characters and their exploits. They therefore contribute to the 'cognitive estrangement' so characteristic of science fiction.[44]

However, three main features of Verne's novels militate against them being classified as science fiction at all. Firstly, diegetic evolution and narrative suspense are often undercut by the fact that the plot of the stories are less concerned with linear action than with the ultimate solution of a mystery (*Vingt mille lieues sous les mers*, *L'Ile mystérieuse*). As we have seen, the situations tend to be played out in isolation and the characters then return to the world 'as we know it', which itself remains largely unchanged and unchallenged (Aronnax, Conseil and Ned Land in *Vingt mille lieues sous les mers*, the five North Americans in *L'Ile mystérieuse*, Lidenbrock and Axel in *Voyage au centre de la terre*, to name but a few). Secondly, and as if to underscore the previous point, elements of the empirical, recognizable world are constantly used as a measure against which to compare and thus the better to comprehend the new environments in which the characters find themselves; thus, the relatively few metaphors that one finds (and they are invariably clichéd) act to make familiar the strange or exotic (e.g. the geological formation of underground galleries as 'les contre-nefs d'une cathédrale gothique'—*VCT*, 161). The hermeneutic process is thus greatly facilitated, contrary to the kind of 'short-circuiting of the signifying process' that, according to Evans, is the hallmark of science fiction as opposed to *scientific* fiction.[45] Thirdly—and this despite Vierne's contention, at least for the characters of *Voyage au centre de la terre*[46]—the characters themselves undergo no fundamental evolution as a result of their extraordinary experiences. In this respect, despite the dramatic nature of the works, the overall impression is one of 'mobilis in *im*mobili' (to subvert the motto of the *Nautilus*—*VMLM*, 80; *IM*, 814). At the end of the novels, the speculative objects and marvellous machines are destroyed, the world returns to comforting order,[47] and the reader, far from being exhorted to weigh up moral problems or even to view contemporary society in a satirical fashion, is encouraged to accept an unproblematical status quo.

With regard to science fiction writing, *Paris au XXe siècle* must rank as an exception in Verne's oeuvre. This text represents a significant departure from the ideology subtending Verne's novels, and clearly points to the fact that the author would have produced a considerably broader range of texts had he not been constrained by Hetzel's 'cahiers des charges', a hypothesis already borne out by a few of the more sombre later works such as *Maître du monde* (1904). Here at last is a text which in fact brings Verne into the direct line of the authors of future-time utopias/dystopias that began in France with Mercier's *L'An-2440* (1771) and continued through Souvestre's *Le Monde tel qu'il sera* (1846) to Robida's *Le XXe siècle* (1883). Recognizably Vernian in the enumerations and didacticism which characterize the descriptions (30, 35, 48, 68, 114–24, 135, 186), the naturalist techniques engendering description in works such as *Autour de la lune* and *Vingt mille lieues sous les mers*[48] are nevertheless missing from *Paris au XXe siècle*, and the judgemental tone of the narrative voice is unerringly dogmatic (35, 185, 195). The text is a strange mixture of satire, melodrama and dystopia. The devaluation of culture and the creative imagination is seen as catastrophic in this society which favours only activities that are mechanical, scientific or technological in nature. Most damningly, the latter prove powerless to deal with such an unexceptional situation as the onset of severe weather conditions (186–7) which ultimately cause the death of the hero, Michel. The traits of facile melodrama and of the *roman-feuilleton* are much in evidence: stereotyped characterization, contrived situations, sentimentality (the meeting between the orphan Michel and his long-lost uncle who understands him and shares his passion for literature, Michel's unrecognized genius, the ideal love of Michel and his sweetheart Lucy thwarted by poverty) and the exaggerated gestures and exclamations which accompany these events;[49] in short, there is more than a passing resemblance to the clichéd Romantic trials and tribulations of 1840s- and 1850s-style Bohemian existence.[50] Such features will undoubtedly make of *Paris au XXe siècle* something of a curiosity within Verne's corpus.[51] Nevertheless, it must be recognized as an example of 'littérature futuriste' of the kind Félix Bodin described and advocated as the way forward in regenerating the novel in his half-novel half-theoretical work, *Le Roman de l'avenir* (1834).[52] Understandably, therefore, much was written at its publication about the prophetic elements of *Paris au XXe siècle*—the allusions to an RER-type network, to the widespread use of the internal combustion engine, to communication by fax machines, to the electric chair as a means of execution.[53] It is also a dystopic vision of a future Paris and shares many of the features of the

more pessimistic science fiction narratives we associate with Wells and his
followers.

This unusual work apart, Verne's narratives overall are
contemporaneous with the time of composition, uphold prevailing
ideology and deny any essential evolution, as we have seen. Much current
criticism has chosen to emphasize the intertextual, self-referential, even
self-mocking nature of Verne's texts. These elements undeniably exist: one
thinks of the intratextual references to the publication of a scientific
account of the journey undertaken by Lidenbrock and Axel, playfully
entitled *Voyage au centre de la terre* (*VCT*, 200 and 371), and of Conseil's
taxonomic activities which are a parody of his master's own enterprise
(*VMLM*, 20, 36, 52, 195, 235, 277, 330)—and indeed of the author's.
Compère has identified a number of other such 'autoréférences',
'autoparodies' and 'autoreprises'.[54] Such textual 'clins d'œil', highlighted
by Vierne and more recently by Meakin,[55] undoubtedly add touches of
'modernity' to Verne's work; they are, however, sporadic and in no way
represent a wholesale debunking or undermining of the essentially serious
enterprise of instruction and high-minded 'divertissement'.

This is not to deny a degree of complexity in Verne's fictions, and re-
readings of his works in the wake of the publication of *Paris au XXe siècle*
will no doubt endorse the contention by some that this corpus is far from
unequivocal and uni-faceted. Certainly this 'new' work underscores—
albeit in dystopic mode—the already vital place accorded in Verne's works
to the possible, the potential. Knowledge is a means of conquering the
world, but belief in the spread of knowledge and technological know-how
also carries with it the assumption that the potential for change exists. In
other words, as in most science fiction, science is portrayed—for better or
for worse—as an 'enabling' force.[56]

Alkon, along with others, defines science fiction as 'the literature of
change'.[57] The case may surely be made that all literature reflects in some
way the evolution of society and the socio-cultural attitudes within that
society. The key to the specificity of different texts lies in defining how
they represent the nature of that evolution. We have seen how the
discourse of Verne's texts is Realist by its positivistic description and
categorization of the world, as well as by its use of Naturalist devices in the
narrative organization and by its didacticism. It is utopian by its depiction
of self-contained 'ideal' communities and paradoxical immobility. It is
science-fictional in the action and pace of the narrative within that static
framework, as well as being a literature of 'open vision' at a time when
fear of the future was not yet synonymous with a fear of science.[58]

Many novelists of the nineteenth century evolved along a line that went from the particular to the universal: Zola from the Gothic *Thérèse Raquin*, through the social fresco of *Les Rougon-Macquart* to the later semi-allegorical—in places utopian—final cycles of *Les Trois Villes* and *Les Quatre Evangiles* and an unrealized project for a drama series, *La France en marche*;[59] Sue from the melodramatic *Mystères de Paris* to the quasi-metaphysical *Les Mystères du peuple* and an over-ambitious project for an all-encompassing final novel *Les Mystères du monde ou l'esclavage, le prolétariat et la misère chez tous les peuples en 1850*.[60] Verne, on the other hand, intercalates the particular and the general from the outset: individual (though often undifferentiated) characters and a collective mass; the smallest technological or scientific elements which together make up futuristic machines or natural phenomena; a particular geographically verifiable point of departure for a global voyage.

Attitudes towards Verne have traditionally been ambivalent. At one end of the spectrum, his works are still dismissed as juvenile literature, a notion borne out by the fact that many Verne novels are still mainly to be found in the children's literature sections of bookshops, while at the other extreme they are hailed as myth-making, even postmodern.[61] A new approach might well be to examine his narratives in the light of newly evolving models of paraliterature.[62] Verne tends to be separated off from his contemporaries (notably the Realist novelists), yet it is surely time to recontextualize his texts, which are, as I have suggested in this study, the site of a number of interconnecting narrative types. What emerges above all from the varying generic narrative strands that I have examined is the interface between the historic (Realist), the a-chronic (utopian) and the futuristic (science fiction). More detailed and wider-ranging studies would no doubt reveal the significance of this interface in the nineteenth century, an era in which the advocacy of progress went hand-in-hand not only with a belief in the importance of history, but, more unsettlingly, with the awareness (implicit or otherwise) of a black hole, a missing link in the concept of universal life as a chain.[63] The recent discovery and publication of *Paris au XXe siècle*, a true example of nineteenth-century futuristic literature, offers an instance of yet one more mode of discourse, and surely means that the reassessment of Verne's oeuvre is set to continue.

Notes

1 *Le Père Goriot* (Paris, Gallimard, coll. Folio, 1971), pp. 21–9.

2 *Le Rouge et le noir*, ed. H. Martineau (Paris, Garnier Classiques, 1960), p. 357; see too p. 376.

3 'L'impossible utopie ou chronos défié', *Bulletin de la Société Jules Verne* (henceforth *BSJV*), no. 108 (1993), 14–25 [15].

4 All Verne's works to which reference is made are from the Livre de Poche

edition. Where page number references appear in the text, the following abbreviations are used:

AL   *Autour de la lune* (1869)
CCMB   *Les 500 millions de la Bégum* (1879)
IM   *L'Ile mystérieuse* (1874–5)
IN   *Les Indes noires* (1877)
RC   *Robur-le-conquérant* (1886)
TL   *De la Terre à la lune* (1864)
VCT   *Voyage au centre de la terre* (1st edn, 1864)
VMLM   *Vingt mille lieues sous les mers* (1869–70)

5 For a stimulating analysis of the distinction and interpenetration of 'type' and 'stereotype' in nineteenth-century fiction, see R. Amossy, *Les Idées reçues. Sémiologie du stéréotype* (Paris, Nathan, 1991), pp. 49–75.

6 Nineteenth-century Realist novelists frequently adapted or had their novels adapted, just as writers of melodrama were also writers of novels, particularly in *roman-feuilleton* form: see J. Best, *Expérimentation et adaptation. Essai sur la méthode naturaliste d'Emile Zola* (Paris, Corti, 1986), pp. 220–3; J.-M. Thomasseau, *Le Mélodrame* (Paris, PUF, 1984), p. 104; J.-L. Bachelier, 'Les combles du mélodrame', *Revue des sciences humaines*, XLI, no. 162, pp. 205–18. Verne's lifelong interest in the theatre is well-known: see D. Compère, *Jules Verne écrivain* (Paris, Droz, 1991), pp. 35–6; his novelistic discourse is imbued with dramatic techniques, as Pourvoyeur has shown: 'Jules Verne, écrivain du théâtre ou romancier dramatique?', *BSJV*, no. 70 (1983), pp. 53–7; and, of course, many of his novels were adapted for stage (and later for screen).

7 F. Raymond reminds us that the names of these two cities formed the original title of the work ('Utopie et aventure dans l'œuvre de Jules Verne', *BSJV*, no. 102 (1992), 26–32, 29).

8 R. Barthes, *S/Z* (Paris, Seuil, 1970), pp. 25–7; see too Ph. Hamon, 'Note sur les notions de norme et de lisibilité en stylistique', *Littérature*, no. 15 (1974), 114–22.

9 J.-M. Adam and A. Petitjean, *Le Texte descriptif* (Paris, Nathan, 1989), pp. 26–33; following these authors, I here take the mathetic function of a description to relate to the distribution and diffusion in the fictional text of diverse forms of knowledge.

10 Although Axel is technically the narrator-focalizer of the story of *Voyage au centre de la terre*, these passages are largely indistinguishable from the didactic pronouncements of the zero degree narrator-focalizer of the great majority of Verne's other novels.

11 They appear in nearly all the novels discussed in this study and are particularly numerous in *De la Terre à la lune*; on the question of Verne's footnotes, see D. Compère, 'Les bas des pages', *BSJV*, no. 68 (1983), pp. 147–53.

12 See D. Compère, *Jules Verne écrivain*, pp. 42–6 for details of Verne's documentation of his novels and pp. 38–42 for what Compère calls the author's 'quadrillage du globe'.

13 Amossy, *Les Idées reçues*, p. 59.

14 Adam and Petitjean, *Le Texte descriptif*, pp. 26–33; see too Ph. Hamon, *Introduction à l'analyse descriptif* (Paris, Hachette, 1981), pp. 234–41.

15 See Compère, *Jules Verne écrivain* (Geneva, Droz, 1991), pp. 17–20.

16 The very title of chapter XI of *Autour de la lune* ('Fantaisie et réalisme',

p. 153) underlines the opposition.

17 See Ch. Bertrand-Jennings, *Espaces romanesques: Zola* (Sherbrooke (Quebec), Naaman, 1987), pp. 125–41.

18 Note in particular the superlative description of Cyrus Smith (as seen through the eyes of his companions): 'un microcosme, un composé de… toute l'intelligence humaine' (*IM*, p. 102). Only in one or two much later works such as *Maître du monde* does the scientist become a demonic force: see J. Noiray, *Le Romancier et la machine. L'image de la machine dans le roman français (1850–1900)*, II (Jules Verne—Villiers de l'Isle-Adam) (Paris, Corti, 1982), pp. 209–15.

19 This rationalization process is somewhat attenuated in the later texts in which a kind of fantastic Romanticism is much more in evidence: see O. Dumas, 'Le fantastique chez Jules Verne', *BSJV*, no. 72 (1984), *passim*; F. Raymond, 'Le Scaphandrier des abîmes', preface to *Le Livre d'or de la science-fiction: Jules Verne* (Paris, Presses Pocket, 1986), pp. 7–26, especially pp. 19–26; and, edited by the same author, *Jules Verne 5: Emergences du fantastique* (Paris, Minard, coll. *Revue des Lettres modernes*, 1987).

20 M. Butor, 'Le point suprême et l'âge d'or or à travers quelques œuvres de Jules Verne', in *Essais sur les modernes* (Paris, Gallimard, 1971), pp. 35–94 (notably pp. 65–7, 75–9). The importance of the centre in alchemy has also long been recognized: see D. Meakin, *Hermetic Fictions. Alchemy and Irony in the Modern Novel* (Keele University Press, 1995), pp. 19–20 and *passim*.

21 I take it here as read that only *textual* utopias can exist given that they represent timeless and spaceless ideals; 'lived' utopias, which have formed the basis of experiments through the ages, cannot but be modelled upon some textual form.

22 See R. Trousson, 'Utopie et roman utopique', *Revue de sciences humaines*, XXXIX, no. 155 (1974), 367–78, [374–6]; Trousson cites the works of the seventeenth-century writers Foigny, Vairasse and Tyssot de Patot.

23 This point has been made by most theorists of utopian writing: see *inter alia* L. Marin, *Utopiques: jeux d'espaces* (Paris, Minuit, 1973), pp. 249–51.

24 Trousson, 'Utopie et roman utopie', pp. 372–3.

25 J. Servier, *L'Utopie* (Paris, PUF, coll. Que sais-je?, 1979), pp. 93–4.

26 The symbolic parallel with the womb is all too obvious: ibid., pp. 101–2, 103–4.

27 Ibid., pp. 94–101.

28 Professor Aronnax's words (repeated by Captain Nemo) in reference to the *Nautilus*, *VMLM*, 261.

29 Interestingly, Verne's original ending to this novel (rejected by Hetzel) emphasizes much more forcefully a nostalgic longing for the lost paradise of 'l'île Lincoln': see O. Dumas, 'La Résurrection de l'île mystérieuse', *BSJV*, no. 77 (1986), 13–14.

30 See S. Vierne, *Jules Verne. Mythe et modernité* (Paris, PUF, 1989), pp. 59–60.

31 This is not to deny some satirical critiques of the possible extremes to which nationalist movements and capitalism in contemporary society could go: see Compère, *Jules Verne écrivain*, pp. 80–5; such critiques are, however, proportionately very few within Verne's overall production.

32 One notable exception is Barbicane's uncharacteristic reference to an after-life: *AL*, 282.

33 T. Unwin, *Verne, Le Tour du monde en quatre-vingts jours* (University of

Glasgow French and German Publications, no. 23, 1992), pp. 12–13, 20–9; see too *inter alia* Raymond, 'Utopie et aventure'.

34 *Le Romancier et la machine*, II, p. 228.

35 *Paris au XXe siècle* (Paris, Hachette/Le Cherche Midi, 1994); see Gondolo della Riva's preface to this edition, pp. 13–15.

36 J. Gattégno, *La Science-fiction* (Paris, PUF, coll. Que sais-je?, 1971), p. 9.

37 Idem., p.9.

38 Ibid., p. 11; here and elsewhere in his study, Gattégno stresses the difference in attitude between Verne's unbounded optimism and H. G. Wells' 'pessimisme lucide et moralisateur' (p. 26).

39 Ibid., p. 10.

40 See Verne's letter to Hetzel, quoted by Vierne, *Jules Verne. Mythe et modernité*, p. 56.

41 Paul K. Alkon, *Origins of Futuristic Fiction* (Athens and London, University of Georgia Press, 1987), p. 12. I am indebted to Prof. C. Crossley of the University of Birmingham, G.B., for bringing my attention to Alkon's writings.

42 Raymond, 'Le Scaphandrier de l'abîme', p. 10.

43 For example, *TL*, 5, 31, 56, 299, 321; *AL*, 287.

44 Angenot's felicitous expression: 'Science Fiction in France before Verne', *Science Fiction Studies*, vol. 5 (1978), 58–66, [62].

45 Arthur B. Evans, 'Science Fiction vs. Scientific Fiction in France: From Jules Verne to J.-H. Rosny Aîné', *Science Fiction Studies*, vol. 15 (1988), 1–11, notably 8–10.

46 *Jules Verne. Mythe et modernité*, p. 136.

47 Many critics have pointed to the essentially cyclical nature of Verne's narratives and concept of time: see, *inter alia*, R. Barthes, '*Nautilus et Bateau ivre*', *Mythologies* (Paris, Seuil, coll. Essais, 1957), pp. 80–2 and W. Butcher, *Verne's Journey to the Centre of the Self* (London, Macmillan, 1990), especially ch. 6, pp. 73–93; A. Martin, *The Mask of the Prophet* (Oxford, Oxford University Press, 1990), notably pp. 191–8.

48 See above, pp. 62–4.

49 See, for example, pp. 89–90, 184–5; pp. 62–3; pp. 130–8, 179–85; pp. 56, 62, 75, 84, 148–9, 151, 157, 183, 204.

50 See Henri Murger's *Scènes de la vie de Bohême* (Paris, Levy, nouvelle éd. revue et corrigée, 1862) and Murger's Préface of 1850, especially the portrait of the type of 'la Bohême ignorée', ibid., pp. 6–7.

51 This is not to say that there are no elements which call for other more complex readings of the text. Among these figure the descriptions of the 'realistic' stage decor and scenery and other features of the 'Grand Entrepôt dramatique' (pp. 167–78), and Michel's grand dying gestures and words in Père Lachaise cemetery which may be seen as an ironic counterpoint to the ending of *Le Père Goriot* (pp. 200–4).

52 See Paul K. Alkon, *Science Fiction before 1900. Imagination Discovers Technology* (New York, Macmillan, 1994), pp. 2–3 and *Origins of Futuristic Fiction*, pp. 6–11.

53 See *inter alia* B. Poirot-Delpech, 'Jules Verne inédit', *Le Monde les livres* (23 septembre 1994).

54 *Jules Verne, écrivain*, pp. 108–21.

55 Vierne, *Jules Verne. Mythe et modernité*, pp. 47 and ff.; Meakin, *Hermetic Fictions*, p. 73.

56 See Alkon, *Science Fiction before 1900*, p. 6.

57 Ibid., p. 16.

58 See Slusser, 'Storm Warnings and Dead Zones: Imagination and the Future', in George E. Slusser, Colin Greenland and Eric S. Rabin (eds), *Storm Warnings. Science Fiction Confronts the Future* (Carbondale, South Illinois University Press, 1987), pp. 3–20, [10 and 19].

59 For details of the latter project, see C. Becker, G. Gourdin-Servenière and V. Lavielle, *Dictionnaire d'Emile Zola* (Paris, Laffont, coll. Bouquins, 1993), p. 414.

60 M. Nathan, 'Socialisme cosmique et métaphysique du feuilleton dans *Les Mystères du peuple*', in *Splendeurs et misères du roman populaire*. Textes réunis et présentés par R.-P. Colin, R. Guise et P. Michel (Presses universitaires de Lyon, 1990), pp. 55–9.

61 See *inter alia* Vierne, *Jules Verne. Mythe et modernité*; Compère, *Jules Verne, écrivain*; Meakin, *Hermetic Fictions*, pp. 63–75.

62 See, for example, A.-M. Boyer, *La Paralittérature* (Paris, PUF, 1982) and D. Couégnas, *Introduction à la paralittérature* (Paris, Seuil, coll. Poétique, 1992).

63 In this connection see M.-H. Huet's stimulating article, 'Anticipating the Past: The Time Riddle in Science Fiction', in Slusser *et al.*, *Storm Warnings*, pp. 34–42.

6

A Hitchhiker's Guide to Paris:
Paris au XXe siècle

DAVID PLATTEN

Jules Verne has been 'saved'. From the late fifties a steady stream of approbatory reviews, articles and books penned by intellectual luminaries such as Roland Barthes,[1] William Golding[2] and Michel Serres,[3] and other notable figures like Simone Vierne[4] and Jean-Yves Tadié,[5] has secured for the most translated of all French writers the literary recognition he had craved during his lifetime but thought beyond reach. Ironically, this posthumous good reception has since rebounded on the author whose name has attracted a certain controversy in the wake of the new complexities found in his work. In September 1994 the publication by Hachette of what was previously a Verne *inédit*, entitled *Paris au XXe siècle*, further stoked what was already a hot debate.

The belated interest in Verne is not especially concerned with the assessment of his literary qualities. As all literature today seems appreciated more for the way in which it defines the prevailing culture than for its intrinsic literariness, so, in relation to Jules Verne, other not strictly literary issues are now at stake: the political and cultural identity of the man; the authenticity of his writings; his status as a national emblem or myth; and above all the diagnostic witness of his vast and original oeuvre to the societies past and present in which it was manufactured and is now read. The resurgence of Jules Verne as a leading light in French literature is also inextricably linked with the emergence of science fiction over the past forty years from cultish sideshow into the mainstream of literary consciousness, a sign of recognition that the collapsing of science into fiction is, in its essential ambiguity, the biggest and most challenging affirmation of the value of literature to the modern world. Perhaps it is by virtue of the questions that now cloud the pristine images of his child-oriented adventure stories that Verne is a little less distanced from this hybrid genre he was supposed to have helped found than he once was. *Paris au XXe siècle* is heralded as an uncannily precise representation of the French capital in

1961, roughly one hundred years on from its time of composition. As such it fits squarely with the central Vernian paradox of a prophetic legacy, of visions sealed into a huge and as yet not entirely untapped corpus of work like predictions in a magician's envelope, awaiting the revelation of their accuracy to an incredulous audience.

This myth of the literary seer, already exposed by numerous Verne scholars, is once again paraded in *Paris*. Notwithstanding the fact that this is a half-baked work of fiction, hardly even a novel, almost totally lacking the narrative verve of the *Voyages extraordinaires*, commentators have unanimously drawn attention to the portentous character of the text. *Le Figaro Littéraire* found little else to say about it, for the content of an anticipatory article in its 21 May issue was largely reproduced in the piece which, four months later, acknowledged its publication. A review article in *The Guardian* newspaper (22 September) was typical of many during this period. Having explained the unusual genesis of the text, the author proceeds to list various inventions that have since materialized and perspectives on a future society that now seem valid contained within it, in each case with supporting citations. Verne is credited with foreseeing the use on a wide scale of electric lighting, 'les candélabres établis par l'électrisation d'un filet de mercure, rayonnaient avec une incomparable clarté … au même moment, les cent mille lanternes de Paris s'allumaient d'un seul coup' (*Paris*, 46); the invention of the internal combustion engine, 'de ces innombrables voitures qui sillonnaient la chaussée des boulevards, le plus grand nombre marchait sans chevaux; elles se mouvaient par une force invisible, au moyen d'un moteur à air dilaté par la combustion du gaz' (48); and the facsimile machine, 'la télégraphie photographique … permettait d'envoyer au loin le fac-simile de toute écriture, autographe ou dessin, et de signer des lettres de change ou des contrats à cinq mille lieues de distance' (70). Likewise he would have forecast the continued decline of the French language, 'la belle langue française est perdue … les inventeurs ont puisé dans le vocabulaire anglais leurs plus déplaisantes appellations … les philosophes pour leur philosophie, ont trouvé la langue française trop pauvre et se sont rejetés sur l'étranger!' (115); the propagation of mass entertainment through his evocation of 'Le Grand Entrepôt Dramatique' (167–78); and the monopolizing of supply-side economics by the state and a small number of multinational corporations, 'Le monopole, ce nec plus ultra de la perfection, tenait dans ses serres le pays tout entier' (29).

However impressive these statements may at first appear, they amount to little more than the sum of knowledge that could easily have been gleaned from the nineteenth-century scientific journals which Verne regularly perused, and by simply keeping abreast of current affairs. The appended notes to *Paris* inform us that the first electric light was produced by Thomas Davy a full fifty years before Verne's book was supposed to have been written, Daimler invented the modern automobile in 1889, though the technology was known a considerable time in advance of its application, and Giovanni Caselli is correctly identified in Verne's text (70) as the inventor of the modern fax machine. With respect to his prognosis on the evolution of society, the French authorities have worried endlessly over a perceived need to protect the national tongue from erosion (normally understood as meaning anglicization) since the foundation of the Académie Française in 1635, and the mass production of culture was underway by the second half of the nineteenth century in the form of the *feuilletons*, in which were published serializations of Balzac (and later Zola) amongst a whole host of other minor writings.

It has become clear that the generally happy juxtaposition of the fantastic with the post-scriptum verifiable in the classic Verne texts has its source in careful planning rather than clairvoyance. The designs of his two most famous machines, the *Nautilus* submarine featuring in *Vingt mille lieues sous les mers* (1867–70) and *L'Ile mystérieuse* (1874–5) and *Albatros*, the aircraft in *Robur-le-conquérant* (1886) and *Maître du monde* (1904), were based on advice given by expert engineers who, in each instance, revised thoroughly the technical descriptions of the vehicle before the text reached its final draft. Other far-fetched claims for the influence of Verne's fiction over future scientific developments are easily dismissed. Jean Jules-Verne's preposterous claim that his grandfather's 'eminently *scientific* fictionalization of moon travel never received a finer consecration than the mission of Apollo 9, one hundred years later' is apparently justified by astronaut Frank Borman's taste for reading science fiction.[6] Remarking that Verne's idea of 'firing a hollowed-out cannon-ball loaded with passengers at the moon' was 'scarcely less fantastic' than H. G. Wells' dream of taking an airship to Mars, Andrew Martin merely restores some badly needed balance to the argument.[7] Verne himself was quite prepared to 'adapt' the laws of science to suit the needs of his fiction. Jean Jules-Verne cites an interesting opthalmic case from *Les Frères Kip* (1902), one of the more obscure works, in which a photographic enlargement of the face of the dead Captain Gibson reveals the image of his murderers.[8] Verne first read about this phenomenon in Villiers de l'Isle-Adam's short story *Claire Lenoir* (1867). According to Jean Jules-Verne he would have then checked in his usual meticulous way the scientific premise stating that on death the retina retains an image of the last thing a person sees. The *Encyclopédie d'opthalmologie* would have informed him that retinal images can be fixed after death by removing the eye and submerging it in a bath of alum. However, not only is there a lapse of nearly twenty-four hours between

Gibson's murder and the taking of the photograph, by which time the image would have long since faded, there is also no mention in Verne's story of any alum-soaking.

Such gobbets of information have led scholars to attenuate the popular notion of Verne as a great scientific visionary. Indeed Michel Serres, a respected voice and novelist in his own right, delivers a damning indictment of Verne's supposed genius for anticipating the scientific discoveries of the future:

> Il n'y a jamais, chez lui, anticipation scientifique, du côté de la technologie ou du savoir naturaliste. Il réactive une science assez vieille, de l'astronomie à la physique de la Terre. Globalement, il est en retard d'un bon siècle. Il n'est à l'heure que pour la communication, et les objets artificiels qu'il met en scène sont toujours des moyens de communication, jamais de production, des véhicules au télégraphe.[9]

Still, the one genuine prophesy in *Paris* is the most important, Verne's evocation of the economic supremacy of the multinationals and the dismal impact of this influence both on the physical environment and on the lives of ordinary citizens. Not only does this vision from afar ring alarming bells, it also foreshadows the preoccupation of much science-fiction writing of the first half of the twentieth century with the dialectic of the modernist utopia and the totalitarian regime. Just as in Greek mythology Hercules found that on slicing one of the Hydra's heads a clutch of new ones sprang instantly from the bereaved stump, so Verne demystified merely makes room for a new set of conundrums.

He is generally regarded as one of the early champions of the technologizing of the world, of the victory of mankind over Nature, a believer in the value of industry, capitalist productivity (he played the Stock Exchange for a short while) and the best-known popularizer of logical positivism, the happy coincidence of Cartesian reason and scientific verifiability associated in France with the nineteenth-century philosopher Auguste Comte. In *Paris*, however, industrialization has resulted in the triumph of Science over the Arts, the veneration of the machine, the transformation of human beings into agents of production, and the death of culture as it was once known and understood. Though it may be a weak novel—Hetzel's eloquent rejection of the manuscript suggests that the publisher was put off by the poor quality of Verne's writing rather than by the negativity of its content—*Paris* is a fascinating document for two interconnected reasons: firstly, it jeopardizes most *idées reçues* concerning Verne and his work, and secondly it raises further questions of authorship and textual authenticity.[10]

Paris is the story of Michel, a young (sixteen-year-old), destitute poet—echoes of the Rimbaud legend, still to come in 1863—who inhabits a world in which the cultural value of what he represents is no longer recognized. In the penultimate chapter, night falls (as it does in Poe's *The Man of the Crowd*) and Michel goes out into the frozen streets of the French capital in search of Lucy, the daughter of his former professor, to whom he has pledged his undying love. Having discovered that father and daughter have been evicted from their lodgings, he carries on walking, aimlessly and without obvious reason. While out on the streets Michel is pursued by the 'démon de l'électricité'. The invention of electricity, or rather the replacement towards the end of the nineteenth-century of the gas lanterns with electric streetlighting is seen in the text as a metaphor for modernity, the historical and ontological step forward which is regretted and ultimately dreaded by the young poet-hero. In this instance he chances upon, in quick succession (96–9), electrically illuminated corpses in the mortuary, the main altar in the cathedral of Notre Dame ringed by Christmas lights instead of candles, an infernal 'concert électrique', and a public execution by electrocution; the latter two events are, naturally, eerie anticipations of distinct aspects of modern (American) culture. His nocturnal peregrinations finally cease at the gates of the Père Lachaise cemetery, where he stumbles over the neglected tombstones of forgotten icons. The narrative closes with the image of this person, who has now become the last hero of Western civilization, standing in anguished contemplation of the metropolis below.

The sequence which concludes the novel offers some important keys to new Verne riddles. For the first time the narrative sounds a truly novelistic note of despair, spiced with touches of black humour. Technology seems at last defeated by the power of nature. The terrible winter of 1961 claims many lives, and decimates agricultural production for the following year; however, the underwater sluices and turbines of the dam on the Seine, ensuring that water is supplied constantly to all Parisians, are not hampered by the thick ice covering the surface of the river. Our poet-hero is poor and therefore victimized, compelled to eat 'pain de houille', a form of bread made from a coal extract. Unable to operate in a technologically motivated environment, he is rendered equally powerless by the force of Nature. The frozen wastes of the Seine deny him even the opportunity of a traditional Romantic suicide, as he peers over the parapet of the Pont-Neuf: 'Mauvais temps pour le désespoir s'écria-t-il! On ne peut seulement pas se noyer' (194).

Michel is, of course, a ludicrous, inflated character. He is incompetent and therefore unemployable. The fact that he valiantly occupies the moral high ground and thus resigns (theatrically)—'Oh! se dit-il! je ne resterai pas un instant de plus dans cette caverne! plutôt mourir de faim!' (177)—from the one job he could perform adequately, working in the vaudeville department of the Grand Entrepôt Dramatique, merely serves to underline his own farcical nature. It is possible that by making his apparent mouthpiece so foppish Verne intended to undermine the thesis presented in *Paris*, thus disarming with irony those who foolishly protest at the advances of science. But here we bump judderingly against a typically Vernian inconsistency, for the destination to which Michel leads us, the equation of material poverty with the industrialization of modern society, is too serious to be ignored.

It is tempting to acclaim Verne's recognition in this text of the failure of a political model. There is some genuine satire. The Société Générale de Crédit Instructionnel, an intriguingly Thatcherite model of education, combines nicely with the character portrait of M. Stanislas Boutardin, the ultimate utilitarian, suggesting an intuitive feel for the positivist age coming to its horrible maturity.[11] Later, satirical intent is conveyed through the person of Quinsonnas, the copyist at the Banque de Casmodage, but also a 'modern' musician and owner of a piano that converts not only into a bed, but also into a commode. Quinsonnas lampoons conspiratorially the ant-like system of labour that reduces all human activity to the purely functional, whilst at the same time participating in it. However, it would be unwise to assume that in the space of a single rejected novel Verne should put to the sword his own hitherto unshakeable faith in bourgeois capitalism and logical positivism, the twin peaks of his intellectual make-up. Jean Jules-Verne records the only time when such scepticism preyed on his grandfather as occurring late in life, when, partially infirm, Verne retreated into what seems a fairly ascetic Catholicism. Even then this new scepticism was considerably mitigated by the genuine reconciliation with his wayward son Michel that took place during his last years.[12] There is also no perceptible gestation of a radical political alternative within the pages of *Paris*, and it would be odd if there were, given that the available evidence defines Verne as a committed, though conservative Republican, typically Gaullist *avant la lettre*.[13] Instead the text focuses on the predicted shape of the city of the future.

This is not the only moment in Verne's fiction when the theme of the city is privileged. In *Les 500 millions de la Bégum* (1879) he sketches out what would become a standard science-fiction topos. The drama revolves around the dualistic antagonism of Christian eschatology, between the Evil and the Good cities, a conceit most notably exploited in the *Star Wars* films of the early 1980s. Stahlstadt, the Evil city, bears a remarkable resemblance to Verne's vision of Paris in the twentieth century. It is an industrialist's Mecca, bureaucratic and absurdly centralized, governed by a bourgeois

élite, militaristic, and trenchantly nationalistic. Nature has been totally
suppressed, and pollution is rife. In contrast, France-Ville aspires to the
status of Plato's Ideal Republic. With its democratically elected rulers and
ecologically minded citizens France-Ville is a pleasant garden-city, with no
industry to speak of, a utopian throwback to the Greek city-state. However,
in spite of the superficial similarities of *Les 500 millions de la Bégum* to *Paris*,
the differences between the representations of the city in each text are
salient. Stahlstadt is an undisguised symbol of Prussian imperialism; the
novel was written in the aftermath of the Franco-Prussian war and the
siege of Paris in 1871 that traumatized many in France, Verne included.
Pre-empted by this allegorical incentive, the authorial voice is strident.
Verne ventures into the realm of the town-planner, using topographies to
wage philosophical and cultural, as well as military, battles. In the end the
duality is dissolved, as the values of each autonomous entity are projected
onto its opposite number. In *Paris* there is only one city and it is a given,
immutable reality. The narrator is equally static. His subject, Michel, is
immersed in the city, as in a prison or a maze, powerless to effect change.
This cityscape is invasive. It controls Michel's sense of identity to such an
extent that he has difficulty in recognizing it as other. As we shall see, he
is a poor spectator. However, whenever mimesis is replaced by diegesis in
this text, Verne's Paris of the future is reconnected to the destiny of
individual. The narrative thus targets a favourite theme of nineteenth-
century literature: the absorption of the individual, defined in Cartesian
terms, into the mass of city life, and consequently his new status and
function in the urban environment. In this context Walter Benjamin's
famous essay on the city-dweller in the nineteenth century seen through
the eyes of Baudelaire, with Engels and Victor Hugo prominent in the
supporting cast, is instructive.[14]

Benjamin describes the historical pre-eminence within a fairly restricted
period of time (before the petty bourgeoisie's enjoyment of the first fruits
of industrialization was superseded by a growing awareness of their
economic power) of a new breed of city animal, the *flâneur*. The *flâneur*
signifies the person who is lost, deliberately or otherwise, in the crowd.
For some this may be a pleasant experience, for others not; in either case,
the detachment effected by this new state of anonymity stimulates a
heightened consciousness within that person of his relationship to the city
environment, which he sees for the first time from a new and different
situation. The *flâneur* is a locus for a new way of seeing.

According to Benjamin, this attempt to appropriate the relatively new
phenomenon of the city first came to light with the emergence in 1830s
Paris of a literary sub-genre called the 'physiologies'. These were paper-
bound, pocket-sized volumes, featuring profiles of street types drawn from

across the class spectrum—Benjamin refers to the street vendor and the opera dandy. The 'physiologies' could be seen as an early handbook for soap opera scriptwriters, written in the condescending tone of the classifier and striking familiar stereotyped attitudes. Once the types were exhausted, the theme of the city itself was exploited, and such titles as *Paris la nuit, Paris à table,* and *Paris marié* abounded. The fashion for 'physiologies' proved to be mercifully short-lived, though in Benjamin's mind the more durable Balzac, with his 'predilection for unqualified statements',[15] is associated with it. New architectural configurations, especially the construction of shopping arcades, and the nocturnalization of Parisian street life during the Second Empire—when shops stayed open until 10 p.m.—created more favourable conditions for *flâneur*-dom. The arcade, an interiorization of the boulevard, provided ideal, idling territory, and as his confidence grew and he became an accepted part of the prevailing culture, the *flâneur* adventured out onto the open street.

Other social and cultural innovations arose as a direct response to living in the city. Benjamin talks of the stimulus given to Napoleonic bureaucracy by the perceived need to identify and control these anonymous citizens through the institution of registers, a process which was significantly facilitated by the advent of photography.[16] However, he chronicles the rise and fall of the *flâneur*, whom he sees as the point of intersection between the individual and the city, primarily through the succession of literatures, literary genres and figures. Thus the individual slipping into the crowd and disappearing without leaving traces is not merely the potential criminal that society as a whole needs to keep tabs on, he is also the elusive figure at the centre of Poe's plots; he signifies the 'origin of the detective story'.[17] Likewise the victim of this social repression is not just anyone, it is Baudelaire, sleeping at different addresses each night in order to keep one step ahead of his pursuing creditors. And if the story of the *flâneur* begins with the 'physiologies', it matures in the great literatures of the period. For Benjamin, the different perspectives of the *flâneur* are reflected contrastingly, in Baudelaire and Hugo.

Baudelaire was intoxicated by the city, but never at home in it, either literally or poetically. Although he revelled in the decadent sensuousness of the *flâneur*, he did not allow this fascination with the spectacle of the crowd to, in Benjamin's words, 'blind him to the horrible social reality'.[18] The anger and terror in the *Spleen de Paris* is not inspired, as most would have it, by the poet's disgust at urban life but by its pornographic attraction to him, by his own enjoyment of what he found to be disgusting. In contrast to Baudelaire's lonely, unrecognized ambivalence, Hugo celebrated the city, seeing in it the amassed legions of his own readership. The city is the canvas for his spiritual and literary universe, the citizen the embodiment

of a new political order of democracy. Benjamin points out that Hugo was
the first great writer to have given his works collective titles: *Les Misérables*,
Les Travailleurs de la mer. Hugo's view of the crowd as a polymorphous entity
means that he was no *flâneur*. Yet, though Baudelaire does distinguish and
separate the individual from the crowd, his model of the city, Benjamin
argues, is no more subtle than Hugo's. In fact Benjamin says that their
model was one in the same, that of the hero, though they each applied it
in a different fashion:

> When Victor Hugo was celebrating the crowd as the hero in the
> modern epic, Baudelaire was looking for a refuge for the hero among
> the masses of the big city. Hugo placed himself in the crowd as a
> citoyen; Baudelaire sundered himself from it as a hero. (66)

If Hugo was simply not a *flâneur*, Michel in *Paris* is the anti-thesis of the
flâneur. For Michel the reality of the city is also identified with the crowd.
However this is not the thriving force for progress and political change
envisioned by Hugo, but an amorphous, elemental mass from which he
would dearly like to extricate himself. From his first appearance the
narrator seems to be warning us that if he were not the privileged character
of this novel, if we were not to be allowed into his head, then he would
be indistinguishable from the masses, 'Michel Dufrénoy avait suivi la foule,
simple goutte d'eau de ce fleuve' (40). The use of the river image is
interesting, for its reflects obliquely on Hugo and the tragedy of his
daughter's drowning at Villequier. Verne's character seizes on the
comparison. Michel feels that he is swept along by the current, 'comme
un homme en train de se noyer' (41), a comparison which the narrator
likes for he then expands on it in exclamatory fashion:

> —me voilà entraîné en pleine mer; où il faudrait les aptitudes d'un
> poisson, j'apporte les instincts d'un oiseau; j'aime à vivre dans
> l'espace, dans les régions idéales où l'on ne va plus, au pays des rêves,
> d'où l'on ne revient guère. (41)

Thus, like the bear from the children's story who is frightened that the sky
will fall on his head, Michel looks dreamily to the heavens rather than at
where he is going. Even then, as he embarks on his grand tour of the city,
his gaze is unfocused, 'l'œil se perdait dans les constellations splendides'
(189). He roams wild-eyed around Paris, 'ses yeux demeuraient hagards'
(191), 'l'œil hagard' (194), and as he mingles with the crowds coming out
of the theatres, he deigns not to observe them, 'Michel ferma les yeux...'
(197), as if hoping to ignore the masses into oblivion. By the time he reaches
the cemetery, we are told that he looks without seeing, 'Michel regardait
sans voir' (201).

Unsurprisingly, Michel's tour of Paris would be of little interest to the prospective tourist, as there are few descriptions of the areas he negotiates or the sites he visits, and those that are there are extremely brief. Properly speaking this is neither tour nor journey, just indiscriminate, random, unplanned movement. But it does have an itinerary, to be formulated from the information supplied by the forty or so names of roads, churches, hospitals, and other institutions that pass in bewildering succession, all within the space of ten pages (189–99). Michel attempts neither to appropriate the city nor to make sense of it. Instead it appropriates him. He is assaulted by light[19] and noise, and tellingly by the passage of time. Belfries dotted around Paris chime out the hours, but Michel still loses track. We are left with the impression that time is running out. Preoccupation with time is very much associated with the nineteenth century and Bergson, with a sense of order and the mastery of chaos, a preoccupation that is personified in Phileas Fogg and the narrative of his wager. Viewed in this sense, as a philosophical and literary tool, then time certainly is running out. The Futurists seeking to abolish time through *simultanéitié*, and Apollinaire and Cendrars merrily disrupting notions of linear time and chronology lurk around the corner. Michel, the twentieth-century creation of a nineteenth-century author, thus covers the distance of his crazy-paved walk rapidly, too rapidly as it turns out. Is this the sign of an altered state of mind, or of naked fear, of 'fear and trembling' before a new Modernist age whose day is due? If so, then Michel's fear is well-founded. His journey ends in nightmare and death, with the visit to the morgue at Montparnasse, the prescient image of public execution by electrocution, and his arrival at the Père Lachaise cemetery, end-point and final resting-place of a putative civilization.

There is, however, a discernible logic which remains intact throughout this chaotic end-game. The apparent surfeit of place-names has a purpose. Once Michel's movements are mapped out, it is possible to see that he tacks across Paris, following a course which is roughly east-north-east. He seems to drift inexorably away from traditional areas of luxury and wealth towards the new poverty zones. The association in this narrative between future worlds and continuing human poverty remains admirably constant. Moreover, if Verne's Paris of the future represents his own dread of modernism, then its obverse is an appeal to tradition. The tragic swerve which takes Michel out onto the streets registers the horror of his realization that the traditions he venerates are no longer meaningful, and possibly never were. The generals of the Grande Armée des Lettres (114) marshalled by the three diners at l'oncle Huguenin's house (ch. 10) constitute an impressive roll-call, but there are too many names. Just as later in the novel we see how the Parisian place-names have lost their evocative power, so the names of the great literary men linger on in the collective memory of the few even when the significance and value of their work has long since subsided. The pretentious l'oncle Huguenin observes the passing of a literary tradition in France with some degree of accuracy, 'En 1978, a dit Stendhal, Voltaire sera Voiture, et les demi-sots finiront par en faire leur Dieu' (117). What all three diners fail to grasp, however, is that to believe in any form of tradition is the equivalent of a philosophical mirage. Nowhere is this more pronounced than in their persistent lament to the passing, of 'la belle langue française' (115). As most linguists appreciate, the regular interference of French governments in matters of national language over the past two centuries has been geared more towards creating 'le français correct' than maintaining it.

Whether or not a naïve faith in monolithic tradition is the cornerstone of Verne's political philosophy must remain a moot point. The narrative of *Paris* presents a number of head-hammering solutions to modern ills, apparently without corrective irony, but this text could easily have been the result of a short-lived obsession on Verne's part. Strangely enough, the effect created is the opposite to the one that appears intended. *Paris* alerts us to the dangers involved in keeping faith with dead traditions. German philosopher Jürgen Habermas argues that any notion of tradition is also a form of ideology. Habermas defines ideology as a systematic distortion of communication. In his thesis communication is most frequently distorted by the interlocutors' recourse to symbols.[20] The figures that people Michel's pantheon are primarily cultural symbols. They are also dead ones. Once a culture stagnates, it invariably dies. Thus these dead symbols are deprived of their ghostly power to haunt and thereby to disturb or affect in some way the present situation. They are the skeletons of Chopin, Dumas, La Rochefoucauld, Banville, Gautier, Balzac, Plouvier, Musset and others, lying beneath their neglected tombstones in the Père Lachaise, reduced in this text to yet another long list of empty names.

At its pinnacle Vernian tradition is the tradition of the family, perpetuated in the real world by the Société Jules Verne, and it is this particular tradition above all others which is exposed and fractured in *Paris*. The extraordinary ceremony surrounding Michel's interview with his uncle, M. Stanislas Boutardin, banker and director of the Société des Catacombes de Paris (see ch. 3), provides an early indication that in the industrial society of the future the family business has become all business and no family. Michel is an orphan. In place of the absent father, there are two uncles. Boutardin and Huguenin represent contradictory and equally absurd view-points, rather like the polar positions occupied by the two cities in *Les 500 millions de la Bégum*. This displacement of paternal relations is reminiscent of the shifting affections, misfortune and ultimate sadness that befell Verne himself in his capacity as a father. His only child, Michel, was born in 1861. Headstrong, independently minded and thus resentful of his father's authoritarian streak, Michel rebelled as a teenager, incurring substantial debts. In 1877 Verne obtained a *correction paternelle* through the jurisdiction of the county court, and in February 1878 Michel was effectively banished to India. Within eighteen months he was back in the family fold, only to elope with an actress the following year.

In the absence until the end of his life of a satisfactory relationship with his own son, Verne turned fatherly attentions in the direction of his nephew Gaston, a brilliant and conscientious student. This relationship too ended disastrously, and in the most bizarre of circumstances. Interrupting a journey from Paris to Blois, Gaston went to visit his uncle in Amiens whom he greeted in a fit of hysteria, claiming that he was being pursued. When Verne tried to reassure him that this was not the case, Gaston promptly drew a revolver and shot at him, injuring his foot. Gaston was taken away for observation, certified insane, and spent the rest of his life in various psychiatric institutions.[21] In *Paris* any form of dysfunction is prohibited. Kinship ties are, like everything else in this Modernist world, mechanized. The progeny of M. and Mme Boutardin is thus characterized with superb precision:

> Quant au fils, multipliez la mère par le père, et vous avez pour coefficient Athanase Boutardin ... C'était un vilain homme, sans jeunesse, sans cœur, sans amis. Son père l'admirait beaucoup. (53–4.)

Not only does Verne anticipate Zola's 'tares héréditaires', but also the common store which is now put in genetics, particularly since the discovery of DNA. The Christian Verne would of course have had the greatest difficulty in accepting this branch of science; developments in genetics have effectively snipped the last remaining strands of sentimental attachment to the idea of the existence of a human soul.

It is perhaps axiomatic that the closer the reader gets to a text, the less it will seem to say about its overt subject matter, in this case Paris or the city of the future, and the more it will reveal about the ambitions and desires of its author.[22] *Paris* is certainly more self-referential than other Verne texts. It alludes symbolically to the literary process through the panoptic Grand Livre operated by Quinsonnas. Moreover, one sequence in which Michel dreams that he has been imprisoned by Le Grand Livre and lies helplessly pressed between its pages seems to offer a fleeting glimpse of the author himself, consumed by his work.[23] The characterization is also less assured than is customary with Verne. It is as if he felt unable to establish the usual distance between the fictional creations and his own anxious predisposition. Gone are the sweeping mythical heroes, the imperturbable Fogg, the supernatural Nemo, the resourceful Cyrus Smith and Robur the Superman, to be replaced with, and this, if anything, is the saving grace of the novel, a more genuine investigation into the relationship of machine to mankind. Then there is the evocation of the Grand Entrepôt Dramatique (ch. 14), less an indictment of popular culture as such than a bitter nod in the direction of Verne's own standing amongst his peers which, as Jean Jules-Verne points out, was a source of great disappointment to him.[24]

This final point would be superfluous to the argument if it were accepted that the novel was written in its entirety in 1863, as at this time Verne was only at the starting-post of his literary career. However, there are indications within the text that suggest it was written at a later date. Certainly, and this is the most important reason to adopt a sceptical attitude concerning this issue, a later dating would modify the supernatural aspect to Verne's 'predictions', bringing them that important step nearer (roughly twenty years) to the realization of the scientific research which would have allowed him to project into the future the vision of a machine-dominated metropolis that we find in *Paris*. Moreover, a later dating would also bear more fruitful comparison with other Verne texts, like *Les 500 millions de la Bégum*, and another posthumous work, *L'Etonnante aventure de la mission Barsac* (1920), which portrays the destruction of the city in an apocalyptic scenario. An important marker is the publication in 1875 of the third volume of *L'Ile mystérieuse*, which, with the dramatic reappearance of Nemo in true guise as anti-imperialist Indian prince and the destruction of Lincoln Island, completes the first round of the 'Empire or bust' cycle within which Andrew Martin expertly situates much of Verne's fiction.

Piero Gondolo della Riva's revelation that Verne's posthumous works were not all his own work—he alleges that many were substantially revised by Michel after his father's death—further complicates the issue.[25] In his book Andrew Martin has turned the controversy to his own profit, using the idea that Verne is 'less an individual than a style, a symbol, a mythology' as a pretext to launch his own highly successful intertextual project.[26] In effect Martin is really saying that questions concerning reliability of source are not worth worrying about. The example of Proust has shown that it is impossible to ascertain exactly how much of any given text is the work of the author, the publisher or in Verne's case, the successor to his estate. It may be that my own anxiety concerning the dating of *Paris*, which was confirmed by the self-same Piero Gondolo della Riva, is misplaced. Jean-Jules Verne describes an extraordinary work which was first published in 1854 and shows that the young Verne was quite capable of the scepticism which would account for the fatalistic strain that runs through the narrative of *Paris*. *Maître Zacharius ou l'horloger qui a perdu son âme* is the story of a

Genevan clockmaker who has invented an escape mechanism which in turn has led him to discover the working union of body and soul, the soul being the spring of life and the body its regulator. This discovery confers mortality on Zacharius, given that his destiny is now linked with the destiny of time itself. Sadly, Zacharius is foiled by a malevolent gnome whose job it is to regulate the sun. His clocks start to go wrong. When he eventually tracks down the one remaining clock which is still in good working order, he finds that its owner is none other than the gnome. Zacharius winds it on a century, but the clock begins to blaspheme. Under exorcism it explodes, the spring is released and bounces around the room pursued by Zacharius who, exclaiming 'Mon âme! Mon âme!', fails to catch it and duly expires.[27]

What separates a story like *Zacharius* from *Paris* is not the obvious distinction between the fantastic and the *vraisemblable*, but the tenor of the humour. *Paris* is the narrative of a tormented, though still brilliantly perceptive, man who saw in the failure of politics, in the relentless march of Progress for the sake of Progress, in the disintegration of his own family unit, and in the onset of old age, the fundamental breakdown of all that he knew and believed in. Typically, this desperation is displaced into a novel about Paris, the city of his student dreams, supposedly written in 1863 but bearing the hallmarks of having been conceived thirty years later. It is still, I feel, a unique voice, if only because it retains that Vernian sense of the uncanny. The conclusion, therefore, brings us full circle. Verne's generalization of Paris as a post-industrial vacuum concords disconcertingly with the thesis recently advanced by historian Alain Minck, in which he diagnoses the imminent breakdown of Western civilization, as the power of nations is progressively diminished and eventually replaced by tribal herdings heralding a return to the feudal lore that characterized medieval society.[28] And secondly, this abandoning of the expansive, confident, empire-building Verne in favour of the mediocre searcher for the human soul is an oblique reflection of the inwards turn taken by science-fiction writing since the moon landings of the late sixties and early seventies, an era which was also characterized by the widespread use of mind-enhancing drugs and the first stirrings of what has since become known as 'virtual reality'. Are there more rabbits, one wonders, still in the hat?

Notes

1 Roland Barthes, 'Nautilus et bateau ivre', in *Mythologies* (Paris, Seuil, 1957), pp. 80–2.

2 William Golding, 'Astronaut by gaslight', *The Spectator* (9 June 1961), 841–2.

3 Michel Serres, 'Le savoir, la guerre et le sacrifice', *Critique* 367 (December 1977), 1067–77.

4 Simone Vierne, *Jules Verne et le roman initiatique* (Paris, du Sirac, 1973), and *Jules Verne, mythe et modernité* (Paris, PUF, 1989).

5 Jean-Yves Tadié, 'Jules Verne', in *Le Roman d'aventures* (Paris, PUF, 1982), pp. 69–112.

6 Jean Jules-Verne, *Jules Verne*, trans. Roger Greaves (London, MacDonald and Jane's, 1976), p. 93.

7 Andrew Martin, *The Mask of the Prophet. The Extraordinary Fictions of Jules Verne*, (Oxford, Clarendon Press, 1990), p. 6.

8 Jean Jules-Verne, *Jules Verne*, p. 207.

9 Michel Serres, 'Le savoir, la guerre et le sacrifice', 1072.

10 Piero Gondolo della Riva, the unimpeachable Verne archivist, estimates in his preface to the text that, on the basis of the correspondence between Verne and Hetzel, it was written, presumably in its entirety, in 1863, the year of Verne's first notable, literary success, *Cinq semaines en ballon*. It is therefore a work of relative youth and not the product of a claustrophobic old age. However, we should also bear in mind Hetzel's recommendation that his protégé should return to the manuscript in twenty years' time. The dating of the novel is a persistent snag. Leaving aside the supposedly predictive slant, it reads, as we shall see, more happily as a late Verne. It is conceivable in my view that the manuscript on which Hetzel commented in 1863 is quite far removed from the complete text published by Hachette more than a century later.

11 *Paris au XXe siècle*, chs. 1 and 3.

12 Jean Jules-Verne, *Jules Verne*, pp. 197–205.

13 Horrified by the events surrounding the Paris Commune in the Spring of 1871 he became disillusioned with national politics, though he remained active in the local sphere, standing successfully for election to Amiens town council in 1888 before going on to repeat this first electoral success on three further occasions, in 1892, 1896 and 1900.

14 Walter Benjamin, 'The *flâneur*', in *Charles Baudelaire. A Lyric Poet in the Era of High Capitalism*, trans. Harry Zohn, (London, Verso, 1983), pp. 35–66.

15 Ibid., p. 39.

16 The first Grand Exhibition of photography took place in Paris in 1855.

17 Benjamin, 'The *flâneur*', p. 40.

18 Ibid., p. 59.

19 This is not as eccentric as it may appear these days. The replacement of the gas lanterns by electric streetlighting brutalized a population who were unaccustomed to such brightness. As Robert Louis Stevenson commented at the time, 'Such a light as this should shine only on murders and public crime, or along the corridors of the lunatic asylums, a horror to heighten horror'. (cited in Benjamin, 'The *flâneur*', p. 51). The instant disorientating effect on people unused to electric lighting would have been similar to the tactic of the interrogator's light beaming relentlessly into his victim's face, associated with authoritarian regimes of the twentieth century. Of course, the welfare of the public came low down the list of priorities for scientists and inventors of the positivist era. One of the proposals submitted to the panel who were to decide how to commemorate the Grande Exposition of 1889 involved the building of an enormous tower, to be ringed at the top by powerful electric light

projectors which would be positioned so as to illuminate the entire city. The idea of constant illumination was rejected and the citizens of Paris had to be satisfied with the Eiffel Tower. Others around this time were less fortunate. In Detroit huge lighting rigs were constructed in several parts of the city and the inhabitants had to endure around the clock electric lighting for a month before the authorities finally yielded to the increasingly desperate pleas of an insomniacal population.

20 See the discussion of Habermas' theory of ideology as tradition in Anthony Giddens, *Central Problems in Social Theory* (London, Macmillan, 1982), pp. 176–7.

21 See Jean Jules-Verne's account of this incident, *Jules Verne*, p. 159.

22 If this value judgment is accepted, then Marcel Moré's autobiographical readings of Verne are *sui generis* foregrounded. See, for example, Marcel Moré, *Les Très Curieux Jules Verne* (Paris, Gallimard, 1960) and *Nouvelles explorations de Jules Verne* (Paris, Gallimard, 1963).

23 *Paris*, p. 73.

24 Jean Jules-Verne, *Jules Verne*, pp. 202–5.

25 Piero Gondolo della Riva, 'A propos des œuvres posthumes de Jules Verne', *Europe* (595–6), (November–December, 1978), pp. 73–82.

26 Andrew Martin, *The Mask of the Prophet*, p. 9.

27 I have merely paraphrased a more extended account of the story of Zacharius, which is given in Jean Jules-Verne, *Jules Verne*, pp. 35–6.

28 Alain Minck, *Le Nouveau Moyen Age* (Paris, Gallimard, 1993).

7

Future Past: Myth, Inversion and Regression in Verne's Underground Utopia

DAVID MEAKIN

In agreement with Jacques Noiray, we can well sense a degree of lucid self-comment in Verne's remark on his ingenious master electrical-engineer Orfanik in *Le Château des Carpathes*, who in fact invents nothing new but 'ne s'occupait que de compléter les découvertes qui avaient été faites par les électriciens pendant ces dernières années, à [*sic*] perfectionner leurs applications, à en tirer les plus extraordinaires effets'.[1] Orfanik is an artist, extracting the 'extraordinaire' (in implicit reference to Verne's global title, the *Voyages extraordinaires*) from established and inherited science, transmuting existing technology by the force of the imagination. Similarly, the mining engineer Cyprien Méré in *L'Etoile du sud* who tries—by the most modern methods he can muster—to make artificial diamonds, turns out not to be the true artist, the true alchemist of the novel, a role reserved for Jacobus Vandergaart (J. V. like his author), the stone-cutter who takes what already exists and transforms it into something extraordinary by the sheer skill of his art.[2]

If Verne does not—as is now well known and fully acknowledged by critics—substantially anticipate the future, his 'inventions', and machines being based on existing and sometimes even already outdated technology, his real relationship to what we know today as science fiction lies in the peculiar ability of his imagination to project a personal cosmos, an alternative universe, often exploiting that limited technology but to poetic rather than scientific or even didactic effect, to create what Patrick Grainville has neatly called a 'Univerne'. In fact, Verne rarely sets his novels in an era later than his own; some of the posthumous stories, of dubious authorship, are exceptions, as is *L'Ile à hélice* placed because of the gigantism of its conception in the twentieth century, but in general we must agree with Noiray again that 'il semble que l'imagination de Jules Verne ait eu le plus grand mal à se représenter l'avenir'.[3] Instead, Verne constructs an imaginary world that coexists but does not coincide with the real, contemporary world, and in this 'et non par sa technologie désuète et trompeuse, se trouve le véritable point commun entre l'"Univerne" et la Science-fiction la plus moderne'.[4] What gives the illusion of a universe is the principle of coherence, and to produce this the rich recurrence of characteristic motifs, particularly connected with initiation of various kinds and bringing with it the well-studied panoply of mazes, volcanoes, grottoes and the like (Bachelard's *imagination matérielle*) is complemented by the equally important combinational structures applied to such motifs, the complex but coherent patterns of symmetry and inversion that Michel Serres rightly valorizes as *l'imagination formelle*.[5] It is the combination of the two that creates meaning. Verne is a mythologist, and his is in Butor's term 'une mythologie singulièrement structurée'.[6] In this—and Butor would be the first to recognize the fact—his work resembles the imaginary world of alchemy, where 'symbols are variable terms, their meaning specified by their grouping'.[7] Now the search for the philosopher's stone and the beginnings of science fiction are one and the same for Butor, and he recognizes Verne's achievement in reworking the synthesis of these two modes in his own apparently positivistic age, largely because of his ability to reproduce in his world much of what Bachelard called 'the remarkable psychological coherence of alchemical culture'.[8]

Yet it is obvious that the ancient hermetic art and science fiction seem at first sight to pull in opposite directions, one essentially regressive and striving to recapture long-hidden truths, the other apparently addressing the future. Their combination must at best have something of a 'timeless' quality, the creation of an alternative universe is likely to take on a utopian (or, in pessimistic mode, a counter-utopian) dimension—for utopia is also uchronia, and utopian vision has a profound relationship with alchemical dreams, the passage from an age of lead to an age of gold (as Butor suggests in his *Portrait de l'artiste en jeune singe*) and with science fiction.

It is for this reason that the focus of our attention will not be a novel such as the *Voyage au centre de la terre*, where for all the mythological density, the alchemical richness, the quest is ironically short-circuited, the journey circular, a mere rite of passage between adolescence and adulthood; but rather *Les Indes noires*, where through multiple initiations we move from the blackness, desolation and chaos (an alchemical *nigredo*) of old, abandoned and exhausted mineworkings to the establishment of a stable, conflict-free underground utopia, lit by the bright artificial sun of electricity. It is a vision remote from the grim social criticism of Zola's *Germinal*, but at the same time far closer to that same novelist's later, utopian *Travail*, also under the sun sign of a redeeming, quasi-mythical electricity. Yet where Zola's romance extends over some fifty or sixty years into a vaguely idealized twentieth century, the action of Verne's tale covers only some three or four years: transformation is melodramatically condensed and compressed into a series of carefully framed initiatory moments where structures, parallels and inversions prove far more important than chronological time, where notions of past and future become relative, and where apparent progress can at the same time be the sign of a regression.

The threshold to the text already embodies a hint of possible inversion, with the 'making-strange' effect of oxymoron in the title of *Les Indes noires* (borrowed from Simonin's *La Vie souterraine*) which is, Verne will be quick to underline, 'un nom très significatif'.[9] Although at this stage the significance he extracts is in terms of a parallel between the wealth Britain has extracted from her colonial empire in India and that which she owes to exploitation of 'ce précieux combustible' in her own depths, the clash between noun and adjective prefigures a transmutation the text will perform, whereby this blackest of settings will become a place of light and abundance, with an exoticism all its own. The tone is set for the 'alchimie à quatre éléments' that Michel Serres has found in this story.[10] Oxymoron is present, too, in the exotic title given to Edinburgh, 'Auld-Reekie' notwithstanding: 'Athènes du Nord' (3). This is also an early indication of how present the past will be in Verne's vision of the industrial world. As William Butcher has remarked, one of his main aims in his exploration of the universe—for all his popular reputation—'is in reality the search for traces of the past, much more attractive to Verne than any conceivable future'.[11] But words are not everything in a Verne text: the illustrations, as we know, are catalysts of desire, fuelling reader curiosity, placed always before the events they picture. Férat's frontispiece, preliminary engraving for *Les Indes noires*, showing a group of elegantly dressed bourgeois figures— complete with parasols!—gazing into a mine shaft, complements the oxymoron effect of the title, suggesting that some of the 'extraordinary' character of this particular journey is to lie in a startling and unique displacement of the notion of tourism and exoticism, the transformation (partly, it will turn out by nature, partly by technology) of a place reputedly of toil, suffering and dreadful darkness into a setting for 'excursions' and 'distractions' for 'aucune mine, en n'importe quel pays du nouveau ou de l'ancien monde ne présentait un plus curieux aspect' (127).

When the story opens we are far from that stage, but the structural principle of reversibility is embodied in the 'deux lettres contradictoires' of the opening chapter's title. Both are addressed to mining engineer James Starr, the first from his former foreman or 'overman' in the Aberfoyle mine, exhausted and closed down ten years before, summoning him to an urgent meeting; the second from an anonymous hand cancelling that summons and telling him it is pointless to attend. Contradiction apart, both establish

the importance in the text of the hermeneutic code, the code of enigmas—
what is the unspoken motivation of the first, who the mysterious author
of the second? Reader and protagonist share the same hermeneutic desire:
'la curiosité de l'ingénieur fut piquée au vif' (2). Now this curiosity is the
typical mental state of Verne's engineers, scientists and explorers generally,
preparing them for all manner of 'astonishment' and 'marvelling' that
Bachelard saw as the most recognizable frame of mind of the pre-scientific
mentality, and not least of the alchemist—a mentality that persists
subconsciously even into the modern technological age in traces of
animism, essentialization projected onto the phenomenal world, revealing
'le vieil homme dans le jeune enfant, le jeune enfant dans le vieil homme,
l'alchimiste sous l'ingénieur'.[12] As we have seen, just such a persistence
will be apparent in that other (younger and rasher) mining engineer Méré,
struggling in vain to elaborate a method of creating diamonds (a variant
of alchemical gold) by an extreme and artificial concentration of that same
carbon which by nature's own prodigiously slower process has made the
precious coal of *Les Indes noires*.

It is noteworthy that although there is no shortage of female presence
in the Scottish novel—the old foreman Simon Ford has his wife Madge,
and above all Harry will find his Nell—the engineer is to all appearances
a bachelor, and there is no reference to a wife in his preparations for the
journey to Aberfoyle, nor in his subsequent life in the underground colony.
He is fully *disponible* for the hermeneutic drive of the quest and in this, like
the scientist Lidenbrock of *Voyage au centre de la terre*, he conforms to
Bachelard's description of the typical alchemist as a middle-aged bachelor,
his 'science' a transference of desire: 'science de célibataires, d'hommes
sans femme, fortement polarisée par des désirs inassouvis'.[13] Starr belongs
to 'cette catégorie de gens passionnés dont le cerveau est toujours en
ébullition, comme une bouilloire placée sur une flamme ardente' (8–10),
and it will be no surprise that when eventually he squeezes—a typical
initiation motif—through a 'narrow orifice' into the hidden realm of coal
unlimited that will be Nouvelle-Aberfoyle, it is with 'une joie complète',
shared also by his companions: 'C'était l'entière satisfaction de leurs désirs'
(90). Subsequently we learn that the engineer, perpetuating the intimist
myths of the mine and grotto that Bachelard described as the Novalis
complex, 's'était donné corps et âme à la Nouvelle-Aberfoyle' (130) (not
unlike the bachelor Nemo in the womanless but womb-like world of his
creation the *Nautilus*, become 'chair de ma chair').[14]

Our engineer, ostensible man of progress, is also president of the 'Société
des antiquaires écossais', and so is turned at least as much to the past as to
the future—just as the alchemist was ever, in Butor's phrase, an
'archéologue mental', longing to discover an occulted truth. He, as well as

the overman Ford (a passing ironic inversion here, since Ford is essentially
an underman, thoroughly wedded, with his family, to the world of below
and living fifteen-hundred feet down in the old workings), is characterized
by nostalgia for the good old days of Aberfoyle: 'oui, c'était le bon temps,
celui du travail, de la lutte— le meilleur temps de sa vie d'ingénieur' (7).
The new mine he will found therefore receives a name that links it directly
and explicitly with the old one, whose sublimated reincarnation it is to be.

Moreover, engineer and overman indulge in the kind of animistic
metaphor that expresses an emotional investment and harks back to those
archaic beliefs concerning mining and minerals that Mircea Eliade has
illustrated and in particular has linked to the alchemical tradition in his
Forgerons et alchimistes; at the heart of those beliefs, and those persistent
metaphors, is the notion of the sacredness of the living Earth-Mother in
whose womb minerals come into being, grow and mature like embryos.
'Si les sources, les galeries des mines et les cavernes sont assimilées à l'utérus
de la Terre-Mère, tout ce qui gît dans le "ventre" de la Terre est vivant,
encore qu'au stade de la gestation'. Miners are implicated in an
'embryologie souterraine'.[15] Needless to say, this lends a very particular
psychoanalytic cast to the engineer's ardent 'desire'. Eliade also explains
by this central archaic notion the tenacious belief that mines—like
volcanoes—can be 'reborn' or regenerated if allowed to rest. Starr's old
mine has been 'dormant' for ten years, since the time when he held in his
hand the last block of coal, 'dernier globule du sang qui circulait à travers
les veines de la houillère' (5). For Simon Ford, too, the mine is 'notre vieille
nourrice' with whom faith must be kept, and who should not be abandoned
simply 'parce que son lait s'est tari!' (7) The faith in question, animated by
the most intimate of associations as we see, and against all reason, is the
'foi du charbonnier' (60) common to all the Ford family. Another
paradoxical inversion, since Simon and Harry are described as
representatives of rationalism, refusing the superstition that is seen as
characteristic both of Scotland and of the mining culture in particular. It
is the faith behind the thoroughly archaic animism that inspires Simon's
enthusiastic sexualization of the mine: 'La vieille houillère va donc rajeunir,
comme une veuve qui se remarie!' (80) As Bachelard insisted, not only is
'le mythe de la fécondité des mines ... de toute évidence incompatible avec
l'esprit scientifique', but, furthermore, 'l'intuition de la fécondité des mines
relève de la psychanalyse' (a cultural psychoanalysis, that is, rather than
an individual one).[16]

In the mythology of the intermittent fertility of the Earth-Mother,
volcanoes naturally have a special place, as they do in Verne's universe:
they provide the most dramatic thresholds, initiatory access to the *point
suprême*. Here the engineer before his descent leans over the silent abyss

of the pitshaft: 'L'ingénieur se pencha sur l'orifice ... Il semblait qu'on fût à la bouche de quelque volcan éteint' (36). It is impossible here not to think of that other, earlier, underground journey, to the centre of the Earth. There, ingress to the mysteries was via an extinct volcano (and, in another typical inversion, exit via a live one), a journey backwards through time-layers, geological strata, culminating in hero Axel's ecstatic dream of origins as he imagined his body melting back into the flux of original chaos. Alchemy, as many authorities have stressed, is a repeat cosmogony.[17] In *Les Indes noires* equally, the engineer and his companions have one face turned resolutely back to the past—and so, too, does Verne's narrative. The chapter 'Le Sous-sol du Royaume-Uni' is on one level the encyclopedic Verne, but it is a poetic didacticism going back imaginatively to the very origins of the planet and echoing the quest for origins, essences and centres that typifies alchemical thinking. The crucial transformation that changes vegetable into mineral to form coal is described as a vast alchemical operation 'dans ce creuset gigantesque où s'accumulait la matière végétale ... Une véritable opération chimique, une sorte de distillation' (21). A quantitative change—intense concentration—leads to qualitative transmutation. And in the process, as a brief *mise en abyme* of the principle of inversion that permeates the text, marine creatures have left their imprint en creux, 'admirablement tirée' (22) like a photographic negative.

This account of the history of coal also contains the seed of a major inversion that the narrative of *Les Indes noires* will perform. Verne is at his most drily positivistic when he explains, with the aid of a table of figures, how industrial expansion worldwide invariably raises the prospect of scarcity. Coal will run out globally, and his statistics give the prediction an air of utter finality. If all the earth were made of coal, Starr remarks with grim humour, it would surely one day consume itself in industry. The Aberfoyle mine is itself a symptom of this pessimism, this spectre of scarcity, and in a curious cyclical reversal of social evolution Starr notices on his return to the region how industry, defunct from loss of energy, has been replaced by agriculture: there is already here, perhaps, a hint of the cyclical pessimism of that late story *L'Eternel Adam* where 'past' and 'future' so disturbingly lose their linear quality. Yet the story itself of *Les Indes noires* proves to be anything but pessimistic, the fable will negate or at least run counter to this trend. The discovery of vast untapped resources creates the impression of unlimited abundance—'la richesse des filons carbonifères était incalculable' (128)—that will be a precondition of the timeless stasis of utopia. Rationalistic pessimism is quasi-magically transmuted into what is essentially a wish-fulfilment dream of plenty, even if the milk and honey of the Ali-Baba's cave of convention receive a curious twist in Verne's version. *Foi du charbonnier* indeed...

Symmetrical with this is a further inversion necessary for the creation of utopia, and a singularly suggestive one in terms of the author's own ideological position. A subsequent passage on the history of mining, going back to Antiquity and, for Scotland, to the thirteenth century, tells us that the Ford family have been miners since those early days, and that the work was originally under the sign of pitiless physical exploitation: 'Ils travaillaient comme des forçats' and were 'de véritables esclaves' in al probability (47). And yet in the next paragraph we are to read that 'Simon Ford était fier d'appartenir à cette grande famille', the last word conjuring up an altogether cosier image, and that he has no greater desire than to carry on working in the traces of his ancestors. In the same way, even the dangers of the mining life become a subject of nostalgia in Starr's and Harry's conversation—'C'était la lutte, et par conséquent la vie émouvante' (32). An all too brief glimpse of the harsh exploitation and dreadful working conditions of miners such as will be the stuff of *Germinal* is immediately eclipsed to provide the conditions for a utopian idealization of the mine. It is a bourgeois idealization in paternalist mode, probably, as Chesneaux suggests, influenced by Saint-Simonian or Fourierist notions.[18] Closure of the Aberfoyle pit produced regret and nostalgia but (unrealistically) no apparent hardship: 'Nous veillerons sur vous', says Starr to the redundant miners, and for him all are part of 'notre grande famille' (5). This impression is to be intensified in the harmonious community of the new mine, where the paternalistic structure is summarized in all its facile sentimentality, in Nell's words: 'J'ai vu ces Bravailleurs, heureux et bons, vénérer M. Starr' (227). The word 'exploitation' will be applied only to coal, never to the workers themselves. Indeed, Verne contrives, after admitting that in the early days they were 'de simples ouvriers', to slip them into a separate and unique category, geographically rather than sociologically situated: 'les mineurs, habitués au calme profond des houillères, affrontent moins volontiers que les ouvriers ou les laboureurs ces grands troubles de l'atmosphère' (16).

This double inversion, this double switch from negative to positive poles—scarcity into abundance, exploitation into fulfilment and harmony—leaves a paradoxical effect, traces of ideological unease behind the alchemy of wishful thinking in the euphoria of the fable.

The simplistic cosiness of wishful thinking is embodied in the evocation, at the heart of the novel, of Coal-City in Nouvelle-Aberfoyle, already thriving a mere and rather magical three years after discovery of the site. Verne, it seems, would have elaborated this curious wish-fulfilment dream of social harmony, had the more positivistic Hetzel not objected,[19] but what remains is suggestive enough. No commuting to the surface for this underground community, cocooned against seasonal change, against weather and time: 'à Coal-City, calme absolu, température douce, ni pluie ni vent. Rien n'y transpirait de la lutte des éléments du dehors' (137). As Michel Serres has noted, the subterranean city is an inverted variant on that privileged Vernian site, the island: built round a great underground lake, it is water surrounded by land rather than land surrounded by water, 'le monde renversé', and typical of the principle of reversal in the text as a whole.[20] It is one of those enclosed spaces of which the hermetically sealed Nautilus or the moon-rocket are the most concentrated examples, where a reassuring image of supreme self-containment can be projected. And like those capsules it is an ambivalent mixture of modern technology and shades and trappings of the past. On the one hand it is lit by the prodigiously bright suns and stars of electricity, that same apparently limitless energy that provides for all domestic and industrial needs. Verne's electricity, 'l'âme de l'univers' in a telling phrase from *Le Château des Carpathes*, is notoriously vague in terms of both its production and its application, but it clearly fulfils the dream of abundance, of virtually inexhaustible energy in a 'modern', technological guise, 'une puissance pour ainsi dire infinie' in a formula that recurs like a refrain in his novels.[21] Most revealing of all in this respect is Nemo's declaration in *Vingt mille lieues sous les mers* that the electricity that so marvellously does everything in his submarine 'n'est pas celle de tout le monde';[22] not *aurum vulgi*, the old alchemists were wont to protest... At the same time, not only is the whole system of caverns of Nouvelle-Aberfoyle described in terms of the evocative vocabulary of prehistory ('une ruche construite sur une vaste échelle et qui ... eût suffi à loger tous les ichthyosaures, les mégathériums et les ptérodactyles de l'époque géologique' (86) but it is stressed that the site is a direct path back to the origins: 'non l'œuvre des hommes, mais l'œuvre du Créateur' (87). It is also a typically incongruous Vernian touch that the 'tourist' entrance to this startlingly new yet prodigiously old place harks back to a pseudo-medieval past, with its 'entrée monumentale, avec tourelles, créneaux et mâchicoulis'—a Disneyland reversion to the period romanticized notably by Walter Scott, whom we shall meet again as a reference point in *Les Indes noires*. This almost surrealist conjunction of modernity and nostalgia recalls Verne's description of his aluminium space projectile: 'avec ses formes imposantes et coiffé de son chapeau conique, on l'eût pris volontiers pour une de ces épaisses tourelles en façon de poivrières, que les architectes du Moyen Age suspendaient à l'angle des châteaux forts. Il ne lui manquait que des meurtrières et une girouette',[23] inspiring Michel Ardan to exclaim, 'Nous serons là-dedans comme des seigneurs féodaux'. It reminds us, too, that one of Verne's most ingeniously 'electrical' novels, *Le Château des Carpathes*, is also his most gothic tale.

The subterranean settlement, with its 'aspect un peu fantastique, d'un effet étrange' (131), enjoys an offbeat 'picturesque' quality all of its own, and its inhabitants (whom we see only at leisure, never at work) are loath ever to leave it. The centre of this centre is the lake, 'cette mer subterranéenne' (131)—another version of the 'mer intérieure' that was so richly valorized in the *Voyage au centre de la terre*, where the wordplay *mer/mère* was more insistent. The journey into the Earth is, as for Goethe's Faust, a return to the Mother, a *regressus ad uterum* that played a key role in the symbolic pattern of alchemy. This utopia is the socialized version of an alchemical dream. We can readily apply to Coal-city what Noiray writes of that other segregated micro-universe, the Nautilus: 'cet univers clos, cette atmosphère ouatée, ce confort définitif, trahissent chez Jules Verne un regret du sein maternel, dont le microcosme offre l'image',[24] and Simone Vierne concurs that in the mining novel the escape from normal time and space represents 'une régression heureuse'.[25] There could be grounds for a fruitful comparison between this 'happy regression' and Rousseau's nostalgic evocation of his timeless island paradise in the fifth *Rêverie*. In fact the *mer intérieure* of Coal-City proves more of an infantile regression, more reassuring in its unruffled calm (it is disturbed only once, by an act of sabotage, but safely absorbs the cascading waters of the surface lake above, thus protecting its children) than the tempestuous equivalent of the *Voyage au centre*: there the storm led to the explorers being expelled from the Earth's womb—via a volcano—in a symbolic re-enactment of the trauma of birth. Here, however, the still waters are a figure of permanent prenatal peace, with no need to be born, no need to return to the everyday world.

If this utopian idealization puts *Les Indes noires* at an opposite pole to *Germinal*, it at the same time makes it an anticipation of Zola's utopian romance *Travail*, which describes the elaboration of an equally paternalistic (and therefore infantilizing) community inspired by Fourier, with the same regressive longing for conflict-free existence and the same transformation of industrial blackness into ideal, season-free light and comfort thanks to the artificial sun of electricity, an occult force under the superficial appearance of forward-looking technology. For Henri Mitterand, 'le langage de la générosité utopique peut être celui de la régression', and these characteristics of *Travail*—which it shares with Verne's tale—combine to make it, in a surprising reversal, an 'anti-*Germinal*'.[26] This coincides with Jean Borie's argument that the retreat from reality and struggle in *Travail* makes it not the most mature, but on the contrary the most infantile of Zola's works.[27] Interestingly enough, Verne's development will take him in a contrary, counter-utopian direction as pessimism increasingly informs his social vision from about 1880 on, to produce for instance the fable of *L'Ile à hélice*, the vast vessel designed as a floating utopia for millionaires, its itinerary planned to avoid the rigours of seasonal change, a perpetual holiday-camp powered and made supremely comfortable by—of course—electricity. That seemingly blissful world will, however, be torn apart by the atavistic force of human conflict, opposing factions on opposite sides of the vessel refusing to coordinate their engines, electric force opposing electric force in a destructive vortex of anarchic energy.

Coal-City, like Zola's utopia, will end up safe from such internal polarization. Its population is characterized by the principle of sameness common to most utopian projections, 'ayant mêmes intérêts, mêmes goûts, à peu pres même somme d'aisance' (136), lending weight to Serres's speculation on the wordplay in Aberfoyle (<*abeille*)—we have already seen that the text itself explicitly evokes the image of the hive. However, the novel does not close with the first evocation of the community in chapter 13, and whereas Zola will describe the gradual withering-away of opposition to Harmony, Verne more melodramatically plots further initiations and confrontations, further patterns of inversion before the 'Other', the external enemy, can finally be eliminated in a ritual that will found and confirm the stability of the city.

For there is a dark, alien force in the depths that must be exorcized. It has already threatened the lives of the heroes, saved from entombment only by a fleeting will-o'-the-wisp figure that has led the search-party through a labyrinth of galleries, and whereas others have found the 'entière satisfaction de leurs désirs', this mystery has lodged with young Harry as a catalyst of desire. He is 'irrésistiblement entraîné' to plumb the enigma by going down into the lowest depths, there to find and save his own saviour, Nell—no spectre, but a flesh-and-blood girl, an orphan of the mine—and to bring her up, perilously, on a fragile rope. It is a neat symmetrical inversion of the familiar myth: Ariadne, in her turn, is brought out of the maze on a thread. And although Harry's first reaction on touching her inert body is 'un vif sentiment de répulsion' (146), this will quickly switch into its opposite as he is 'irrésistiblement attiré par l'étrangeté même de Nell' (152). Just as he had been driven to seek out 'les plus lointaines *profondeurs* de la houillère' (141), so now he is 'troublé jusqu'au plus *profond* de son cœur' (163, my italics) by the young girl. The depths without and the depths within are clearly in close correlation. Harry is supremely a man of the vertical axis that dominates this novel, and it is fittingly he who takes charge of Nell's ascending initiation, corresponding dialectically to his own descending one, as a vital precondition of their union, *coniunctio* or *coincidentia oppositorum* in the hallowed alchemical expression. Adaptation to the light and community of Coal-City is one stage, but just as Harry delved below to find her, so Nell must ascend above it to experience for once the spectacle of the outside world.

This initiative comes to light in a chapter that invites interpretation as a *mise en abyme* of the concern for symmetricality and inversion throughout. Entitled 'Sur l'échelle oscillante', it portrays Harry's meeting with his friend, the piper Jack Ryan, on the system of oscillating ladders or 'enginemen'. Harry is on the way up, Jack on the way down, and this reverses their first encounter in the text when Harry was descending, Jack ascending. It is here, at this mid-way point of passage, that Harry explains his aim for Nell, his plan of upward revelation to complement, no doubt, his own downward initiation. The ladder system itself emphazises not only the vertical axis, but also the principle of reversibility—'une de ces échelles qui, en se relevant et en s'abaissant par oscillations successives, permettent de monter et de descendre' (164). The effect of complementarity is compounded by the fact that the two young men are complementary alter egos, the piper given to superstition, his friend to rationalism, caught here in balance and dialogue on their reciprocating ladders.

If Harry is such a suitable guide for Nell's revelation, this is related to his ability to correlate the surface and underground worlds, to chart their symmetrical relationships. For above the inner lake is the outer one; as that founding text of esoteric alchemy, the Emerald Tablet of Hermes, had it, 'What is below is like that which is above, and what is above is like that which is below, to accomplish the miracle of one thing.'[28] So by the law of inversion, the touching of opposites, Harry is compared in his knowledge of the underground with an Alpine guide on his sunlit, snow-white summits. But to complete the revelation he also takes with him songster Jack (the aesthetic dimension) and his own initiatory 'second father', James Starr, whose name predisposes him for the role he is to play here. He it is who reveals the third spatial dimension of this vertical text, the marvels of the firmament. Height and depth match symmetrically, inversions of the same, as Nell undergoes the dizziness of a reverse 'leçon d'abîme' by gazing upwards, and the engineer concludes, 'Il semble alors que le firmament soit comme un profond abîme dans lequel on est tenté de s'élancer' (183). This heightened 'tourist' trip on the outside (inverting the subterranean but less initiatory tourism we have already met) confirms another *coincidentia oppositorum*, a matching of those apparent vertical opposites, mountains and mines: both stimulate the imagination, Verne claims, both heights and depths are prime sites for myth, legend, story, and if the Greeks had been a people of the plains, they would never have invented their mythology. The principle had been established earlier:

> Si les montagnes des Hautes-Terres sont peuplées d'êtres chimériques, bons ou mauvais, à plus forte raison les sombres houillères devaient-elles être hantées jusque dans leurs dernières

profondeurs ... Qui allume le grisou et préside aux explosions terribles, sinon quelque génie de la mine? (58)

Just such a malevolent spirit, rising up as from the depths of the mythopoeic imagination is Silfax, Nell's grandfather, the ancient 'fireman' or 'penitent', whose garb and function in the pre-Davy-lamp days are more reminiscent of the sinister figures of gothic romance than of the nineteenth century. Though a creature of flesh and blood, Silfax maintains mythic qualities, an inverted figure of God: 'partout et nulle part'; 'Il est invisible, lui, mais il voit tout'; 'dans sa folie, un homme puissant par l'esprit' (225). He is the opposite of our benevolent, constructive engineer—a symmetry suggested by the ambiguity of 'génie' in the quotation at the end of the last paragraph: the word can denote 'engineering' as well as 'genius' and 'spirit' technology as well as magic. As malevolent spirit, Silfax is an ingenious anti-engineer. He is also an intertextual inversion of the alchemist guide Saknussem of the *Voyage au centre*—he does not open paths, but blocks them, strives monomaniacally not to stimulate but to prevent initiation. His name richly essentializes him: Serres sees *sileo* and the principle of silence (*sileo* is also to conceal) plus *fax*, the flaming torch that was his function and will now be his ultimate threat.[29] We might add that fax is also passion, fury; and that the name overall suggests *silex*, the flinty hardness of the *pierre à feu*. What is Silfax but a perversion, a perverse inversion of the *maître du feu* in whose tradition Eliade places the alchemist? 'Silfax se proclamait le roi des ombres et du feu' (223): this is a malevolent, paradoxical fire that is wedded to darkness, in stark contrast with the benevolent, sublimated fire of electricity. That sublimated, even aestheticized fire shines resplendent— and safe, for it cannot ignite fire-damp—for the wedding.

> les disques d'électricité, ravivés par des courants plus intenses, resplendissaient comme autant de soleils. Une atmosphère lumineuse emplissait toute la Nouvelle-Aberfoyle.
>
> Dans la chapelle, les lampes électriques projetaient aussi de vives lueurs, et les vitraux coloriés brillaient comme des kaléidoscopes de feu. (232)

Silfax's ultimate menace is the malign naked flame to ignite the gas he has released and Verne seems about to appear once again as the 'apocalyptographe' extraordinary,[30] but for the intervention of Nell, the 'good genie' of the mine. It is thanks to her that Silfax's sinister bird—for the anti-God has an anti-dove—drops its deadly flame into the same waters into which Silfax plunges. Malign fire is extinguished for ever, and the way is open for the 'happy-ever-after' of integrated, conflict-free utopia bathed in purified light, and promising even something at least approaching the ancient alchemical dream of eternal life: 'Qu'y avait-il d'étonnant à ce que,

sous le climat de la Nouvelle-Aberfoyle, dans ce milieu qui ne connaît pas
les intempéries de dehors on devînt deux fois séculaire?' (236).

The wish-fulfilment dream of womb-like happiness is all the more
complete for the definitive elimination of the Other, and the mythic
dimension of the text is all the more effective for the patterns of
polarization, symmetry, and inversion of which we have seen many
examples. Only one ambiguity remains, as Silfax's bird, the *harfang*—
embodying, it seems, the promised longevity of the underground—
continues to pay fleeting visits. To a degree it has passed from a negative
to a positive pole, but remains a marginal element, the one outsider to the
city, problematic: does it return to visit Nell, or rather the site of its master's
death as 'un signe maintenu de la disparition du Dieu fantastique, anti-
colombe planant sur les eaux calmes de l'utopie'?[31] The ambiguity itself
feeds legend, and it is with legend, its continuation and enrichment, that
the text closes: 'on chante encore dans les veillées écossaises la légende de
l'oiseau du vieux Silfax'. A closure—especially in view of the 'encore'—
that for all the vaguely futuristic use of electricity places the whole fiction
firmly in the past, and even in the tradition of folk legend.

And just as there is a paradoxical tension of nostalgia and anticipation,
past and future, so too the text embodies a tension of positivism and
superstition, rationalism and myth. Verne seems to nail his colours to the
positivist mast in his comment on the Scottish propensity for the fantastic:
'L'instruction, quoique largement et libéralement répandue dans le pays,
n'a pas pu réduire à l'état de fictions ces légendes...' (58). But for all this
education, and for all the declared rationalism of the Fords, myth still
flourishes in utopia, as Madge and Jack elaborate 'histoires bien dignes
d'enrichir la mythologie hyperboréenne' (132). No sooner does Nell appear
than instant legend is created around her, 'un nouveau texte à leurs récits
légendaires' is added to the stock. True she is a mere mortal, but she still
fulfils the function of the *fée des mines* archetype, and Verne typically has
it both ways—rationalism and a thrill of superstition, the merely strange
plus a hint of the fantastic, as when he remarks: 'Jack Ryan *avec quelque
raison* la compara à un farfadet *un peu* surnaturel' (150, my italics). Silfax
likewise is human, but we have seen how his spirit seems to live on in the
harfang, and there is a paradoxical twist in that the 'rational' explanation
for his long malevolence is, precisely, unreason, madness. 'On ne raisonne
pas avec la folie', admits Starr (220).

The engineer-antiquarian is himself, in his oscillation between past and
future, anything but closed to legend. It is mainly via him that the most
explicit intertext, the works of Walter Scott, enter the novel, for he is
steeped in those historical romances, and Scott is the real guidebook in
Nell's tour of the surface, advising the travellers on the best spot from which

to view the sunrise (and Verne bows to his precursor by having the sun catch in a gleam of gold the top of the Scott Monument which 'brillait comme un phare' (186). They can almost imagine they see, on the surface of Loch Katrine, the shade of 'la belle Hélène Douglas' like an 'ombre légère' (199)—but we may remember being informed that Nell is short for Helena (150), so that, as one lake above mirrors one below, so does one 'ombre légère', one Helen, echo another. As above, so below (in hermetic shorthand), and thus is legend reincarnated. Verne's text is less a systematically positivistic account of the present—let alone a scientific prediction of the future—than a cultural mine in which he reworks and dialogues with the world of myth and with the writings of his literary forebears. If Scott is the most explicit here, it is, ironically, because he is the most superficial influence, his novels invoked for effects of local colour. At a deeper level in the cultural mine is, as ever, the more disturbing Poe (the horror of entombment) and especially Hoffmann, whose *Bergwerke zu Falun*, with a similar complex of main characters, also involves a malevolent spirit of the mine who fiercely opposes the marriage of a young couple, to the point of murder.[32]

Verne's explorers are rediscoverers, his writings inevitably follow the traces of earlier writings, and like the texts of alchemy themselves his novels are a paradigm of the intertextuality of all literature. His inspiration lies in the past, and looming behind the apparent dismissal of fantasy and legend is a powerful valorization of such non-rational discourse—with which, as we have seen, the novel ends. Jack Ryan, singer, conteur, fantasist, is a vital figure in the work's economy and an essential member of the trio of guides in Nell's initiatory journey with his refrain:

> Gardez à jamais
> Vos légendes charmantes
> Beaux lacs écossais!

It is he who, having had to work on the surface in farming after the closure of Aberfoyle, hankers for the mine, where the acoustics were better: 'il y avait des coins sonores, des échos joyeux qui vous renvoyaient gaillardement vos chansons, tandis que la-haut!' (40). What are we to conclude, but that the underground and its echoes—mythic, literary—are more propitious for art than superficial reason, rationalism of the surface, positivism of the plains? *Les Indes noires*, with all its utopian regression, its myths and inversions, its intertextual echoes and harmonics, is surely ample testimony to that belief, that *foi du charbonnier* that is, deep down, the *foi de l'écrivain*.

Notes

1 J. Noiray, *Le Romancier et la machine*, vol. 2 (Paris, Corti, 1982) p. 95.

2 D. Compère, 'Jules Verne en ses miroirs', in J. Bessière (ed.), *Modernités de Jules Verne* (Paris, PUF, 1988) p. 28. See also D. Meakin, *Hermetic Fictions: Alchemy and Irony in the Modern Novel*, Keele University Press, 1995, pp. 63–75.

3 Noiray, *Le Romancier*, p. 92.

4 F. Raymond, 'Pour une connaissance appliquée', in *Jules Verne 3* (Paris, Lettres Modernes, 1980), p. 10.

5 M. Serres, 'Un Voyage au bout de la nuit', in *Critique*, XXV, no. 262 (mars 1969), 302.

6 M. Butor, 'Le point suprême et l'âge d'or à travers quelques romans de Jules Verne' in *Répertoire* I (Paris, Minuit, 1960), p. 132.

7 M. Butor, 'L'Alchimie et son langage', in *Répertoire* I, p. 18.

8 G. Bachelard, *La Formation de l'esprit scientifique* (Paris, Vrin, 1986), p. 46.

9 J. Verne, *Les Indes noires* (Paris, Hachette, 1967), p. 3. Subsequent page references to this edition are given in brackets in the text.

10 Serres, 'Un Voyage', p. 302.

11 W. Butcher, Introduction, Jules Verne, *Journey to the Centre of the Earth* (Oxford University Press, 1992), p. xiv.

12 G. Bachelard, *Psychanalyse du feu* (Paris, Gallimard, 1987), p. 16.

13 Ibid., p. 96.

14 J. Verne, *Vingt mille lieues sous les mers* (Paris, Hachette, 1986), p. 134.

15 M. Eliade, *Forgerons et alchimistes* (Paris, Flammarion, 1977), p. 34.

16 Bachelard, *La Formation de l'esprit scientifique*, p. 158.

17 Fulcanelli, *Les Demeures philosophales et le symbolisme hermétique dans ses rapports avec l'ésotérisme du Grand Œuvre* (Paris, Editions des Champs-Elysées, 1960), p. 111.

18 J. Chesneaux, *Une lecture politique de Jules Verne* (Paris, Maspéro, 1971).

19 S. Vierne, *Jules Verne et le roman initiatique* (Paris, Editions du Sirac, 1973) p. 258.

20 Serres, 'Un Voyage', p. 291.

21 See Noiray, *Le Romancier*, p. 96.

22 Verne, *Vingt mille lieues sous les mers* , p. 119.

23 J. Verne, *De la Terre à la lune* (Paris, Hachette, 1978), p. 176.

24 Noiray, *Le Romancier*, p. 132.

25 S. Vierne, 'Jules Verne et la mine fantastique des *Indes noires*', in *Actes du 98e Congrès national des sociétés savantes*, vol. 1 (Saint-Etienne, 1973), p. 159.

26 H. Mitterand, *Le Discours du roman* (Paris, PUF, 1980), p. 163.

27 J. Borie, *Zola et les mythes ou de la nausée au salut* (Paris, Seuil, 1971), p. 113.

28 J. Read, *Prelude to Chemistry* (Cambridge, MA, MIT Press, 1966), p. 54.

29 Serres, *Le Romancier*, p. 300.

30 P. Mustière, 'Jules Verne et le roman-catastrophe', *Europe*, no. 595–6 (novembre–décembre 1978), 43.

31 J. Delabroy, '"La Pierre du dernier salut": *Les Indes noires*', in *Jules Verne 5* (Paris, Lettres Modernes, 1987) p. 54.

32 V. Dehs, 'Inspiration du fantastique? Jules Verne et l'œuvre de E. T. A. Hoffmann', in *Jules Verne 5*, pp. 169–71.

8

Measurement and Mystery in Verne

TREVOR HARRIS

'Non, je ne peux pas dire que je sois particulièrement emballé par la science': not the kind of remark one might naturally associate with Verne. And yet, when interviewed in 1893, this is how the author sums up his position.[1]

Given the general perception of Verne's work and the almost universally accepted assumption that his novels may be categorized as science fiction or, at the very least, fictions grounded in science, Verne's 1893 comment necessarily seems enigmatic. We might even be tempted to see it as a piece of *senilia*, although the author's general health in 1893 was not really in question; the first serious symptoms of the diabetic illness which Verne suffered from in the last years of his life not appearing until 1895. Moreover, his intellectual vigour at the time can scarcely be questioned: 1893 was a busy year in terms of composition and publication. No: Verne may love science 'un peu', but certainly not 'passionnément' and the aim of the following discussion is to show that Verne, far from singing the unqualified praises of positivism and progress, is actually writing against science, *à rebours*, indeed, of smug Second Empire and—subsequently—Third Republic scientific orthodoxy.

Science fiction, after all, is a blanket term all too easily thrown over Verne's work. The titles of recent critical literature on the author can still tend to reinforce this reading,[2] and, although understandable to the extent that the *Voyages extraordinaires* are packed with all manner of contraptions and imagined machines—some of which accurately prefigure more modern counterparts[3]—the reflex is none the less misleading. At the opposite end of the scale, one recent assessment of Verne rejects categorically the view of him as science-fiction writer: 'contrairement à l'idée reçue, Verne ne cherche à anticiper sur son époque. L'avenir n'intéresse pas l'écrivain, et l'anticipation n'est pas son fait'.[4] Even if we do not follow Picot all the way in rejecting, out of hand, the importance of utopianism in Verne's work, it has to be said that other labels, although nearer the mark by virtue of their less strict categorization—'littérature conjecturale', 'roman d'anticipation'—are equally apt to skew our approach. Suffice to say that the basic facts of Verne's output do not support the view of him as a writer fundamentally, or even frequently, obsessed with the future, or even one engaged in dreaming of idealized, alternative societies. Much of his writing, although brimming with exotic adventures, is placed within a thoroughly contemporary setting: when it is not, it invariably comes under the heading of pure fantasy (for example, *De la Terre à la lune* of 1865). Moreover, the deformation of that contemporary reality through some highly speculative, yet plausible invention, does not seem to be Verne's yardstick here. In this respect, in terms of the history of the science fiction genre, the utopian, More–Swift–Voltaire tradition of science fiction is far less influential where Verne is concerned than the fantastic, Gothic, Walpole–Poe–Mérimée tradition of scientized fantasy fiction, or 'merveilleux': as, for example, in *Le Château des Carpathes* (1886).

Putting this same point differently, one need only consider those cases where Verne allows himself to indulge in science fiction *stricto sensu*, to realize that it does not constitute the happiest choice of genre for the author. *La Journée d'un journaliste en 2889* (or 2890, depending on the source one consults) first published in 1891, was in fact a text originally produced by Verne's son, Michel. As for the ill-fated *Paris au XXe siècle*, the reactions of Verne's publisher, Pierre-Jules Hetzel, were so discouraging as to ward Verne off the genre very early in his career.[5] The manuscript, indeed, has only recently come to light, found languishing at the bottom of a dusty trunk belonging to Verne's son. The romantic circumstances of the discovery of Verne's manuscript, however, do little to conceal—or rather, do everything to underline—what was clearly perceived by Hetzel as an embarrassing aesthetic failure and something of a marketing nightmare.[6]

Finding the right niche in the market, indeed, was not a minor consideration for Hetzel and one which underlines the extent to which Verne's apparent enchantment with science was imposed upon him.[7] Verne's actual orientation, carefully guided in its initial stages by Hetzel, brings together the exotic elements of both the adventure story and the 'merveilleux', while simultaneously drawing on Second Empire, Cousinian positivism to give resonance and pedagogic purpose to the writing. In this Verne is in perfect harmony with the orientalist/realist tensions of the middle of the century. Verne's first major novel, *Cinq semaines en ballon* (1863), for example, appears in the same year as Renan's *Vie de Jésus* and the first volume of Littré's *Dictionnaire*, while closely following the rich, African 'ailleurs' of *Salammbô*[8] and the sombre, pagan otherness of Leconte's *Poèmes barbares*. Hetzel's flair, then, was perhaps used to best commercial advantage by keeping Verne firmly in the mainstream, clear of risky, futuristic science fiction, but also away from the use of science to investigate the Parisian or the parochial—a vein which Verne might well have been tempted to open, but which the Goncourt brothers were to exploit with their *Germinie Lacerteux* in 1864, and which Zola, of course, was shortly to explore so fully, in a career chronologically parallel to Verne's and yet in singular non-competition with it.

Rather than science fiction, then, Verne, from the very beginning of his career, produces what Arthur Evans has dubbed the 'scientific novel'.[9] Why not, and with some justification, speak of 'the novel of Progress', so imbued does Verne's style appear to be with an About-ian faith in forward movement?[10] Or could one term such writing—from 1870 onwards—'the novel of the Republic'? After all, this very tricolour writer, stockbroker by training, liberal by nature, honest-to-goodness 'bon bourgeois' by his working methods, is comfortably close to what Huysmans, in *La Cathédrale*, called 'une époque de bedon et de bidet'. Indeed, Verne's quintessentially positivistic approach—his ever-presence in the Bibliothèque impériale/nationale, his voluminous card-indexes—put him squarely within the scientific, industrial, solidly liberal bracket. Furthermore, the avowed aim to educate and entertain via the *Magasin d'éducation et de récréation*, Hetzel's strict censorship of the Verne texts and the conspicuous, pious, wholesome moral cleanliness of Verne's plots: all these tend to make of the Verne/Hetzel tandem, an eminently Victorian couple.

Indeed, educate, entertain; but also, protect. Aside from the commercial implications for Verne and Hetzel of the immense success of the *Voyages extraordinaires*, this utilitarian, moral dimension looms large. The mission—Hetzel's, at least—is to bring to the reader new and exciting facts, but to soften the blow of this potentially disturbing paradigm shift, to feed the strange through the familiar, the unknown through the known. This essentially childlike vision, mixing fantasy with safety, removing the dangers and placing them in a virtual reality, reduces any 'frisson' to manageable proportions. The shift for Hetzel, indeed, must never amount to an earthquake. The 'frisson' must not, as it were, make the earth move, must remain a minor tremor and never a 'petite mort' for Verne's innocent little readers. Knowledge, that is, for such tender young consumers, needs to remain virtual, not carnal, and Verne's bedtime reading, as corrected and censored by Hetzel, is something of a literary 'bouillotte'.

Having accepted the inappropriateness of classifying Verne as a science fiction author and, further, gained a glimpse of how science was, to an extent, foisted on Verne, we might wish to qualify his own brand of exotic realism as the novel of *movement and measurement*. In the same interview in which Verne describes himself as lukewarm towards science, he also underlines the extent to which 'la géographie est à la fois [sa] passion et [son] sujet d'étude'.[11] Verne often speaks of his love of maps and the moral 'bouillotte' alluded to above, vies with the physical 'bougeotte', a natural wanderlust, unsurprising enough in one born in the busy port of Nantes and raised on the exotic allure of—among others—James Fenimore Cooper. Travel is, indeed, such a key value in Verne that the lines which structure his imagination are—precisely—imaginary lines: the meridians, circles around the world, which so fascinate Verne and whose recurrence in his work already points to the problematical status of 'Progress' there. The circular structure of many of his narratives produces 'great circle' stories, as it were, yarns spun out to encompass the globe: literally, in the case of Phileas Fogg. But even straight lines, here, are circular: Michel Strogoff, for example, returns to Moscow along the same line which he had taken to reach deepest Siberia, moving smoothly back along that space-warp which he had so painfully strung out, while ducking and leaping his way under and over the dangerous weft of Tartar rebellion.

The web thus woven is less a sinister, arachnid trap or pre-modernist, narrative snare, than a convenient, tightly woven string bag in which to deliver the narrative goodies to Verne's expectant child readers. There are no narrative jitters or self-consciousness here, only the confident industrial-age clatter of the author's narrative shuttle. These unselfconscious stories produce artefacts which are well-wrought urns, no doubt, having a crushing sense of an ending, certainly. Rather than experimental novels, however, Verne—more honestly, more unashamedly—indulges in elaborate countdowns, the distance covered by the hero or, as it were, the elapsed time (or pages read) of the adventure accumulating with a regularity and order which appears, to this reader at least, to be the very inverse of suspense.

For Verne, productivity counts more than anything else. Size matters. Each of his texts is an Olympic game in which the characters—all record breakers in their way—attempt to breathe proleptic life into the motto: *citius, altius, fortius*. The author seems to have no concept of the common measure and his writing lumbers forward with, at times, a ponderous precision, the redeeming feature for the reader being the epic dimension, the sheer vastness of the vision. The following passage from chapter 4 of *Michel Strogoff*, is not untypical:

> Le territoire russe, en Europe, en Asie, en Amérique, s'étend du quinzième degré de longitude est au cent trente-troisième degré de longitude ouest, soit un développement de près de cent degrés, et du trente-huitième parallèle sud au quatre-vingt-unième parallèle nord, soit quarante-trois degrés. On y compte plus de soixante-dix millions d'habitants. On y parle trente langues différentes.[12]

Movement, distance, speed: these are the values written through Verne's pure adventures. Verne's heroes, accordingly, are required to indulge in constant calculation and measurement. Strogoff repeatedly reassesses the distance to be covered between himself and his ultimate goal:

> 'A huit heures du soir, soixante-quinze verstes de plus avaient été dévorées ... A minuit, quarante-cinq verstes au-delà ... le bourg de Novo-Saimsk était atteint ... Deux cents verstes environ séparent Novo-Saimsk de la ville d'Ichim ... Le lendemain ... les deux tarentass n'étaient plus qu'à trente verstes d'Ichim' (175).

Doctor Fergusson, in *Cinq semaines en ballon*, performs similar calculations: 'En pointant sa carte, il trouva que sa route latitudinale était de deux degrés, ou cent vingt milles dans l'ouest' (88); 'Le [ballon] dérivait dans le nord-est d'une trentaine de milles depuis deux heures environ' (105), and so on. As for Stanislas Boutardin, in *Paris au XXe siècle*, 'il s'exprimait par grammes et par centimètres, et portait en tout temps une canne métrique, ce qui lui donnait une grande connaissance des choses de ce monde; il méprisait royalement les arts' (51). Even a limited acquaintance with Verne throws up a mass of such examples. Whether French or English, Scottish, Siberian or Transylvanian, Verne's characters are in the permanent grip of a *libido calculandi*. The distances, times and averages which form such an obsessional part of Verne's narrative scheme—is it not possible, indeed, to claim that the digits 0–9 are the main character in any Verne novel?— make his typical plot a cross between popular adventure story and modern endurance race, and his typical hero, a correspondingly hybrid figure: Michel Strogoff is thus a kind of Indiana Indurain, participating in a 'tour de Russie', or more appositely perhaps, a trans-Siberian excess.

Verne's gigantism, however, as well as his atomic-clock precision are never quite gratuitous. The brief to educate and entertain inevitably brings an inveterate bookworm like Verne to include a solid pedagogic apparatus in his novels. His calculations are never performed in a vacuum, but rather explained and converted for the young French reader. For example, at the beginning of *Le Château des Carpathes*, when describing Transylvanian topography, Verne informs his reader in a footnote that 'le mille hongrois vaut environ 7500 mètres' (4). Similarly, recondite cultural information is glossed: thus, in *Les 500 millions de la Bégum*, we are informed at some length about the origin of the term 'grotte du Chien' (120). Information is also sometimes presented in tabular form,[13] the overriding concern being the exhaustiveness of the information provided. Narration thus constantly rubs shoulders with enumeration, so much so that one is tempted to speak of Verne's style of writing as the enumer-narrative, a list of lists, a vast accretion of details, of the concrete, the palpable, the substantive: like Dickens's 'Coketown', Verne's narrative, so overladen is it with the material, seems to be nothing more than a 'triumph of fact'.

Verne's narratives are obsessed, then, with the *where* and the *when*, with the precise physical dimensions of their environment. They are equally preoccupied with the *how*. The Vernian journey, that is, is not merely a timed, carefully measured excursion. Each voyage requires, in addition, its own particular type of conveyance, its very own manner of displacement: the *Voyages extraordinaires*, taken collectively, might indeed invite the alternative title, 'Around the World in Eighty Ways'. From humble horses and carts, to the more futuristic 'ascensoir', via the whole gamut of flying and floating, digging and diving, Verne's characters use a bewildering array of means of transport to move along, up, down, through and round his much plodded globe, tying it up, strapping it down, in a neat bundle or package to be delivered, following Hetzel's predilection, for the 'étrennes'.

Verne's usual line of approach, therefore, is this all-encompassing 'paquet-cadeau' grasp of the voracious nineteenth-century, positivist, 'géographe'—or, as Jean-Paul Dekiss has it, 'géophage'.[14] It is also, necessarily, an all-seeing one. Verne's method, that is, is panoptic as well as panoramic. Michel Strogoff, for example, despite his supposed blindness, returns from Siberia having seen all. Doctor Fergusson, in *Cinq semaines en ballon*, scuds across Africa, in the bulbous, eyeball-shaped mass of the *Victoria*, all-seeing, all-dominating, in a truly aerial perspective.

Indeed, it is in this sense that Verne's travellers can be said to supervise, literally, the development of those they see. And it is through characters such as Fergusson, that we can measure not only the implicit impact on Verne's writing of colonialist expansion and competition with Britain, but also the extent to which that theme reveals Verne's anxieties concerning the 'foreign' and his consequent ambivalence towards Knowledge.

It is not simply that, for example, Doctor Fergusson is turning himself into an airborne cartographer, as he floats across the African continent, but also that his inexorable advance connotes the unstoppable onward march of science—Fergusson's east to west route effectively causing the landscape to move from left to right beneath him, the balloonist and his neo-colonialist crew 'reading off' the landscape as they pass over it, consuming the book of the world, categorizing, taxonomizing as they go. 'Géophages' Verne's characters may often be, but in comparison with the anthropophagi whom they oversee, Fergusson and his companions always operate at this superior contemplative distance and with scientific detachment.

Through Fergusson, indeed, we meet with a vision of alterity which is clearly central to Verne's preoccupations from the very beginning of his writing career, and which, even in *Cinq semaines en ballon*, is already evidence of positivism entering into its negative phase, already a clear indication of that unease and morbid fascination in the face of otherness, which were to characterize the last two decades of the century. The detachment and distance which typify the Vernian hero's voy(eur)age—in respect of the generally uncouth races (namely, all except white Europeans) he must have commerce with—are generated by a fear of otherness and, ultimately, a dubitative relationship with time and Progress, rather than the straightforward, confident command of these concepts which the wonderfully controlled, 'scientific', materialist 'épaisseur' of his writing often seems to impart and which many readers still assume to be his natural mode.

For Verne's depiction of the foreign, or of the alien other, reveals, beyond the apparently anodine Gallocentric, not to say 'franchouillard', discourse, a far more sinister taxonomy of race types. Whatever the theoretical sources for Verne's summary classifications,[15] his foreigners are little more than crude stereotypes. True, some are benign: the pair of genial journalists, Harry Blount and Alcide Jolivet, in *Michel Strogoff*, for example. Even here, however, one suspects that Verne's caricatures are not entirely innocent. Blount, 'L'Anglo-Normand', is 'compassé, froid, flegmatique', while Jolivet, 'le Gallo-Romain', is qualified as 'vif, pétulant' (7). But Verne's characterization is not limited to this tendency to describe them in much the same way as one might classify church columns. His constant allusions to Blount's touchiness or his 'raideur toute britannique' (100) and to Jolivet's resourcefulness and intellectual rigour, to his wit and 'sa bonne humeur, que rien ne pouvait altérer' (153), provide permanent comic relief no doubt, notably in chapter 11 of part 1 of the novel. But they also constitute a ludic inversion of Anglo-French colonial rivalries—a 'mésentente cordiale'—a wish-fulfilling distortion in which Jolivet constantly has the upper hand over his British colleague.

But perhaps the real value of reading *Michel Strogoff* through this paradigm of racial stereotypes is that one is better able to see that the real threat Verne is writing against is the ethnic dilution of the European racial 'type', whether in its French or British manifestations. Strogoff, himself, is clearly the genetic limit beyond which Verne is not prepared to go. The Tsar's courier presents 'les beaux caractères de la race caucasique' (32), while Strogoff's companion, Nadia, is already at one remove from the most desirable chromosomic recipe: although 'véritablement charmante', she represents 'le type slave dans toute sa pureté,—type un peu sévère' (56). As the tale unfolds and we advance eastwards with Strogoff, beyond the Urals, the stereotypes become increasingly threatening. Ivan Ogareff, the traitor, the fallen angel, is genetically perfidious: 'Ayant en lui un peu de sang mongol par sa mère, qui était d'origine asiatique, il aimait la ruse' (199). The further east Strogoff goes, the more reductive and the more anonymous these ethnic stereotypes become. The Uzbecks, for example, 'race dominante en Tartarie', are reduced from human to animal, by being juxtaposed with their horses, 'de race usbèque, comme ceux qui les montaient' (236–7)[16]—a description which seems subtlety itself when placed alongside the presentation of the prelinguistic, black natives in *Cinq semaines en ballon*, whom Dick Kennedy and Joe believe they see attacking Doctor Fergusson's balloon. The assailants prove to be apes: 'la différence n'est pas grande', admits the doctor (103).

For Verne's explorers, difference *is* distance. Fergusson, for his part, manages to escape from the degenerate identity/sameness of the tribal warriors by floating skyward. Alcide Jolivet, as one might expect, wriggles out of such uncomfortable thoughts by way of a merry quip: 'Il ne faut pas trop se tartariser!' (290). The basic issue remains the same and Verne's repressed nightmare vision of alien invasion returns soon enough during his description of the Tartar march on Tomsk:

> Les cavaliers tartares pullulaient, et, parfois, il semblait qu'ils sortissent de terre, comme ces insectes nuisebles qu'un pluie d'orage fait fourmiller à la surface du sol. (304)

This apocalyptic, catastrophist vision of alien invasion, is what Strogoff seeks to avert in his latter-day crusade, fighting the good fight at the very limits of 'civilization'. Jolivet, in what seems a classic statement of colonialist ideology, points out: 'Le beau rôle est encore à ceux dont les armes civilisent' (290).

But through the colonialist hype, anxiety constantly lurks on the horizon to threaten Verne's hero. Indeed, one is justified in wondering about the extent to which Verne is confident regarding his crusaders, or about the ultimate worth or success of their 'mission civilisatrice'. Michel Strogoff, after all, seems a strange case. For, despite being helped by a whole series of secondary characters, notwithstanding his unparalleled knowledge of the territories he crosses (as well as the languages spoken there), in spite of the privileges afforded by his special courier status and even though he has apparently limitless funds and a wodge of passes and podaroshnas, Strogoff somehow manages to lay himself in the path of the invader and be taken prisoner by the Tartar soldiers, coming within a whisker of failure on his crucial mission. In the end, it is only a series of fortuitous circumstances (431, 439, and 455) which prevent his chestnuts from being roasted beyond recognition. The bumbling Blount and the jolly Jolivet, invariably beat Strogoff from A to B, not to mention from B to C and C to D. What, exactly, is the status of a figure like Strogoff, who always contrives to be headed off by two journalist-buffoons?

One frequently has the impression that Blount and Jolivet are reporting—at most—on some grand, imperial war game, or less seriously still—on an elaborate sporting encounter. Where Doctor Fergusson and his happy crew are concerned, there is no ambiguity at all: they are floating over Africa, because it is there, three amateur sportsmen on an early package tour.[17] 'Je ne suis pas fâché d'avoir vu un orage d'un peu haut. C'est un joli spectacle!' (132), remarks the buoyant Joe Wellington: 'Quel pays de chasse!' (125), exclaims Dick Kennedy. Before the off, there is even a weigh-in, 'comme des jockeys' (40), as well as a healthy book opened on the event: 'On engagea des sommes énormes au livre des paris, comme s'il se fût agi des courses d'Epsom' (13). Fergusson's balloon journey, it has to be said, was from the outset placed in a ludic context, rumoured to be nothing more than a hoax by Barnum, 'qui, après avoir travaillé aux Etats-Unis, s'apprêtait à "faire" les Iles Britanniques' (11).

Verne, for all his arch-positivist accuracy and even in his most 'heroic' tales (*Michel Strogoff*), presents the 'voyage' as 'extraordinaire' to the extent that it invariably contains an element of 'fantaisie' as a bit of a joke. That is, there is often a sense in which the ludic level of the ideology Verne is representing shows through, in which Verne, notwithstanding his best efforts, ends up catching colonialism with its ideological trousers down: an aspect of Verne's thought which becomes clearer if we briefly reconsider some of the points made, above, in respect of the author's apparent worship of the facts.

Where the learned conventions of his narrative are concerned, he is not above throwing in the odd ludic footnote. In *Le Château des Carpathes*, for example, while musing on the development of the telephone and the clarity with which two people can understand each other, Verne adds in a spurious (if far-sighted) reference to the videophone: '[Ces personnes] pouvaient même se voir dans des glaces reliées par des fils, grâce à l'invention du téléphote' (214). This is Verne at his most science fictionesque, no doubt. But the conflation of 'éducation' and 'récréation' at the pedagogic level of his text, as well as highlighting a tension inherent to the genre, also underlines Verne's willingness to discard fact for fun. In the same way, while many of Verne's methods of travel are inevitably fantastical, given his themes, some are so farcical as to smother man's technological prowess: for example, the 'éléphant remorqueur' episode in chapter 17 of *Cinq semaines en ballon*. Or again, in the opening pages of the same text, Verne's enumer-narrative reaches a degree of exhuastivity which borders on the satirical, if not on self-parody: I am referring to the A to Z of 'célèbres voyageurs qui s'étaient illustrés sur la terre d'Afrique' (8), which occupies pages 8–9. How many readers, one is forced to wonder, actually bother(ed) to read through Verne's list?

The hyperbole is surely ironical. Its rhetorical *vis-à-vis*, litotes, is equally

ludic. Consequently, when we learn that the toasts proposed to these
famous travellers are 'portés avec les vins de France' (8), we are justified—
notwithstanding the historical accuracy of British love of claret—in being
suspicious of Verne's intention. Is this merely an innocuous detail? Our
suspicion tends to be confirmed when we learn, a little further on, that in
preparation for Fergusson's daring journey, 'les fabriques de Lyon avaient
reçu une commande importante de taffetas pour la construction de
l'aérostat' (11). At one level, Verne's brief clearly requires him to promote
the domestic product whenever he can. But contemporary Franco-British
rivalries simply cannot be ignored here and Verne's ironical approach to
them underscores his doubts, not only concerning the colonial contest
alluded to, but also about the very status of Progress. Taking another
hyperbole to illustrate the point further, we can look again at the
description, in *Paris au XXe siècle*, of Stanislas Boutardin, who

> s'exprimait par grammes et par centimètres, et portait en tout temps
> une canne métrique, ce qui lui donnait une grande connaissance des
> choses de ce monde; il méprisait royalement les arts, et surtout les
> artistes, pour donner à croire qu'il les connaissait; pour lui, la peinture
> s'arrêtait au lavis, le dessin à l'épure, la sculpture au moulage, la
> musique au sifflet des locomotives, la littérature aux bulletins de
> bourse. (51)

Verne's industrial villain is, of course, a 'poncif' for science-fiction writers
of the period.[18] But the satirical excess of the description once again calls
Verne's commitment to progress into question. So does Huguenin's ironical
diatribe on industrial pollution later in the same novel:

> —Vois-tu, Michel ... à dix lieues autour de Paris, il n'y a plus
> d'atmosphère! Nous étions jaloux de celle de Londres, et, au moyen
> de dix mille cheminées d'usine, de fabriques de produits chimiques,
> de guano artificiel, de fumée de charbon, de gaz délétères, et de
> miasmes industriels, nous nous sommes composé un air qui vaut
> celui du Royaume-Uni. (153)

All of which is at once another mocking reference to the more farcical
aspects of Franco-British industrial competition and a singularly
unenthusiastic response to material progress and the supposed benefits to
modern society of scientific enquiry.

In short, Verne is writing in nostalgic and not proleptic mode. Although
this does not amount to a palpably original statement concerning the
origins of science fiction or scientific novels, it sheds a certain light,
nevertheless, on Verne's own bent in his earliest work for disguised satire
on Progress. He is profoundly suspicious of development and anxious about

the future, even through his most positive and optimistic characters. Fergusson, for example, muses on the likely emergence of Africa as the future centre of the civilized world, 'quand les régions de l'Europe se seront épuisées à nourrir leurs habitants' (123). Dick Kennedy, Fergusson's sceptical companion, goes one better by formulating a vision of cataclysmic destruction at the hands of science: 'Je me suis toujours figuré que le dernier jour du monde sera celui où quelque immense chaudière chauffée à trois milliards d'atmosphères fera sauter notre globe!' (124). The narrator of *Le Château des Carpathes*, adds to this catastrophist view, the vision of time as essentially sterile, bereft of the capacity for renewal and of scientific progress as a leading force in the creation of the necessary conditions of that sterility: 'Nous sommes d'un temps où tout arrive—on a presque le droit de dire où tout est arrivé ... D'ailleurs, il ne se crée plus de légendes au déclin de ce pratique et positif XIXe siècle' (2). Knowledge, one is forced to conclude, far from liberating humankind, is a serious impediment to happiness. And we arrive at the paradox of the world-weary positivist, whereby Progress in fact topples over into degeneration, advance becomes decline and—as in Herbert Spencer's famous image—increased knowledge ironically connotes a vaster ignorance.

Verne's endings frequently underline the point: his greatest heroes never reach, nor do they dispense perfect, complete knowledge, since if that knowledge is an end (*finis*), both limit and cessation, then its attainment or revelation effectively stops Vernian history. We never 'see', for instance, the letter which Strogoff carries east from the Tsar. Phileas Fogg's victory depends on a *mis*calculation: his number-crunching fails to take account of an eternal cosmic reality. Captain Nemo, Robur-le-conquérant, and Rodolphe de Gortz, all take their most powerful knowledge with them to the grave. Positivism, *in fine*, Verne seems to be saying, threatens to produce absolute *stasis* and it is only the artfully flawed genius of Verne's latter-day romantics which ensures the survival of an information gap, an imperfection, a blemish which generates man's quest. Knowledge cannot be allowed to conquer all if it is not simply to negate itself. In the words of Robur, such total knowledge has to be held back from humanity until 'le jour où elle sera assez instruite pour en tirer profit et assez sage pour n'en jamais abuser' (247).

Hiding knowledge in this fashion means that one cultivates the occult. Everything remains possible, since nothing, at the end of a novel like *Robur-le-conquérant*, has actually happened.

In the final analysis, Jules Verne's use of science places a bracket around self-satisfied republican materialism, feeds off it, but only to nourish a latter-day Romantic disillusion, or to stress those elements in his imagination which might be more accurately classed as 'fin de siècle', in the sense that they deny the possibility of genuine betterment or evolution towards some destiny forged by human enquiry. What is denied in Verne's writing is, precisely, change, revolution and what is preserved is a space for mystery and faith. Science and civilization must win, of course, in the battle against superstition and savagery. But total victory is anathema, since the complete absence of the alien would destroy the need for enquiry which is a synonym of self.

Notes

1 Quoted by Jean-Paul Dekiss, *Jules Verne. Le rêve du progrès*, (Paris, Gallimard, 1991), p. 145.

2 For example, Jean Bessière (ed.), *Modernités de Jules Verne*, (Paris, Presses Universitaires de France, 1986).

3 Although Michel Serres in a recent French television programme—*Arte*, December 1994—was adamant that Verne had invented nothing, but had simply embroidered on existing inventions.

4 J.-P. Picot, 'Jules Verne et la constellation Thanatos', in G. Ponnau (ed.), *Fins de siècle . Terme-évolution-révolution*? (Actes du congrès de la société française de littérature générale et comparée, Presses Universitaires du Mirail, 1989), pp. 465–74 (473).

5 In a letter to Verne written in late 1863 (or perhaps early 1864), Hetzel writes: 'Mon cher Verne, je donnerai je ne sais quoi pour n'avoir pas à vous écrire aujourd'hui. Vous avez entrepris une tâche impossible—et pas plus que vos devanciers dans des choses analogues—vous n'êtes parvenu à la mener à bien', *Paris au XXe siècle*, (Paris, Hachette, 1994), p. 15.

6 Hetzel, later in the same letter, adds: 'C'est la littérature ... qui me blesse—inférieure qu'elle est à vous-même presqu'à toutes les lignes', ibid., p. 16.

7 A point explored, in greater detail by Simone Vierne, 'Hetzel et Jules Verne, ou l'invention d'un auteur', *Europe*, 619/620 (November–December 1980), 53–64.

8 Strange, in the midst of one of Verne's most ideologically laden, pedagogical texts, to come upon the following passage, in some ways evocative of Flaubert's narrative:

> De nombreuses tentes, faites de peaux, de feutres ou d'étoffes de soie, chatoyaient aux rayons du soleil. Les hautes houppes, qui empanachaient leur pointe conique, se balançaient au milieu de fanions, de guidons et d'étendards multicolores... Un pavillon spécial, orné d'une queue de cheval, dont la hampe s'élançait d'une gerbe de bâtons rouges et blancs, artistement entrelacés, indiquait le haut rang de ces chefs tartares.

At the beginning of the next paragraph, however, we are firmly back with the quantity-conscious Verne: 'Le camp contenait au moins cent cinquante mille soldats ...' (*Michel Strogoff*, (Paris, Livre de Poche, 1966), p. 263).

9 'It is the *explicitly* pedagogical signifying structure of Verne's basic narratological recipe that serves to differentiate his 'scientific novel' from most modern SF' (Evans's emphasis). Arthur B. Evans, *Jules Verne Rediscovered* (Greenwood Press, 1988), p. 104.

10 Edmond About's *Le Progrès* appeared in 1864. Indeed, About himself, had it not been for his preference for political journalism, might have constituted a serious competitor for Verne, given the success of *Le Roi des montagnes* (1857) and *L'Homme à l'oreille cassée* (1862).

11 Dekiss, *Jules Verne*, p. 146.

12 *Michel Strogoff*, p. 53. Other quotes from Verne novels are made from the Poche editions in each case (with the exception of *Paris au XXe siècle*) the page reference being given in brackets after the quotation.

13 See *Cinq semaines en ballon*, pp. 47–8.

14 Dekiss, *Jules Verne*, p. 72.

15 Verne (*Michel Strogoff*, p. 28) refers to Rémusat (1788–1832). Gobineau (1816–82), whose *Essai sur l'inégalité des races humaines* appeared in 1853–5, is another possible source. Verne has to be seen, indeed, as contributing already to that pseudo-scientific orthodoxy, with its attendant racial taxonomy, which was soon to be such an important element in arguments for revenge over Prussia and, a little later, purification of the French military.

16 Curiously enough, Verne's consistency in respect of the Uzbecks, is less than scientific: described on p. 236 as 'd'une taille au-dessus de la moyenne', they revert, on p. 263, to being 'petits de taille'. Is this a mere slip of the pen? Or is it evidence of the arbitrary nature of the classifications Verne establishes? Does the latter not induce the former?

17 Thomas Cook's first tour, by train, was in 1841.

18 And, indeed, of later writers. In respect of dashed romantic hopes for the artist in a hyper-industrialized world, one can usefully juxtapose Verne's 1863 'Grand Entrepôt Dramatique' (chapter 14 of *Paris au XXe siècle*) with, say, René Barjavel's 1943 vision of sterilized, state-regulated artistic production in Part One of *Ravage*.

9

The Science is Fiction: Jules Verne, Raymond Roussel, and Surrealism

TERRY HALE and ANDREW HUGILL

The name of Jules Verne is mentioned less often than it deserves to be in relation to the French avant-garde of the early and mid-twentieth century. Indeed, the influence of his work is clearly to be seen in not only the writing of Raymond Roussel, and as a consequence in the internal publications of the Collège de Pataphysique (whose members, let us recall, have included Boris Vian, Eugène Ionesco, Raymond Queneau, and Michel Leiris), but also, though to a slightly lesser degree, in numerous productions of the writers and artists generally associated with the French and Belgian Surrealist movements. However, Verne's presence is even more strongly manifested in the writings of the Greek Surrealists, particularly those of Andreas Embirikos.

As Michel Leiris confided in his diary, Raymond Roussel's admiration for Jules Verne is in need of some elucidation.[1] The same might be said of the equally unlikely affection with which the Surrealist movement viewed Verne. After all, the author of scientific adventure stories is frequently regarded as the spokesman of the very causative system which Surrealism set out to abolish. The present article will seek to present an overview of the manner in which these various writers and movements have perceived the author of *Les Voyages et aventures du capitaine Hatteras* (1866), *Michel Strogoff* (1876), *Les Naufragés du 'Jonathan'* (1909), and *L'Etonnante aventure de la mission Barsac* (1919).

Verne and Roussel

'Je voudrais aussi, dans ces notes', wrote Raymond Roussel in *Comment j'ai écrit certains de mes livres*, 'rendre hommage à l'homme d'incommensurable génie que fut Jules Verne' ['I would also like, in these notes, to pay hommage to that man of incommensurable genius, namely Jules Verne'].[2] He continues:

Mon admiration pour lui est infinie.

Dans certains pages du *Voyage au centre de la terre*, de *Cinq semaines en ballon*, de *Vingt mille lieues sous les mers* , de *De la Terre à la lune* et de *Autour de la lune*, de *L'Ile mystérieuse*, d'*Hector Servadac*, il s'est élevé aux plus hautes cimes que puisse atteindre le verbe humain.[...]

O maître incomparable, soyez béni pour les heures sublimes que j'ai passées toute ma vie à vous lire et à vous relire sans cesse.

[My admiration for him is boundless.

In certain pages of *Voyages to the Centre of the Earth*, *Five Weeks in a Balloon*, *Twenty Thousand Leagues Under the Sea*, *From the Earth to the Moon*, *Trip to the Moon*, *Mysterious Island* and *Hector Servadac*, he raised himself to the highest peaks that can be attained by human language.

O incomparable master, may you be blessed for the sublime hours that I have spent endlessly reading and re-reading your works throughout my life.]

Comment j'ai écrit certains de mes livres—or, rather, the essay which gave rise to the title of the posthumous volume in which it later appeared—was first published in the April 1935 issue of the *Nouvelle Revue Française*, some twenty months after Roussel's death at the age of fifty-eight in Palermo following an overdose of barbiturates. The significance of Roussel's essay, however, is not limited to the simple acknowledgement of Verne's importance to him as a writer. In *Comment j'ai écrit certains de mes livres*, Roussel also provided the key to his own unique manner of composition— a procedure which at first sight would seem to have little or nothing in common with that of Verne.

The basis of Roussel's method is provided by the pun, usually culled from the alternative definitions of words given in his favourite dictionary: Bescherelle's *Nouveau dictionnaire national*. In *Comment j'ai écrit certains de mes livres* he cites two main types of example. The first is a phrase or sentence, sometimes a popular saying, whose meaning can be entirely altered by the substitution of one letter for another, for example:

> Les lettres du blanc sur les bandes du vieux *b*illard
> Les lettres du blanc sur les bandes du vieux *p*illard

This is given as the generic phrase of the basic scenario of *Impressions d'Afrique* (1910), in which both cryptography (chalking the letters of a message one at a time around the north, south, east and west cushions of a billiard table), and the capturing of whites by an old plunderer (King Talu) play a part.

The second is a substitution method in the standard French construction '—à—' (e.g., machine à coudre = sewing-machine). Thus, 'sabot à dégrès' becomes both a 'stepping-clog' and a 'thermal-violin', which partly gives rise to the chemist Bex's 'orchestrion': a thermally controlled music-machine which produces clog-dances for violin according to changes in temperature to which the imaginary chemical *Bexium* (so named after its 'inventor') is sensitive. Likewise, the curious stage performance—which commences with him scooping up copper coins and building them into a strange construction at the back of the stage—of the clown Whirligig derives from *tour* (tower) *à billion* (copper coinage). This same construction may also be found in the names of various characters: thus the four-year-old Bob Boucheressas (from 'bouche à ressasse') is able to reproduce any sound he hears.[3]

All the incredible machines and scenarios in Roussel's work, and much of the 'action' and dialogue, are constructed from such plays on words. Roussel's creative task was to develop the results of the collisions of meaning in his imagination. One consequence of this is that narrative tends to crumble under the weight of such a conception while Roussel's tendency to an extreme concision means that any narrative *device* proclaims itself even more loudly than in Verne. But the most perplexing aspect of the 'poetic method' is that, even after its revelation and explanation, the enigma of Roussel's work remains in tact. This effect may be directly experienced by reading *Impressions d'Afrique* in which the first half of the book—designed to 'set the scene' and causally explain the various bizarre events described in the second half—is shifted to begin *after the second half ends*, apparently offering the reader first a mystery, then a revelation. In point of fact, however, the revelaion succeeds only in deepening the mystery, leaving the reader still more perplexed by the end of the book. This same puzzlement operates between Roussel's work taken as a whole and the revelation of the 'procedure'.

In *Comment j'ai écrit certains de mes livres*, Roussel further notes:

> J'ai beaucoup voyagé. Notamment en 1920–21 j'ai fait le tour du monde par les Indes, l'Australie, la Nouvelle-Zélande, les archipels du Pacifique, la Chine, le Japon et l'Amérique. Je connaissais déjà les principaux pays de l'Europe, l'Egypte et tout le nord de l'Afrique, et plus tard je visitai Constantinople, l'Asie-Mineur et la Perse. Or, de tous ces voyages, je n'ai rien tiré pour mes livres. Il m'a paru que la chose méritait d'être signalée tant elle montre clairement que chez moi l'imagination est tout.[4]

> [I have travelled a great deal. Notably in 1920–21, I travelled around the world by way of India, Australia, New Zealand, the Pacific archipelagi, China, Japan and America. ... I already knew the principal countries of Europe, Egypt and all of North Africa, and later

I visited Constantinople, Asia Minor, and Persia. Now, from all these voyages I never took a single thing for my books. It seemed to me that the circumstance deserves mention, since it proves so well how imagination counts for everything in my work.]

Roussel completed his world tour in under three months. Asked by a Parisian friend to send back a present which would be 'rare and evocative of the local colour [of India]', he sent an electric fan. In China he never left the hotel bedroom. In Tahiti he avoided watching the spectacular sunsets. He professed great admiration for Pierre Loti, whose books of foreign travel such as *Aziyadé* and *Le Mariage de Loti*, inspired many Parisians with longings for the Orient but, unlike Loti, Roussel never felt tempted to dress up in regional costumes or to become part of the local life. The most he managed was to eat kangaroo soup in Australia.

In 1925–6, he took things a stage further and constructed the world's first mobile home, a motorized *roulotte*, or gypsy caravan: an automobile thirty feet long by eight feet wide containing a sitting-room (complete with armchairs, wireless set, electric heating and a safe), bedroom, bathroom and even servants' quarters! The *Revue du Touring Club de France* published a feature article about his vehicle under the heading: 'La maison roulante de M. Raymond Roussel'.[5] In his Paris-on-wheels, Roussel could avoid the tiresome business of checking-in to foreign hotels, dealing with the natives, or even seeing the local landscape.

Given this indifference to place, what could have been the motivation for Roussel's meanderings? There do not seem to have been any undue personal pressures upon him at that time which might have caused him to flee. He was not undertaking any obvious research, in the way that Verne did during his trips around the world, or up in a balloon. As a millionaire, perhaps Roussel was bowing to some such social pressure as: 'since money is no object why not see the world?' But it seems hardly likely that a man of Roussel's fixity of purpose would have gone to such lengths in the interests of social conformity. The only explanation which bears scrutiny seems to be that, contrary to his statement above, he did indeed 'take something for his books' from all this travel. However, this 'something' was not information about the real world, but rather an understanding of the inner world (the world of Conception, Roussel would have called it) and, crucially, its *interaction* with the act of travel.

As we have seen, that Verne was the model for his work was fully if implicitly acknowledged by Roussel, but the precise nature of this indebtedness can be understood on several levels. It is important to establish first that the most obvious and straightforward way in which Verne could have influenced Roussel is *not* one of them. However 'fantastical' and imaginary Verne's tales may have been, he went to great lengths thoroughly to research factual details, in order to give as much appearance of verisimilitude as possible. Indeed, he went to astonishing lengths in this regard. English translations of Verne's works are often heavily edited, to remove the interminable lists of flora, fauna, place-names, geologies, local customs, and so on, with which they are filled. Since these lists frequently occur at the beginnings of chapters, with the incentive of the 'action' driving the reader on through them, it was a relatively straightforward job to make the necessary cuts. Verne's information was obtained from a variety of sources, including newspapers, libraries, journals and word-of-mouth, and not all the 'facts' he presented to the reader were beyond question. Nevertheless, Verne's books undoubtedly had an educational value and the thrill of adventure they describe was as much a thrill of the discovery of *information* as of discovery of new worlds, or the quest for self-knowledge which drives many of his characters.

There is considerable divergence between the two writers at this point, for Roussel's works, although obsessed with detailed description, shun any connection with the world of external reality, and so contain no 'factual' content whatsoever. Also, although informed by learning, they contain no educational material and are of no potential 'use' to society at large. The various machines and inventions they describe have no prospect of ever coming into existence, unlike those of Verne, whose predictive powers are legendary. The anthropological content of Roussel's work is at best irrelevant and at worst a travesty of reality, whereas Verne's does ring true to some extent, at least as an accurate depiction of the way in which the colonialist powers saw the world. Finally, Roussel had no discernible political or social agenda, whereas Verne's works are informed by his political ideas and several are, in effect, political tracts.

Given such an apparent gulf between the two, how can Verne's all-pervading influence upon Roussel be so confidently asserted, not least by Roussel himself?[6] In what sense can Roussel be said to have modelled himself upon the older writer?

The first and most obvious direct influence is in the prose style. Both writers employ a prose which is deliberately flat, neutral and sparing in its use of adjectives. This is the case even at the most 'sensational' moments of the narrative, for which a single expression of amazement by one or more characters, plus a key adjective from the narrator, normally suffices. Apart from encyclopedias and dictionaries, the major stylistic precedent for this technique is de Sade, whose detailed cataloguings, fantastic machines, predictive powers and boundless imagination rival those of Verne and Roussel. But of course, the inaccessibility of de Sade's work rules him out as a serious *influence* upon either writer.[7]

The effect of this stylistic neutrality is to throw the objects and events being described into sharp relief, in the manner of a catalogue. Unobtrusive prose supports description, of which there is a great deal in both writers' works, often presented under the guise of dialogue or reported speech. Consider the following examples:

> — [...] Vous avez certainement remarqué que [le] sommet [de cette tour] est surmonté d'un pylône métallique très élevé. Ce pylône est un "projecteur d'ondes". La tour est, en outre, hérissée sur toute sa surface d'une multitude de pointes, qui sont autant d'autres projecteurs de taille réduite.
> —Projecteurs d'ondes, dites-vous?... —demanda le docteur Châtonnay.
> —Je ne voudrais pas vous faire un cours de physique, répondit Marcel Camaret en souriant. Quelques explications de principe sont cependant nécessaires. Je vous rappellerai donc, si vous le savez, je vous apprendrai, si vous l'ignorez, qu'un célèbre physicien allemand du nom de Hertz, a remarqué, il y a de cela déjà longtemps, que, lorsqu'on fait éclater l'étincelle d'une bobine d'induction dans le petit intervalle séparant les deux branches d'une condensateur, résonateur ou oscillateur, selon le mot qui vous conviendra le mieux, cette étincelle provoque, entre les deux pôles de cet instrument, une décharge oscillante, ce qui revient à dire qu'il est parcouru par un courant alternatif, ou, en d'autres termes [...].

['] You have undoubtedly noticed that [the] summit [of this tower] is surmounted by a very tall metal pylon. This pylon is a 'wave projector'. The tower bristles, moreover, with a number of points; these are smaller projectors.'

'Wave projectors, you say?' asked Dr Châtonnay.

'I'm not going to give you a course in physics,' said Marcel Camaret smilingly. 'But a few explanations of its principles are however necessary. I will remind you, then, if you know it already, or tell you, if you don't, that a celebrated German physicist called Hertz noticed some time ago that when an electric spark from an induction coil flashes across a short gap between the terminals of a condenser—or a resonator or oscillator, whichever word pleases you best—that spark sets up between the two poles of the instrument an oscillating discharge. The gap is crossed by an alternating current, or, in other words [...].']

Canterel pris alors la parole pour nous expliquer la raison d'être de l'étrange véhicule aérien.

Le maître avait poussé jusqu'aux dernières limites du possible l'art de prédire le temps.[...] Pour mettre en saisissant relief l'extrême perfection de ses prognostics, Canterel imagina un appareil capable de créer une œuvre esthétique due aux seuls efforts combinés du soleil et du vent.

Il construisit la *demoiselle* que nous avions sous les yeux et la pourvut des cinq chronomètres supérieurs chargés d'en régler toutes les évolutions—le plus haut ouvrant ou refermant la soupape, tandis que les autres, en actionnant les miroirs et la lentille, s'occupaient de gonfler avec les feux solaires l'enveloppe de l'aérostat, grâce à la substance jaune, qui, due à une préparation spéciale, exhalait sous tout ascendant calorique une certaine quantité d'hydrogène.[8]

[Canterel then began to speak and explained to us the purpose of the strange aerial vehicle.

The professor had developed the art of weather-forecasting to the furthest possible limits. ... In order best to accentuate the extreme perfection of his forecasts, Canterel conceived a device capable of creating an aesthetic object solely on the basis of the combined efforts of the sun and wind.

He constructed the beetle standing before our eyes and furnished it with five highly accurate chronometers designed to regulate all its operations—the top one opened or shut the valve, while the task of the others, which worked the mirrors and the lens, was to use the rays of the sun to inflate the aerostat's envelope by means of the yellow substance which, because of its special preparation, released a certain quantity of hydrogen whenever there was an increase in temperature.]

Both these episodes last several pages, and it is characteristic of both writers' main protagonists to embark upon lengthy exegeses of this type. In fact, many of the books are themselves entire monologues or journals, 'narrated' by one or a number of the characters. This can result in episodes of Chinese boxes of reported speech. The character/narrator's desire to be objective and factual is then implicitly given as the reason for the flatness of the prose. Sometimes, when the narrative reaches a particularly tense moment, this can be signalled by the neutral tone beginning to waver. Frequently the narrator him- or herself emerges as less than heroic, but in these cases the reader is supposed to accept their word all the more readily since they display, often humorously, human failings.

A number of the scenarios described are astonishingly similar. Verne's *Les Naufragés du 'Jonathan'* (1909; but not translated into English, as *The Survivors of the 'Jonathan'*, until the 1960s) has precisely the same starting-point as Roussel's *Impressions d'Afrique*: a group of western travellers is shipwrecked and thrown into a foreign situation surrounded by 'savages' (who turn out to be as, or even more, civilized than themselves) and are confronted with the need for organization. In Verne's story, this turns into a series of social and political experiments, each system failing until anarchism (which Verne sees as freedom from government, rather than insurrection) finally triumphs. In Roussel's version the 'rules' explored apparently govern the ordering and construction of entertainments devised to while away the time until a ransom is paid. This in turn proves to be a pretext for a more mysterious set of rules governing the elements of each entertainment and, ultimately, the tale itself. Both worlds are entirely imaginary: Verne's is located on an imaginary Tierra del Fuego, Roussel's in an imaginary Africa. The geographical details are precisely given in both cases, the difference being that Verne's accord with the known facts of real geography, whereas Roussel's are plainly impossible.

Another such parallel exists between *Locus Solus* and the second part of *L'Etonnante aventure de la mission Barsac*. In the latter story, a mysterious *place* is created in an unknown location somewhere in the middle of the Sahara desert. The scientist-genius who builds the city, Marcel Camaret, is an unwitting collaborator in the creation of Blackland: a society gone wrong, which eventually brings about its own destruction. Through Camaret, Verne predicts the invention of the helicopter and other scientific devices. Martial Canterel is plainly another version of the Nemo-Camaret archetype, and his *place alone* strongly resembles Blackland, except that it lacks the sense of morality and social commentary. Furthermore, its inventions prefigure no subsequent developments in science. Interestingly, both of Verne's stories cited above—*Les Naufragés du 'Jonathan'* and *L'Etonnante aventure de la mission Barsac*—were published posthumously, which suggests either that Roussel saw sketches or discussed them when the two writers met, or that their minds worked along parallel tracks.

That this latter suggestion is most likely is demonstrated by an examination of the profound similarities which occur at the level of formal construction of the tales. In both cases, this has a remarkable similarity to music (Roussel actually trained as a musician) in its quasi-symphonic development of a key motif, in the integration of the ideas, in the substrating opposition of what one might call tonalities. Verne explores this connection overtly in a story—commissioned for the Christmas number of *Le Figaro Illustré* in 1893—'M. Ré Dièze et Mlle Si Bémol'.[9] Both writers often employ a chaining or linking device which drives the narrative forwards. In Roussel's play *La Poussière de Soleils*, for example, the device is buried treasure, each scene culminating in the revelation of a new clue. Verne's work is almost entirely constructed in this way, and it is no accident that he admired Poe, the inventor of the detective story, for the 'treasure' that is discovered at the end of the book is often a truth, either about a person (e.g., Captain Nemo, Captain Hatteras, etc.) or the world (e.g., the international dateline in *Le Tour du monde en 80 jours*). Music, too, employs this stratagem: the first movement of Beethoven's *Symphony No. 3*, 'Eroica', for example, only reveals its unadulterated principal theme at the end, thus making the movement a journey of discovery.

Underlying this narrative device, however, is that enigmatic method based upon wordplay which, as we saw earlier, Roussel called his 'procedure' or, to distinguish it from Verne's technique, his 'poetic method'. An indication of its existence lies in the names given to characters and the titles of the books. Captain Nemo is, of course, 'no-one' or 'no-name', in the manner of Ulysses hiding his identity from the Cyclops, but he is also 'omen' in reverse; Marcel Camaret (*L'Etonnante aventure de la mission Barsac*) is the great scientist/inventor, oblivious to the use to which his inventions may be put by the evil, and evilly named, Harry Killer (which itself turns out to be a pseudonym); the Kaw-Djer (*Les Naufragés du 'Jonathan'*) is the embodiment of a savage wisdom, a mysterious being of entirely non-European culture who instinctively understands both Nature and himself, just like J.-J. Rousseau's 'noble savage'.

In Roussel's work, similar types are linked to similar names: in the unfinished tale *Flio*, characters are referred to simply by initials;[10] in *Locus Solus*, the scientist hero is Martial Canterel; in *Impressions d'Afrique*, the 'savage' Seil-Kor is the intelligent, sensitive son of the brutal King Talu. The titles of these books are themselves wordplays: *Impressions d'Afrique*, for example, also puns as *Impressions à fric*—in slang, a book published a the author's own expense, which was indeed the case—and the entire narrative scenario, anything but an example of travel writing, is derived from the chance collision of the meanings of three words. *Locus Solus*, too, has several meanings. Roussel himself points out that there is a 'lake' on the moon named Lacus Salus.

Verne's fondness for codes and ciphers was a matter of public knowledge.[11] At one point, he published a challenge in a national newspaper to any member of the general public to decipher an 'insoluble' cryptogram of his own invention, and was most surprised and disappointed when the solution was discovered quickly and rather easily. Characters in the novels often have to unravel or decode hidden messages and the word 'mystery' is much employed. For Verne, the greatest mystery was the world or, indeed, the universe and so, taken as a whole, Verne's writing may be seen as an attempt to map and decipher 'universal meaning'. The Earth itself is circumnavigated, penetrated, viewed from space and the moon. Lines are drawn across its surface as if to expose its hidden order: North by Captain Hatteras; longitudinally/latitudinally by Captain Nemo; through time by Phileas Fogg; and so on. Like the Qaballah's dissection of scripture, this constant delineating and mapping seeks to uncover, anagrammatically or crypographically, the Word of God. The cryptanalyst, presented with a page of apparently random letters, seeks to discover patterns, trying to isolate first the letter 'e' (the most common letter in both French and English), then 't' and so on. Lines are drawn across the cryptogram. Connections and resemblances are noted. Eventually, with a mighty jolt, the whole structure tumbles into meaning. Through his characters and his work, Verne tries to apply a similar method to the fundamental questions of all the disciplines of philosophy: ethics, epistemology, physics, and metaphysics. The wonder is that narrative survives such a grand endeavour: indeed, sometimes it does not. The apocalyptic ending of *L'Ile mystérieuse* (1875; tr. *The Mysterious Island*, 1875) is as much the immolation of narrative as of Captain Nemo and the *Nautilus*.

Verne and the Avant-Garde

Pierre Janet, who treated Roussel for a range of psychological disorders towards the end of World War I, has claimed that Roussel considered himself to be the equal of Dante, Shakespeare, or Victor Hugo.[12] Although such a claim might have seemed absurd at the time, by the time of his death in 1933 Roussel was already being seen by some as a major precursor of the avant-garde. As Michel Leiris noted in an essay which served as a preface to the posthumous publication of *Comment j'ai écrit certains de mes livres* in the *Nouvelle Revue Française* in 1935, Roger Vitrac and Jean Lévy had already come close in print to discovering the key to Roussel's enigmatic procedure of composition.[13]

Vitrac, of course, was a member of the Surrealist movement almost from the outset (though by 1935 he had long been excluded by Breton) while Jean Lévy, who would later sign himself Jean Ferry, in the future would distinguish himself not only as a Roussel scholar but as an author in his own right. Nor were Vitrac, Leiris, and Ferry—and it is perhaps not coincidental that Leiris (like a number of other dissidents of Surrealism after their exclusion by Breton) and Ferry would later become active members of the Collège de Pataphysique—isolated examples. Already, in 1911, Marcel Duchamp, Picabia, Gabrielle Buffet (Picabia's wife), and Apollinaire had attended a performance of *Impressions d'Afrique* together at the Théâtre Antoine. In 1924, André Breton, Michel Leiris, Benjamin Péret, Paul Eluard, and Robert Desnos attended the first night of *L'Etoile au front* at the Théâtre Vaudeville.

All these writers would, of course, also have been familiar with Verne from their youth—as Guillaume Apollinaire admitted when he described *Les Malheurs de Sophie* as 'un des plus célèbres livres de cette bibliothèque rose, délices de notre enfance, comme l'œuvre de Jules Verne le fut de notre adolescence' ['one of the most famous books in that romanesque library which was the delight of our childhood, just as the works of Jules Verne were for our adolescence'].[14] Thus, even though Breton never accorded to Verne the same formal importance as a precursor of Surrealism as he did to Roussel, the Surrealists did not know of Verne only through Roussel. This formal lack of acknowledgment—Verne is not mentioned, for example, in the list of precursors drawn up by Breton in the *Manifesto* of 1924, a list hardly intended as definitive in any event, nor among the twenty-six additional names suggested in 1932— is probably responsible for the current failure to recognize the place occupied by Verne in the movement's background.

Christian Robin has recently gone some way to rectifying this situation. At the beginning of 1916, he reminds us, Breton found himself stationed as a temporary intern at the neurological centre situated on rue du Bocage in Nantes, the city where Verne was born in 1828 and spent much of his childhood.[15] It was in this city—the only one in France, Breton would later remark in *Nadja* (1928), where he felt a certain sense of expectancy—that Breton first met Jacques Vaché, whose notion of black humour would rapidly establish itself as one of the central tenets of Surrealism. It was in Nantes too that Vaché killed himself in 1919. Several years after his death, *La Révolution surréaliste* published a nihilistic little tale written by Vaché under the pseudonym of Michel Strogoff, the central character of Verne's 1876 novel of the same title. Verne's novel depicts the adventures of a courier of the Tsar sent with an important message for the governors of Irkutsk; Vaché's story concerns a Russian student who has his hands cut off by a German officer who then reads to him the day's increasingly improbable headlines.[16]

One could multiply instances of this kind at will: the section casually entitled by Breton and Soupault '80 Jours' in *Les Champs magnétiques* (indeed, the very title of this firstly characteristically Surrealist novel would seem to have a Vernian quality);[17] Soupault's reminiscences in *Mémoires de l'oubli* of reading Verne in his youth;[18] Breton's later oblique reference to Verne in his description of the hollowed rock at Gaspé in *Arcane 17* (1944).[19] Indeed, there is also the curious coincidence by which the heroine of *Nadja* has almost the same name as that of *Michel Strogoff*.

The debt is more clearly marked in the case of Robert Desnos. Although the subject of nearly all his early writing is that of inner adventure (the dream), the images which are employed—particularly in *La Liberté ou l'amour!* (1927; tr. *Liberty or Love!*), generally considered one of the masterpieces of early Surrealism—for its representations are largely those associated with external adventure of the kind described by Verne: the voyage, the sea, the yacht, the shipwreck, the forest, the desert, the North Pole, the night, the stars. To these might be added such refinements, analogous to the technical passages Verne included in his works, as the sponge, the anemone, the starfish, the sea horse, the mermaid. Obviously, *La Liberté ou l'amour!* is not constructed along the same lines as Verne constructed his adventures—as a pure product of automatic writing (the novel is claimed, and there seems little reason to dispute such a claim, to have been written while in a state of self-induced hypnosis)—nor do the characters behave in a rational manner.

But then again, it could be claimed that a character such as Captain Hatteras hardly behaves rationally either. At the end of *Les Voyages et aventures du capitaine Hatteras* (1866; tr. *The Adventures of Captain Hatteras*, 1874–6), the eponymous captain, having travelled to the North Pole and having been transformed by the process, is incarcerated in a lunatic asylum near Liverpool.[20]

> Depuis quelques temps, le capitaine Hatteras [...] se promenait chaque jour pendant de long heures; mais sa promenade s'accomplissait invariablement suivant un sens déterminé et dans la direction d'une certaine allée de Sten-Cottage. Le capitaine, une fois arrivé à l'extrémité de l'allée, revenait à reculons. Quelqu'un l'arrêtait-il? il montrait du doigt un point fixe dans le ciel. Voulait-on l'obliger à se retourner? il s'irritait [...].
>
> Le docteur observa attentivement une manie si bizarre, et il comprit bientôt le motif de cette obstination singulière; il devina pourquoi cette promenade s'accomplissait dans une direction constante, et, pour ainsi dire, sous l'influence d'une force magnétique.
>
> Le capitaine John Hatteras marchait invariablement vers le Nord.

> [For a considerable time the captain had been in the habit of walking in the garden for hours, ... but his promenade was always in one direction in a particular part of the garden. When he got to the end of this path, he would stop and begin to walk backwards. If anyone stopped him he would point towards a certain part of the sky, but let anyone attempt to turn him round, and he became angry ...
>
> The Doctor, who often visited his afflicted friend, noticed this strange proceeding one day, and soon understood the reason for it. He saw how it was that he paced so constantly in a given direction, as if under the influence of some magnetic force.
>
> This was the secret: John Hatteras invariably walked towards the North.]

Like Hatteras, the two principal 'characters' of Desnos's novel, Sanglot the Corsair and Louise Lame, are driven on by a higher purpose: not on this occasion the influence of the magnetic north, however, but that of desire. Thus, Corsair Sanglot (who has occasionally been likened to Captain Nemo) can travel just as easily beneath the sea as on land, even when plunged neck-deep in a field of sponges. Indeed, nothing—not even death—may impede the progress of those who are imbued with that sense of freedom conferred by the erotic.

The influence of magnetic force becomes even more confused with sexual attraction in Michel Leiris's *Le Point cardinal* (a title to which it is worth drawing attention in this context) written in October 1925 but not published until 1927.[21] At one point in the story, the narrator is induced to make love four times 'with an attractive enough girl' on the dial of enormous compass below a swaying metallic pendulum which marks time like a metronome. The lovers unite once with their heads facing in each of the four cardinal directions. In the end though, the narrator parts for the north again ('preferring the torment of the ice and polar mirages to that of artificial fires and sullied fantasies'). As in *La Liberté ou l'amour!*, such scientific trappings, though profoundly evocative, are largely subverted by the text which surrounds them. Although Surrealism is generally thought of nowadays as primarily a visual movement, it is worth reminding ourselves that it began as an essentially literary one. Texts such as *Le Point cardinal* prefigure the paintings of Ernst, Dali, and Tanquy with their worlds of glassy rigidity and hard strangeness. With their strangely lit contours, the landscapes of *Le Point cardinal* resemble nothing so much as heightened dream images. The peculiar juxtaposition of the mathematical tools of the causative system and the dream element is emphasized by Leiris in an entry from his diary about this time:

> Le monde de mes rêves est un monde minéral, dallé de pierres et bordés d'édifices sur le fronton desquels je lis parfois des sentences mystérieuses. C'est une longue suite d'esplanades, de galeries et de perspectives à travers lesquelles je me promène, comme dans un espace entièrement abstrait, dépouillé de toute réalité terrestre. Le fil à plomb, le compas, la balance y sont maître, car ce monde nocturne est pour moi beaucoup mieux organisé que celui de mes veilles. La poursuite d'une pensée, son élucidation par la dissection minutieuse des mots qui la formulent, la recherche des axes de l'esprit, toute tentative de défi au vertige, cela je ne puis guère l'effectuer que dans mes rêves, quand je ne suis plus qu'un point mathématique se déplaçant le long d'une ligne, dans le désert de la cité pavée de mots.[22]

> [The world of my dreams is a mineral world, paved with stones and

bordered with edifices on whose façades I occasionally read mysterious sentences. I wander through a long series of esplanades, galleries and perspectives as if in an entirely abstract space, deprived of any earthly reality. Plumblines, compasses and scales rule here, because this nocturnal world is for me much better organized than that of my waking day. The pursuit of an idea, its elucidation by the most minute dissection of the words in which it is formulated, the search for the axes of the mind, every attempt to defy the giddiness, that I can hardly effectuate except in my dreams, when I am no more than a mathematical point moving along a line, in the desert of the city paved with words.]

Nor are the causative fantasies of at least in part Vernian inspiration to be found only during the 'heroic' early period of Surrealism: as late as 1971 Paul Delvaux exhibited a painting entitled *Hommage à Jules Verne*. In a recent interview, Delvaux explained that his father's secretary had given him a copy of *Vingt mille lieues sous les mers* following his first communion in 1909.[23] The main character to strike Delvaux's imagination, however, was the geologist Professor Otto Lidenbrock from the *Voyage au centre de la Terre* whom he first incorporated into one of his own works in the 1939 *Phases de la lune*.[24]

The fascination of the French avant-garde with Jules Verne was memorably celebrated in issue 16 of the *Dossiers du Collège de Pataphysique* in 1961. Indeed, the entire issue is devoted to the centenary of the discovery of the North Pole by Captain Hatteras on 11 July 1861. According to the 'psychological' reading of Verne's *Les Voyages et aventures du capitaine Hatteras* proposed by the Satrape Lutembi, for example, the captain's 'folie polaire' is concomitant with, or even anterior to, his adventures. More significantly, however it is not only Captain Hatteras who is in the clutches of polar madness: 'Autour de lui, tous la partagent, avec des nuances diverses' ['Around him, every one shares it in different degrees'].[25] He continues:

> Les matelots eux aussi, même ceux qui se défient, admettent les mythes polaires et les superstitions qu'ils qualifient de "degrés de latitude": ils entrent dans le jeu d'Hatteras qui les ancre dans leur crédulité barbare en leur distribuant au prétendu passages de ces pistes illusoires les symboles incomestibles de vos religions monétaires (pratiques d'autant plus délirantes que, l'auteur le souligne, dans les marécages solidifiés où ils se trouvent, ces rites naïfs ne peuvent plus entrer dans le jeu de vos simagrées sociales). Bref, il apparaît que Jules Verne a voulu faire ici une étude générale de ce que j'appelle [...] l'humanité.[26]

[The sailors too, even those who are mistrustful, admit the polar

myths and superstitions which they qualify by "degrees of latitude":
they enter into Hatteras's game who anchors them in their barbarous
credulity by handing out at the so-called passes on those illusory
tracks the incomestible symbols of your monetary religions (practices
all the more insane since, as the author stresses, in the frozen swamps
in which they find themselves, these naïve rites can no longer play
a part in your social pretences). In short, it would seem that what
Jules Verne intended here was a generally study of what I call [...]
humanity.]

Verne and Greek Surrealism

Surrealism made its way to Greece during the 1930s where Andreas
Embirikos (1901–75) became the movement's main spokesman and one
of its leading exponents. The extent of Verne's impact on Greek Surrealism
did not become manifest until much later, however. In 1964, Embirikos
published a considerably censored version of a novella entitled (in the
French translation) *Argo ou vol d'aérostat*.[27] The dramatic (and sexual)
climax of the story coincides with the gala launching of a balloon in
Columbia in the early years of the present century before a group of
Russian, English and French aristocrats. As in the case of Robert Desnos's
La Liberté ou l'amour!, Embirikos' novella represents a strange amalgam of
science-fiction fantasy in the manner of Verne and erotic descriptions in
the style of the Marquis de Sade.

Embirikos' masterpiece, however, is generally considered to be *The Great
Eastern*.[28] This monumental work (it consists of a total of nine volumes,
amounting to over two thousand pages) occupied thirty-five years of the
writer's life from 1940 to 1975. The novel records the events which take
place on the maiden voyage of an ocean liner called *The Great Eastern*, sailing
in May 1867 from Liverpool and destined for New York. As the writer
himself suggested, the ship itself may be considered a character in the novel
which not only carries 'its passengers and crew from the Old to the New
World' but 'also carries them into a utopian world of sexual licence, of
freedom and of love'.[29] The latter, of course, are three classic Surrealist
themes.

Embirikos himself was born into a well-known Greek family of ship
owners, and this may go some way to accounting for his fascination with
sea travel. However, Verne is a central presence in the novel. The last
volume, for example, includes two illustrations from the French Hetzel
edition of *Une ville flottante*. More significantly, it has been claimed that the
language of the entire novel sequence resembles that of nineteenth-
century Greek translations of Jules Verne.[30] This feature is likely to render

any attempt at translating the novel into other languages highly problematic.

Verne himself does not make an appearance in *The Great Eastern* until the fifth volume (chapter 61), where he is portrayed as a mysterious passenger sitting in the ship's library reading a chapter of a book by the Danish explorer Malte-Brun dealing with the United States of America. The work by Malte-Brun praises the free spirit and impressive achievements of this young country that its writer sees as the new centre of civilization, replacing Europe and the East. Carried away by what he reads, Verne falls into a daydream in which he sees himself as the captain of a steamship called the Cape Hatteras that is sailing from northern France to the US. As soon as the ship (which is carrying such passengers as Phileas Fogg, Michel Strogoff, and Captain Nemo) reaches its destination, where it is enthusiastically greeted by President Grant, the dreamer launches into a detailed description of the social, political and financial institutions of the country. Verne is obviously being press-ganged by Embirikos into acting as a spokesman for the author's own vision of an international confederacy, a totally emancipated world which is free from conventional morality and ruled by pleasure. Verne's identity is only revealed in the following chapter when the Swiss philosopher Hans Edelmann approaches him. It transpires that the two men are keen philatelists.

In the seventh volume (chapter 72), Verne appears during a tremendous storm to witness silently an act of sexual congress taking place on deck. Embirikos, praising his purity of mind, comments that Verne's own intensely sensual nature is never betrayed in any of his writing. Verne later participates in a conversation between Edelmann and the French painter Emile Berthier (who fulfil a similar philosophical function as Sade's libertines). Among the various topics they discuss are female hysteria (a subject of some considerable interest to the Surrealists) while Verne interjects that the scientist and the artist can coexist in the same person. Verne also expresses his fears about Edelmann's vision of a world of absolute sexual freedom, concerned that such a liberation could endanger the whole of civilization and the Christian Church and lead back to a primitive state of society. Significantly, by the end of their conversation, Verne has been convinced by his companions' arguments and gives his consent to their theories.

Finally, in the eighth volume (chapter 91), Verne is actually described, inspired by his own experiences on the trip, writing the opening pages of his novel *La ville flottante* on board *The Great Eastern*. This opening chapter commences with a sexual phantasy, and Verne undergoes an inner struggle with regard to whether he should physically give in to his sensual nature and obey his sexual instincts. The voice of reason finally prevails and he pauses outside the door of one of the beautiful temptresses on board the ship and turns back. Thus, in Embirikos' version, Verne writes *La Ville flottante* as an act of Freudian sublimation.

In an addendum to the first volume of *The Great Eastern*, Giogis Yatromanolakis comments on the ingenious manner in which Embirikos integrated his basic source of inspiration into his own creation. *La Ville flottante* was written in 1868, the year after Verne himself travelled to the United States, and deals with a similar subject matter. In many ways *The Great Eastern* crystalizes the manner in which Verne was central to the Surrealist endeavour—and the manner by which the Surrealists sought to recast that influence. In the work of Embirikos the universe of Jules Verne is immediately recognizable but it is also a universe which has become thoroughly eroticized. The closed world of the ship has become an enchanted arena of sexual encounter; the Marquis de Sade is an ever-present passenger; events are controlled by subconscious forces rather than conscious ones; and the physical laws of time and space (not to mention the literary laws of narrative and character) are abolished at a stroke.

Conclusion

Through Roussel, we reach not only Surrealism but also pataphysics, which, as Alfred Jarry states in *Les Gestes et opinions du docteur Faustroll*, 'est la science de ce qui se surajoute à la métaphysique' ['is the science of that which is superinduced upon metaphysics'][31] It is here that the depth of Roussel's indebtedness to Verne becomes clear, for he modelled himself not so much upon the older writer himself, but more upon his *characters*, as the exponents of a hidden and mysterious order. The chain of reasoning behind this is obvious enough: to Roussel, Verne's characters seek a truth, which they apparently discover; this truth then forms the basis for Roussel's own explorations. To model oneself upon fiction in this way is destructive of both oneself (and Roussel was a suicide) and of the external world (hence Roussel's insistence upon Conception as opposed to Reality). It affirms the supremacy of a truth discovered in fiction, and by fictional characters, over any truths isolated by 'science'. The plays on words in which these truths reside become doorways both to a superior and parallel world and to the properties of that world, in much the same way that the veils which surround the mysteries of alchemy turn out to be those mysteries themselves.

Modelling himself upon Hatteras, Roussel allows his external state to mirror his internal life. His conceptual journeyings are echoed in his physical travels. He is offering an image of apparently irrational behaviour, behind which is concealed a deep and mysterious knowledge. It is for us to decipher this, and it is this which makes Roussel a science-fiction writer in an absolute sense, for his knowledge, his *science*, is fiction.

A similar point might be made with respect to Surrealism which was an attempt, amongst much else, to abolish the supreme authority of the causative system. One of the realms of experience claimed by Surrealism was that of dreams, and it is in this world—a world in which logic, time, and space are eliminated—that Verne managed to colour the imagination of the movement's founders.

Notes

1 *Michel Leiris: Journal, 1922–1989*, ed. Jean Jamin (Paris, Gallimard, 1992), pp. 601–2.

2 *Comment j'ai écrit certains de mes livres* (Paris, Pauvert, 1963), p. 26; tr. Trevor Winkfield, *How I Wrote Certain of my Books* (New York, SUN Press, 1977), p. 13. In a footnote, Winkfield cites a letter written to Roussel's friend and financial adviser, Eugène Leiris (the father of Michel Leiris) in which he writes: 'Ask for my life, but don't ask me to lend you Jules Verne! I'm so devoted to his work I'm positively "besotted". Should you read him again I beg you never, ever, even to mention his name in my presence, since I regard it as blasphemy to pronounce it other than on bended knee. He is by far the *greatest literary genius of all time* ...'

3 All these examples are drawn from *Impressions d'Afrique* (Paris, Lemerre, 1910; repr. Paris, Pauvert, 1963). The most complete study to date of Roussel's procedure in this work remains Jean Ferry's *L'Afrique des Impressions* (Paris, Pauvert, 1967).

4 *Comment j'ai écrit certains de mes livres*, p. 27.

5 *Revue du Touring Club de France* (August 1926), tr. Anthony Melville in *Raymond Roussel: Life, Death and Works* (London, Atlas Press, 1987), pp. 148–51.

6 There appears to have been much less of an influence the other way round, although it would be interesting to know the details of the discussion when Roussel and Verne met in 1899. This meeting is alluded to by Roussel in *Comment j'ai écrit certains de mes livres*, p. 26. Roussel, who would have been 22 at the time, was doing his military service in Amiens; Verne would have been in his early seventies. Trevor Winkfield, however, notes that in Verne's *Bourses de Voyage* (Paris, Benett, 1903) 'Rosam angelum letorum' is distorted into 'Rose a mangé l'omelette au rhum' (28). In *Le Très Curieux Jules Verne*, moreover, Marcel Moré drew attention to 'le rôle que jouent les logographes, anagrammes, métagrammes ou autres' in Verne's works (Paris, Gallimard, 1960), p. 55.

7 Cf., however, Annie Le Brun, *Vingt mille lieues sous les mots, Raymond Roussel* (Paris, Pauvert, 1994), pp. 313 and 327.

8 The first extract is taken from Verne's posthumous *L'Etonnante aventure de la mission Barsac* (Paris, Hachette, 1919; repr. Paris, Les Humanoïdes Associés, 1977), p. 342; the second is taken from Roussel's *Locus Solus* (Paris, Lemerre, 1914; repr. Paris, Gallimard, 1963), pp. 35–6.

9 'M. Ré Dièze et Mlle Si Bémol' was first published in book form in a collection of stories entitled *Hier et demain* (Paris, Benett-Myrbach and Roux,

1910); tr. as 'Mr Ray Sharp and Miss Me Flat', in *Yesterday and Tomorrow* (London, Arco, n.d.).

10 First published in *Bizarre*, 34–5, (1964), 2–13.

11 On this subject, see Marcel Moré.

12 Extract from Dr Pierre Janet, *De l'angoisse à l'extase* in *Comment j'ai écrit certains de mes livres*, pp. 127–32 (p. 129); tr. as 'The Psychological Characteristics of Ecstasy', in *Raymond Roussel: Life, Death and Works*, pp. 38–42.

13 'Documents sur Raymond Roussel', *NRF*, no. 259 (April 1935). Now in *Roussel, l'ingénu* (Paris, Fata Morgana, 1987), pp. 7–21 (p. 11). Leiris, incidentally, knew Roussel reasonably well through his father: Roussel was one of the principal benefactors of the Dakar–Djibouti scientific mission (1931–3) in which Michel Leiris participated.

14 Cited by Christian Robin, 'Jules Verne et le surréalisme', in *Le Rêve d'une ville. Nantes et le surréalisme* (Musée des Beaux-Arts de Nantes, 1994), pp. 123–41 (p. 125).

15 Ibid.

16 'Le sanglant symbole', *La Révolution surréaliste*, no. 2 (15 January 1925), 19.

17 Particularly in the light of the 1874 story *Le Docteur Ox*.

18 Robin, 'Jules Verne et le surréalisme', p. 124.

19 Ibid., p. 126.

20 *Les Voyages et aventures du capitaine Hatteras*, 2: *Le Désert de glace* (Paris, Hetzel, 1866), p. 463. It is to be assumed, incidentally, that Verne was familiar with the phrase 'mad as a *Hatter*' as appropriate for an Englishman. Perhaps, too, one may detect a pun on 'n'a terre as' or something similar, meaning 'not of the Earth'.

21 Now in *Mots sans mémoire* (Paris, Gallimard, 1969); tr. Terry Hale as *The Cardinal Point* in *The Automatic Muse* (London, Atlas Press, 1994).

22 *Journal, 1922–1989* (Saturday, 24 January 1925), p. 93.

23 Maurice Debra, *Promenades et Entretiens avec Delvaux* (Paris, Duculot, 1991), p. 242.

24 Ibid., pp. 104–5.

25 'Lettre du Trt Satrape Lutembi sur le pôle et la politique', *Dossiers du Collège de Pataphysique*, no. 16 (1961), 5–12 (7). Among other contributors to this publication were Jean Dubuffet, Jean Ferry, and Raymond Queneau.

26 Ibid.

27 (Avignon, Actes Sud, 1991), tr. Michel Saunier. A short extract is available in an English translation by Amy Mims as 'Argo (or Voyage of an Airship)'. *London Magazine*, vol. 36, 1 and 2 (April/May 1996), 118–25.

28 With regard to Embirikos and *The Great Eastern*, the authors of this article are greatly indebted to Xanthi Stefanidou's unpublished MA dissertation, 'Andreas Embirikos's *The Great Eastern* from a Surrealist Perspective: Translation and Study' (University of East Anglia, 1996). We would also like to thank Ms Stefanidou for so courteously answering our many other queries concerning the role of Jules Verne in Embirikos' novel. The first volume of *The Great Eastern* was published posthumously in 1990 (Athens, Agra Editions), subsequent volumes following at short intervals, and would seem to have attained something of the status of a cult work, particularly among the younger generation.

29 Stefanidou, 'Andreas Embirikos's *The Great Eastern*', p. 6.

30 Roderick Beaton, *An Introduction to Modern Greek Literature* (Oxford, Clarendon Press, 1994), p. 220.

31 In *Alfred Jarry: Œuvres complètes*, ed. Michel Arrivé *et al.*, 3 vols (Paris, Gallimard, 1972–1988), I, p. 668; tr. Simon Watson Taylor in *Selected Works of Alfred Jarry*, ed. Roger Shattuck and Simon Watson Taylor (London, Methuen, 1965), p. 192. It should not be forgotten that *Voyage au centre de la terre* was one of Dr Faustroll's 'livres pairs'.

10
Mysterious Masterpiece

WILLIAM BUTCHER

'Edom': the disturbingly modern short story published after Jules Verne's death in 1905. Its brilliant rehearsal of the whole *Voyages extraordinaires* in fifty dense pages has generated considerable controversy. But the short story published as 'L'Eternal Adam' still remains largely unknown. There has been little examination to date of, for example, the links with *Vingt mille lieues*, the real-world references, the ethnic allusions, the biblical borrowings, or the linguistic and evolutionary ideas. Nor has external evidence as to the tale's authorship been produced to date. The present essay will accordingly survey the background to 'Edom' before attempting to decipher the tale itself.

Until recently Verne studies were dominated by research in French, often carried out by non-literary specialists. Many imaginative and wide-ranging studies have thus been produced, revealing a multi-layered complexity and depth in what was once considered a straightforward corpus. Verne is now amongst the French writers generating the most critical material, in marked contrast with the situation only twenty years ago. What is surprising, nevertheless, is that the most basic extrinsic research has not been carried out. Whereas writers of lesser significance, however measured, have been minutely edited and had their least source investigated, even Verne's pivotal works still suffer from a lack of detailed exploration. Thus the correspondence has not been systematically collected; not one of the manuscripts of the pre-1905 works has been thoroughly studied to date, let alone published; nor is there available a systematic indication of published variants for any of the novels.[1]

We should not be too surprised, therefore, at the lack of textual information on 'Edom'. This story of about 13,200 words was first published in *La Revue de Paris* of 1 October 1910 (no. 19), under the title 'L'Eternal Adam' and with the subtitle 'Dans quelque vingt mille ans...' It was republished by Hetzel *fils* in the volume *Hier et demain* (1910) with the subtitle now an epigraph and with seven illustrations by Léon Benett. The proofs, edited by Louis Ganderax, *normalien*, are in the Bibliothèque nationale (B. N. n.a.fr. 17000, fo. 1–61), with the amended proofs generally corresponding to the published versions.[2] The manuscript of 'Edom' was seen by scholars before 1981, but no information about it has been published to date.[3]

In the pre-1978 critical literature on 'Edom', many commentators expressed surprise at its brilliance and density, in contrast with most of the *Voyages* published between 1895 and 1905.[4] Two main explanations were proposed: that Verne's son Michel might have contributed to its composition, or that the novella might date from a more vivacious earlier period and that Verne had held back its publication because of its radical nature. Jean Jules-Verne, Michel's son and the inheritor of the family papers, deliberately muddied this posthumous question when he wrote, in *Jules Verne* (1973) (pp. 374–6), that 'Au XXIXe siècle' (1889) was 'écrite en collaboration avec Michel qui a tenu la plume', that in Michel's work on *L'Etonnante aventure de la mission Barsac* (1914) 'il ne s'agissait que de retouches mineures', and that 'Edom' was entirely Jules'.

Then, on 11 July 1978, a dusty Italian sports car drew up at the Colloque de Cerisy. Piero Gondolo della Riva gave a paper claiming that complete chapters of eight of the posthumous works, including virtually the whole of *L'Agence Thompson and Co.* (1908), were in fact written by Michel. His arguments were based on correspondence between Michel and Hetzel, on the manuscripts in Jules' hand, and on five posthumously prepared typescripts. Manuscripts and typescripts were almost identical, but radically different from the published versions, thus allowing Michel's changes to be identified. Apart from Jean Jules-Verne, no one has substantially contested Gondolo della Riva's published conclusions that Michel was responsible for substantive parts of the eight novels and one collection of short stories.[5] Further proof came with the publication of five typescripts between 1985 and 1989.[6]

However, for two of the posthumous works, *L'Agence Thompson and Co.* and 'Edom', there is no surviving typescript—and 'Edom', in particular, is not even alluded to in any known extant material.[7] In his paper Gondolo della Riva indicated that these two manuscripts were in Michel's hand, and so concluded that the two works 'furent vraisemblablement écrits par Michel' (76).

Reactions have varied. Writing about 'Edom' in 1979, I pointed out that 'un doute subsiste néanmoins, car personne ne sait si Michel Verne n'a pas, par exemple, recopié une version antérieure', and similarly Porcq maintains that, most probably, 'l'œuvre est de Jules Verne, remaniée par Michel'.[8] Boia, on the other hand, accepts Michel as the author; and Dumas categorizes the tale as 'écrite par Michel'.[9] In 1991, however, Dumas 'discovered' the proofs in the Bibliothèque nationale and decided that 'Edom' was by Jules after all, declaring: 'vers 1910, Michel Verne ... recopie le manuscrit original'.[10] Unfortunately, his only evidence is ... a misquotation of my phrase above!

Critical opinion is equally divided about Michel's literary ability. One problem is that the only publications he signed appeared in 1888, were in the field of journalism, and seem generally unexceptional.[11] Also, the only work for which we have an explicit listing of Michel's changes is 'Le Humbug',[12] where we can observe that very little was added and that original ideas were excised, although some overall coherence was gained. Gondolo della Riva points out that Michel 'altered' the works from Jules' intentions, perhaps in order to 'get his own back' on his father; he praises, however, the philosophical conclusion of *Les Naufragés du 'Jonathan'* (1909). Dumas, for his part, prefers Jules' original manuscripts on principle,[13] even when most editors might have amended them as inconsistent or distasteful. Without 'Edom', in sum, it is difficult to argue for Michel's credentials as a writer of the first order.

We thus have a work whose brilliance is not in dispute, but which cannot easily be ascribed to either Jules or Michel. We have no information from the documentation, no author's proof corrections, and no definite information about a surviving manuscript.

There remains 'Edom' itself, and accordingly the rest of this study will concentrate largely on an internal analysis of this strange tale.

Its order of publication within *Hier et demain* may not be innocent. The collection opens with 'La Destinée de Jean Morénas' and 'Au XXIXe siècle', both first published before 1905, implying that the other four stories may also be in approximate order of Michel's contribution (as well as chronological setting and amount of scientific content). The title of each of the six narratives has a footnote, the last four footnotes being signed 'M.J.V.'.[14] In these, 'Le Humbug' is characterized as a 'boutade', 'Au XXIXe siècle' as a 'fantaisie', and 'Edom' as a 'nouvelle ... sous une forme assurément fantaisiste'. Michel indicates only 'Morénas' and 'Edom' as being by Jules Verne, and merely admits that 'Morénas' has been 'considérablement modifiée' and 'Au XXIXe siècle', slightly revised. However, in these few lines, the only properly literary output carrying Michel's signature, there are several mystifications, including the erroneous claims that 'Au XXIXe siècle' was written in English and that a 'fier optimisme' inspires Verne's works. The opposite of what Michel says may generally therefore be closer to the truth.

The internal construction of 'Edom' further indicates its uniqueness within the collected works. It is the only *Voyage extraordinaire* fully to justify a use of first- and third-person narrators in equal proportions. The dual structure also motivates complex, self-reflecting debates on such ideas as the nature of repetition, the importance of writing, the role of science, the origin of civilization, and the future of mankind. The whole tale seems to resemble an anonymous 'récit d'outre-tombe' (262), a message without a return address assigned to the hazards of an indefinite sojourn underground (260). Even the questions the critic might ask, such as the reliability of interpretations based on etymology, mythology, or extrapolation, are mockingly present in the text.

What does seem clear in 'Edom', nevertheless, is the existence of a very large number of affinities and allusions to the whole *Voyages extraordinaires*, whether from the beginning, middle, or the period 1905–14.[15] Similarities with *Vingt mille lieues* (1869) appear particularly sustained. Both involve: a hint of the pleasure of smoking; an allusion to the famous battle of 1862 between the *Virginia* and the *Monitor*, the first semi-submerged ironclad; the idea of limbs becoming cold as a sign of approaching death; an overwhelming dominance of the oceans and an exclusive diet of seafood; the incorporation of Old Testament language into the text; an interest in archaeological remains as a way of investigating the truth of legends or biblical narratives; a fascination for the lost continent of Atlantis, destroyed by volcanic action, with descriptions of its arches and broken columns giving rise to heady contemplations on human destiny; the idea of the ruins being brought up from the depths by volcanic activity; an interest in the word 'Edom'; an invented language containing teasing hints of European and non-European languages; a new and totally masculine society; a contrast between a French narrator and his mainly Anglo-Saxon companions; uncertainty as to what language is used in the dialogues; a surprising re-emergence of French to convey a personal message; the idea of entrusting a written narrative to a random, even aleatory, destination; and the contrast between a scientific composition, written by men of superior learning but destined to be lost, and a personal narration, composed by a slow-witted and self-centred author but surviving many vicissitudes to great effect.

This brief summary demonstrates, then, that the two works, although separated by thirty-six years, have a great deal in common. It would undoubtedly be possible to establish a similar density of borrowing, allusion, and pastiche with a number of other *Voyages*. 'Edom' forms part of a closely knit network of literary themes and structures, with its author(s) demonstrating a quite remarkable knowledge of the collected works.

Another Vernian topos pervading 'Edom' at all levels is that of the principle of alternation. A first example is the successive civilizations which have risen and fallen. We know little about the initial setting of the twenty-third millennium, apart from the single tantalizing illustration showing a Chinese-style circular arch, possibly a pagoda, and three pillars crowned with capitals. We know little about the Atlanteans either, except for ruins of the identical 'chapiteaux' (224) and 'colonnes' (255). And we know virtually nothing about the civilization *before* the Atlanteans, hardly even its existence; just as the twenty-third millennium is barely aware of the third-millennium civilization (our own). In other words, of the four stages, each hardly knows the previous one, which is highly dissimilar, but each demonstrates clear affinities with the last-but-one civilization.

Island and ocean constitute a more developed alternation. Mountain-tops and sea-chasms, landslides and rising seas form inseparable couples. For third-millennium mankind to be wiped out by the cataclysm, all land must sink below the ocean; but, for instantaneous plant and animal evolution to come into play, the new lands must come from the ocean— and so on with each succeeding upheaval.[16] The rise and fall of both civilizations and continents are, in sum, as regular as Fogg's dining habits or Hans' pay-days en route for the Centre of the Earth.

More generally, careful permutations are established within 'Edom' between such varied themes as technology and humanism, desire for immortality and incidence of mortality, stasis and change, reductionism and transcendence; as well as structures like present- and past-tense narration and anonymous first-person narrator and third-person Sofr in the twenty-third millennium. After being established, however, any alteration is often duplicated or divided and then superimposed on itself, in a never-ending series of intersecting, self-reflecting forms. It is almost as if the simpler, two-way alternation of the earlier works were being parodied.

Given this eternal oscillation, the precise link between the two main protagonists is clearly important. The fact that Sofr learns about the first-person narrator and the immediately preceding civilization represents a unique bridge across the 20,000-year abyss, and so can be considered the nub of the tale. In contrast with the previous phases of history, the surviving civilization is thus warned of the fate its predecessors suffered—and may therefore be able to do something about it. The careful symmetry of man's ups and downs, his 'vains efforts accumulés dan l'infini des temps' (263), can perhaps be broken after all (as Fogg's and Hans' routines are). The tale may not be nearly as pessimistic as critics have claimed.

But how does the first-person account in fact reach Sofr? Clearly, the anonymous narrator would not have survived without the high technology of the 35-H. P. 'double phaéton' (231) and the lowish technology of the steam-and-sails *Virginia*. Again, had Sofr not wished to expand his *scientific* laboratories, the message would not have been unearthed. But the proximate cause of survival is the message's container, 'une sorte d'étui, fait d'un métal inconnu, de couleur grise, de texture granuleuse' (227)— aluminium we later learn (260). Because the paper was rolled up in it, we know that the container is cylindrical and relatively small; also, 'au tiers de sa longeur, une fente indiquait que l'étui était formé de deux parties s'emboîtant l'une dans l'autre' (228). In other words, it must be a cylindrical cigar-case! The case must somehow have been taken on to the motor-car, on to the *Virginia*, on to the new land, and then kept for several decades. In fact, nowhere is tobacco mentioned in the tale, except for the pre-cataclysmic 'au moment des cigares' (232). Such is the ingenuity of the description that this important realization of the means of transmission of the central message does not seem to have been made to date.[17] The irony throughout the tale as to the usefulness and durability of high technology may apply especially to the unconventional purpose the aluminium container is put to. Considerable pathos derives from the retention of the useless case through all the colony's vicissitudes—even after the death of virtually all its original members—and its reminder of fallen grandeur and the frivolity of smoking luxury cigars.

Nor do the possible consequences end there. The names of characters in the *Voyages* are often highly revealing. Those of the postprandial three wise men, Bathurst, Mendoza, and Moreno (231), all seem to refer to precise nineteenth-century events.[18] Also, the surname of the women who will give birth to three-quarters of the colony is the rare Raleigh (231). It is surely associated with Sir Walter and his famous introduction of tobacco. Raleigh was also responsible for the first British attempt to colonize America: 121 settlers were left on an island in Virginia, but three years later they had disappeared without trace, apart from the word 'Croatoan' found carved on a tree.[19] A lost colony leaving only a single, obscure name behind it: the parallel with 'Edom' is striking. The case of the missing cigar, without even considering what Freud might have made of it, leads us to striking historical resonances.

Other details also become significant when assembled. Thus Sofr-Aï-Sr has a monosyllabic tripartite name with the surname first (cf. 'Mogar-si' (217) = 'cigare-mo(u)', as Porcq has pointed out) and lives in the capital on the east coast of the Empire (214). Sons are identified by numbers not names. His is a cultured classical civilization which invented printing and has an uninterrupted history of thousands of years; it seems advanced in some respects but closed and backward in others. It is dominated by a 'race ... prolifique' (216), the so-called 'Hommes-à-Face-de-Bronze' (note the article-less syntax). These features concord with the only other 'Empire' mentioned in the tale, of 'quatre cents millions d'âmes' (245). Sofr's homeland is central in both geographical position and importance, a middle

kingdom as it were. The opening sentence describes it as surrounded by
'Quatre-Mers', situated north, south, east, and west. But 'Four Seas' is a
stock expression in Chinese: the Northern, Southern, Eastern, and
Western, corresponding to the English 'Seven Seas', but also collectively
signifying 'the world united in brotherhood'. The 'Fixed Star' is referred
to rather than the 'North Star'. In other words, every detail quoted in this
paragraph refers to China and the Chinese.[20] The evidence is
overwhelming.

'Someone', then, has ingeniously strewn clues throughout 'Edom',
including the names Raleigh and *Virginia*, the cigar-less cigar-case, and a
systematic reference to the Chinese. The survival of themes and sources
from the past seems to depend on gratuitous and frivolous details. But to
date, no one seems to have deciphered them. The past has remained dead
and buried for ninety years.

> Edom saith, We are impoverished, but we will return and build the
> desolate places; thus saith the Lord of hosts, They shall build, but I
> will throw down. (Malachi 1:4)

The tale's title is also highly symbolic. In *Vingt mille lieues*, Nemo explains
that the 'Red' of 'Red Sea' is a translation of the Hebrew 'Edom' (meaning
both 'rouge' and 'roux').[21] Genesis says of Jacob's twin brother that 'Esau
is Edom' (36:8), that he is 'red' and 'hairy all over' (25:25), and that his
name also comes from the 'red' colour of the mess of pottage he sells his
birthright for (25:30, 27:21–4). The name, which occurs eighty-eight times
in the Old Testament, then applies to Esau/Edom's second-millennium-
BC descendants in the Wilderness of Edom, south-east of Israel. As cousins
to the Jews, the Edomites were subject to great hatred. The Book of Obadiah
is particularly indignant about their collaboration with the Babylonian
conquerors, with the prophet Obadiah calling down a Day of Judgment
on them.[22] The particular connotations of the name of Edom for the turn
of the twentieth century may be that of a civilization without written traces,
described in an unverifiable oral tradition but with archaeological evidence
beginning to be dug up.

In 'Edom' the surviving tribe is described as 'couvert de poils rudes,
err[ant] dans ce morne désert' (259). In addition to this almost direct
biblical quotation, the name may have generated such elements as the
various archaeological excavations in the tale, the theme of disinheritance,
and the repeated cataclysms. Further resonance is added with Sofr's final
realization of the truth of the linguistic legend transmitted down from
man's origins, that 'Edom' is a deformation of 'Adam': 'Edom, Edèm, Adam
[replaced in the published version by the illogical 'Hedom, Edem, Adam'],

c'est le perpetuel symbole du premier homme' (261). The theme of repeated alternation is again apparent here, for 'Edom' has two distinct identities: the name in the Bible; and as a twenty-third-millennium derivative, and replacement, of 'Adam'. The derivation is invented ('Adam' in fact means 'man' in Hebrew, itself possibly derived from 'earth'); but since 'Adam n'était peut-être que la déformation de quelque autre mot plus ancien' (261), the implication may be that *Eden* and even 'Iten' (213) are also variants of the same word. 'Rien que sur cette petite difficulté philologique, une infinité de savants avaient pâli, sans trouver de réponse satisfaisante' (227). The word 'Edom' is thus at the heart of interrogations about the past and even the origin of man—or lack of origin. The tale is producing radical ideas about the Bible, allowing itself to comment on religious ideas and on man's prehistory more freely than the previous *Voyages* did.

But another surprising deduction follows on concerning another long-hidden clue. What language does the lost colony speak? The answer is not evident, but a passing remark concerning Bathurst's pronunciation of the word 'Adam' reads: '(naturellement, en sa qualité d'Anglo-Saxon, il prononçait Edèm)' (232). The forms 'Edom' and 'Hiva' (226) that are transmitted down to Sofr's civilization are therefore (corrupt) English ones, making English the spoken language of the colony's descendants. However, although logical as far as it goes, this idea will ultimately be turned upside-down, for the two degraded forms are apparently the *only* words to survive. The written English and Spanish languages, as presumably recorded by Bathurst and Moreno, are in any case lost. And the discovered manuscript, deliberately written in French (230), changes everything: it accurately transmits a complete idiom, effectively resurrecting a lost language.[23] 'Edom' seems to be arguing that, once again, seemingly ineluctable tendencies can be reversed. The turn-of-the-century fear of linguistic decline and fall is turned inside out: French survives at the expense of English.

The tale's concern about linguistic evolution proceeds in parallel with an anxiety about biological evolution, and about progress in general. In a nutshell, the *Voyages* manifest a distrust of the idea of Darwinian evolution, and produce repeated rearguard arguments against it. In 'Edom' the terms 'darwiniste' (232), 'loi de l'évolution' (220), and 'sélection naturelle' (232) put in an appearance, and the truth of short-term evolution is apparently accepted. The concept is even exaggerated in the extraordinary acquired-characteristics accelerated-evolution scene of the marine animals 'en train de devenir terrestres' and the flying fish turning into birds (256).[24] Even man seems to be able to lose any of his characteristics, such as speech or intelligence. But this is just a narrative feint: the characteristics he loses or acquires mask, but do not substantially remove, his uniqueness. Man has always survived each successive disaster and retains in particular a mysterious mechanism allowing him repeatedly to climb out of the morass (218). The conclusion, or rather initial axiom, is that animals can and do evolve, but man cannot. While undoubtedly putting a strong case for late-nineteenth-century *social* Darwinism, 'Edom' ultimately seeks out the precise conditions which allow the evolutionary applecart to be overturned. In the face of the realization that the earth's history is infinitely longer than conventional biblical views would allow, the tale maintains that man always will remain, and always has remained, the same as he is now. Darwinism is partly bunk.

Two final themes exhibit a similar structure. 'La véritable supériorité de l'homme ... c'est, pour le penseur, de ... faire tenir l'univers immense dans le microcosme de son cerveau' (236). This sententious, unVernian, definition, produced at the height of the central cataclysm, highlights the unlimited capacity of consciousness: it has, on the one hand, the power to produce a one-to-one mapping between itself and the whole of the universe. But contrariwise, the one-to-one mapping may map the mind back on to itself: the mind can *always* imagine a remedy to events, or at least an antidote: 'La véritable supériorité de l'homme ... c'est, pour l'homme d'action, de garder une âme sereine devant la révolte de la matière, c'est de lui dire: "Me détruire, soit! m'émouvoir, jamais!"' (236). Consciousness—the word occurs four times in the tale—is thus a direct link between an individual's finite mind and his 'theory-of-everything'.

A similar function which focuses, by turn, on 'everything' and on itself is the instance of narration. The French first-person narrator occupies the centre of all sorts of symbolic representations. Thus he—ironically—outlasts the two doctors, and even his own son, becoming the living memory of the whole colony; he controls the destinies of the writings of the other two, and so is a quasi-divine three-in-one; in the event, he accords special treatment to his own word; he has no name, as if symbolizing his own 'immanen[ce]' (233); he is even depicted as God in the final illustration (259). His self-generating, all-englobing written production could be defined as 'I am that I am'. The mystery of ends and origins is reproduced in—and generated by—the mystery of written creation.

The varied themes studied here are, I would claim, closely linked. The religious arguments, linguistic anxiety, evolutionary debate, and many of the other concerns show common morphological characteristics. All draw attention to the origin—whether of mankind or of language—and all point to an all-englobing metaphysical theory: briefly, that there is nothing new under the sun.

ce dernier problème resterait à résoudre: cet homme, maître du monde, qui était-il? D'où venait-il? Vers quelles fins inconnues tendait son inlassable effort? (220)

il s'interdisait de [le] discuter (232)

We can conclude that 'Edom' asks questions about man and life and everything, but provides highly ambiguous answers. But the very asking is revealing; and so 'Edom' serves to summarize a tendency visible throughout the *Voyages*. In this tendency, a positivistic, limited-context argument typically forms the thrust of the main narrative, easily gaining the assent of public opinion. But in each case this theory has two Achilles' heels: the 'inductive fallacy', where observing even a very large number of instances of a phenomenon does not allow one to determine the next instance; and the essential subjectivity of any theory proceeding from an individual. Current discoveries can always be reversed by future discoveries. Anything lost can always be found—and vice versa. Invariably, therefore, the argument ends up being hung from its own petard and undergoing a sort of 'eversion'. Because of the Achilles' heel in the first-level argument, a subjective element in its own objectivity, the argument can be re-applied to its own basis, and hence produce diametrically opposed conclusions. This process exists at many levels throughout the *Voyages extraordinaires*—even the conventional wisdom embodied in stock expressions and metaphors is typically undermined and 'demetaphorized'. The self-eversion of arguments explains the difficulty of finding consistent 'messages' in Verne's works: even the doubting process may be subject to doubt. Clearly also, the process is trying to jump out of the fiction into the real world.

Verne's grossly inappropriate public reputation has, from the beginning, been the symptom, and even the cause, of a limited first-level analysis: a deeper reading leads to the appreciation of a number of receding levels. The works produce complexity as if to spite the simplistic interpretation placed on them. The contribution of 'Edom' may thus be to make the regressive argument all-inclusive and hence systematize the process of re-evaluation. Adam is the vital missing link to 'une infinité d'autres human-ités' (234), a universal peg to hang indefinitely recurrent arguments on.

There are then only three means of escape from the indefinite recurrence: all, as we have seen, find objects which *incorporate* the self-doubting into the process: the process of writing as a way of understanding the writer, the medium as message about the medium; consciousness, aware of its own consciousness, and therefore of its own powers and limits; and man, looking at his own past existence so as to better understand his present.

Two ideas marked the beginning of the twentieth century. Einstein's essential innovation in the Special Theory of Relativity (1905) was to assume space and time were not unalterable givens, but to take them *into* the equations, as variables subject to transformation and to higher-level analyses. In 1910 Bertrand Russell destroyed the coherence of the foundations of mathematics by considering the set of all sets that contain themselves: a third-level object which analyses an impossible second-level object. The essence of modernity, captured in various forms in the period 1905–10, may therefore be in the failure of any totalizing symbol—a failure produced by applying the would-be totalizing symbols to themselves. In these terms, 'Edom', itself torn between 1905 and 1910, is hauntingly modern.

But where does this leave the question of authorship? The first and third sections of the tale do display a more abstract and theoretical vocabulary, with the use of regular subordinate clauses making for a more formal style. Furthermore, the average word, sentence, and paragraph lengths are significantly greater in the first and third sections.[25] They seem more philosophical and modern than the rest of the corpus, more linked to Michel's known writing. But what remains is the tale's striking coherence—around the dual focus—and its allusion to the problems both of the previous corpus and of concluding the previous corpus. The crux, then, of the problem of internal analysis is that no other *Voyage* written after, say, 1873 seems to show the same quality; but many elements of the work seem to post-date, for example, 1890, and some seem characteristic of the vital 1905–10 period. Any internal ascription to Jules would in any case be hazardous, since what one writer can do, another can always imitate. On the other hand, it is impossible to prove a negative, that Jules did *not* contribute.

In sum, hardly any progress has been made at this stage on how such a singular masterpiece came to be written. Just like Edom, 'Edom' seems to have no recorded history, no clear author, but simply roots trailing back indefinitely. If we argue by analogy with 'Au XXIXe siècle', perhaps the closest work, we may suspect alternating accretions from the two authors. 'Edom' seems simultaneously imitative, parodic, and innovative—as if its overriding aim were to obscure the authorship question. Both theme and structure seem to add to the mystery, taunting the exegete with an infinite regress of hypotheses-within-hypotheses. The questions of rebellion and conformity, filiality and paternity, inherited wisdom and creative originality seem to circle endlessly round one another. Because the previous seventy works do not reach a synthetic conclusion, 'Edom' goes out of its way to try to conclude. But things seem to have been arranged by the author(s) in such a way that any conclusion contains in germ its own contradiction. The answer, if any, would be obtained by seeking the first cause. But any seeming origin refers back to the totality. The truth lies within. The only clear conclusion is that of a mysteriously self-aware masterpiece.

Or, as Roudaut puts it: 'l'issue du labyrinthe est une nouvelle entrée dans le labyrinthe, ce qui sera plus tard est ce qui fut jadis' (207).

Appendix

Such was the state of play when I sent the proofs of this article to Piero Gondolo della Riva. His reply produced another bombshell, which brings vital understanding to the posthumous question, and is therefore worth quoting textually:

> Depuis quelques mois j'ai retrouvé chez un membre de la famille Verne ... ce fameux manuscrit qui est *absolument* de la main de Michel. [C'est le] texte complet (51 pages recto-verso) ... C'est un *véritable manuscrit* avec un nombre extraordinaire de ratures ... Je dispose d'ailleurs de documents inédits qui me font croire que cette nouvelle (ainsi que *L'Agence Thompson*) a été écrite par Michel du vivant de Jules et que ce dernier l'a lue et, peut-être, corrigée.

This scholar, whose previous claims have proved justified, further adds that the modified manuscript corresponds to the unedited proofs; and that Simone Vierne and the Verne family are now convinced that the handwriting is indeed Michel's.

One conclusion thus immediately stands out: that 'Edom' was, after all, at least partly composed by Michel, but also, in all probability, partly by his father. The correct authorship ascription seems to lie somewhere between 'Michel and Jules Verne' and 'Michel with Jules Verne'. The debate is thus likely to continue, trying to remove the onion layers of each author's contribution.

Notes

All French books cited are published in Paris unless otherwise indicated.

1 Olivier Dumas has published most of Verne's letters to his family (*Jules Verne* (Lyon, 1988)). The *Bulletin de la Société Jules Verne* (*BSJV*) has published extracts from the pre-1905 manuscripts, especially the conclusions. The manuscripts are studied in detail in *Around the World in Eighty Days* and *Twenty Thousand Leagues under the Seas* (tr. and ed. William Butcher (Oxford University Press, 1995 and 1998)). As another indication of the work yet to be done, the existence and location of a manuscript of *Voyage au centre de la Terre* were unknown until 1995.

Twenty Thousand Leagues under the Seas (tr. and annotated Walter James Miller and Frederick Paul Walter (Annapolis, Maryland, 1993)) provides details of some of the published variants. *Journey to the Centre of the Earth* (tr. and ed. William Butcher (Oxford University Press, 1992, revised 1998)) gives full information about the different editions.

An additional obstacle to detailed textual study is the lack of machine-readable versions of Verne's works, which would aid stylistic analysis and cross-referencing of the large number of proper names across the canon.

2 Throughout this study, the tale is referred to as 'Edom', apparently closer to the intention of the author(s) than 'L'Eternel Adam'. The proofs have been transcribed by Christian Porcq (*BSJV*, no. 100, 4e tri. (1991), 21–48), but without the footnotes and with the words 'Jules VERNE' added at the beginning and the end! All quotations here are taken from this transcription, using, however, page references from the more accessible Livre de poche *Hier et demain* (1979).

Before Porcq's transcription of the proofs it had not generally been realized that the corrections to them, including the change of title, were carried out by an editor. It is also interesting to note that in the proofs the tale is divided into three parts, headed 'I', 'II', and 'III', corresponding to the alternation between Sofr and the anonymous narrator. However, nearly all of the other changes in the proofs are minor, and were presumably carried out with Michel's consent—or at least knowledge!—and in any case do not throw light on the origin of the tale.

3 Simone Vierne writes 'Nous avons pu consulter le manuscrit, *de la main de Jules Verne*' (*Jules Verne et le roman initiatique* (1973), p. 736); Piero Gondolo della Riva states 'le manuscrit original [d' 'Edom'] qui appartient aux héritiers de Jules Verne *est de la main de Michel*' ('A propos des œuvres posthumes de Jules Verne', *Europe*, novembre–décembre 1978), 73–82). The town of Nantes acquired the surviving manuscripts from Verne's descendants in 1981, with the notable exception, however, of 'Edom'. The manuscript has therefore disappeared from public view—to such an extent as for Christian Porcq to imply that there is no manuscript (*'Edom*, ou l'arche de Noé de tous les *Voyages'*, *BSJV*, no. 100, 4e tri. (1991), 49–57 (49)).

4 Most notably Michel Butor, 'Le Point suprême et l'âge d'or à travers quelques œuvres de Jules Verne', in his *Essais sur les modernes* (1960), pp. 36–94; François Raymond, 'Jules Verne ou le mouvement perpétuel' (*Subsidia pataphysica*, vol. 8 (1969), 21–52); Jean Roudaut, '"L'Eternel Adam" et l'image des cycles', *L'Herne: Jules Verne*, ed. P. A. Touttain (1974), pp. 180–212; and Françoise Gaillard, '"L'Eternel Adam" ou l'évolutionnisme à l'heure de la thermodynamique', in *Colloque de Cerisy: Jules Verne et les sciences humaines* (1979), ed. François Raymond and Simone Vierne, pp. 293–325.

5 Jean Jules-Verne, 'Une Lettre de Jean Jules-Verne', in *Europe*, (novembre–décembre 1978), 89–93; Gondolo della Riva, 'A propos des œuvres'.

6 *Le Secret de Wilhelm Storitz* (version originale) (1985), *La Chasse au météore* (version originale) (1986), *En Magéllanie* (1987), *Le Beau Danube jaune* (1988), *Le Volcan d'or* (1989).

7 Michel does say in 1905 that *Hier et demain* will contain 'deux nouvelles absolument inédites' (quoted by Porcq, p. 50): these are presumably 'Pierre-Jean' (published as 'La Destinée de Jean Morénas') and either 'Le Humbug'

or 'Edom'.

8 William Butcher, 'Le Sens de "L'Eternel Adam"', *BSJV*, no. 58, 2e tri. (1981), 73–81 (73); Porcq, p. 57. Similarly Arthur Evans characterizes 'Edom' as 'undoubtedly much revamped by ... Michel' (*Jules Verne Rediscovered* (New York, 1988), p. 97).

9 Lucian Boia, 'L'Eternel Adam et les fins du monde', *BSJV*, no. 67, 3e tri. (1983), 127–32, and 'Un Ecrivain original: Michel Verne', *BSJV*, no. 70, 2e tri. (1984), 90–5; Dumas, *Jules Verne*, p. 514. Similarly Andrew Martin says 'mainly—perhaps wholly by Michel' (*The Mask of the Prophet* (Oxford University Press, 1990), p. 192).

10 'Les Avatars d'*Edom*', *BSJV*, no. 100, 4e tri. (1991), 15–18 (15).

11 Nine pieces under the general title *Zigzags à travers la science* in the *Supplément littéraire* of the *Figaro* in 1888 (some pieces were subsequently reprinted). Michel Verne also signed a twenty-seven-line song entitled *Dans le cloître* (*s.d.* 1911–15, reproduced by Piero Gondolo della Riva in *BSJV*, no. 106, 2e tri. (1993), 4–5): interestingly, it refers to 'l'éternel hiver', a general Michelian trait being to antepose 'l'éternel'.

It is now known from the correspondence that 'Au XXIXe siècle', of considerable interest, was entirely written by Michel (although borrowing from Jules' unpublished *Paris au XXe siècle* (written in 1863, but published only in 1994) and Albert Robida's *Le XXe siècle* (1882), and although subsequently revised by Jules). Jules himself commented that Michel has 'une remarquable facilité d'écrire' (letter to Paul Verne of 12 October 1895, reproduced in Dumas, *Jules Verne*, p. 481) and 'writes ably on scientific themes' (reported by R. H. Sherard, 'Jules Verne at Home: His Own Account of his Life and Work', *McClure's Magazine*, no. 2 (January 1894), 115–24 (120)).

12 In *Humbug*, (tr. and ed. William Butcher (Edinburgh, 1991)).

13 'Les Avatars d'*Edom*' and countless other articles in the *BSJV*.

14 The repeated 'M.J.V.' ('MJV' in the proofs), which was often interpreted as 'Monsieur Jules Verne', must now be understood as 'Michel Jules Verne', and is therefore misleading, for Michel is referred to as 'M. M. Verne' in the correspondence.

15 In particular, many technological ideas are shared across several works. Thus the concept of fax visible in 'Edom' (233) already occurs as 'photo-télégraphie' in *Paris au XXe siècle* (1863), although the term is recorded (as 'téléphotographie') only in about 1890; again neither the strange term in 'des tubes pneumatiques ou *électro-ioniques* sillonnant tous les continents' ('Edom' (233)) nor its English equivalent 'electro-ionic' are recorded in the dictionaries: 'ionique' (in the electrical sense) is first recorded as 1907, although it appeared in English in about 1885–90. The phrase 'tubes pneumatiques' (233) is borrowed from 'Au XXIXe siècle' (p. 188) and from the 'pneumatic Tubes' [*sic*] in Michel's seventh 'Zigzag'. 'Immanente énergie' (233) seems to refer to the equivalence of matter and energy, more fully developed in *La Chasse au météore* (1908); the famous equivalence '$E = mc^2$' was first formalized by Einstein in 1905. These cross-borrowings over more than forty years have not been identified to date, but are surely an important subject for future research.

16 As a result, exceptions like the remaining islet above Rosario must be compensated for by land at the Canaries and Azores. This in turn necessitates a double upheaval: one to kill the present inhabitants off, and one to bring signs of the former inhabitants back up from the depths.

This alternation also explains third-millennium Captain Moris's intuition of seeking land by heading south-west from a submerged Europe: a distant memory of Atlantis, combined with the despairing thought that since land isn't where it should be...

17 I.O. Evans, for instance, translates 'étui' as 'container', Arthur Evans (*Jules Verne Rediscovered*, p. 99) as 'canister'.

18 Bathurst, in New South Wales, where a 'mine d'argent' (230) was discovered in 1830; Mendoza, a city in Argentina almost totally destroyed by an earthquake in 1861; Moreno, Gabriel García (1821–75), president of Ecuador 1861–5 and 1869–75.

19 Interest in the 'Lost Colony' was renewed towards the end of the nineteenth century, when a group of mixed-blood Indians claimed to be descended from the colonists and the Croatoan tribe.

The name Moris (242) may refer to Robert Morris (1731–1806), a prominent leader in the War of Independence and the sole American tobacco purchasing agent for the French Farmers-General.

20 The mention of the 400 million souls is possibly part of a belief in a 'yellow peril' (*Oxford English Dictionary* (1900)), the turn-of-the-century fear that the West could be overwhelmed by numerically superior Orientals. 'Au XXIXe siècle' describes the fear more directly: 'la prolification [sic] chinoise est un danger pour le monde' (201). Further evidence of Michel's interest in China is his final 'Zigzag', entitled 'Intelligence et douleur: Un Anesthésique anglo-chinois', an article which anticipates such ideas in 'Edom' as the correlation between brain size and intelligence and the invention of printing, etc., by the Chinese while the West was still primitive. On the other hand, Jules Verne was approached for a 'prophecy' on the 'yellow peril' in 1895 by Félix Fénéon, author of an article 'Blancs, jaunes, noirs' in *La Revue blanche* (1889); Verne, however, replied that 'les temps des prophètes sont passés (Fénéon, *Œuvres plus que compètes*, (Geneva, Droz, 1970), vol. 2, p. 548). Even the name Mendoza could be that of a seventeenth-century Chinese missionary.

China already had a population of 430 million in the census of 1850, so the 'quatre cents millions' is puzzling. Is it a sign of part of the tale being written in the 1860s—or of an attempt to make it look so?

21 Part 2, ch. 4. However, in reality the Bible's Hebrew for 'Red Sea' is 'Yam Suf' ('sea of reeds'), which in any case is not now considered to be the modern Red Sea.

22 Obadiah is the name of the judge in *Le Tour du monde*.

23 Hiva is in fact a French name, from Nouka-Hiva, an island referred to in *Vingt mille lieues* (part 1, ch. 17) as being in French Polynesia (itself mentioned in 'Edom' (245)).

24 In an interview in 1902, significantly, Jules Verne jokes: 'According to the general terms of the survival of the fittest and the growth of muscles most used to the detriment of others, a herd of cattle inhabiting this district [the Klondyke, full of 'distressing' mosquitoes and horse-flies] would be all tail and no body in the far future' (unsigned interview, *The Commercial Appeal*, Memphis (30 November 1902), repr. by Henry Sharton in *Extraordinary Voyages* [sic], vol. 1, no. 2 (June 1994) 1–8 (3)).

25 An average of 5.0 letters per word in section II, 5.4 letters in sections I and III. Similarly, the average sentence lengths are respectively approximately 15 and 21 words, and the average paragraph lengths, approximately 46 and

64 words. Finally, the longest sentences have, respectively, 68 and 105 words. If we compare the average word-length in Jules Verne's *Les Aventures de la famille Raton* (1891) with that in 'Au XXIXe siècle' (1889), mostly by Michel Verne, we get: 4.8 and 5.2 letters per word; 14 and 17 words per sentence; 28 and 29.2 words per paragraph; and longest sentences of 106 and 138 words. In other words, all the evidence is consistent with Michel's contribution being in every case stylistically distinct and with his being mainly responsible for the first and third sections of 'Edom'.

Index